WE Remember IT WELL!

Stories from Our Lives

*Wishing you joyful memories —
Earl and Vivian Ziegler*

by
Earl and Vivian Ziegler

We Remember It Well

by
Earl and Vivian Ziegler
3001 Lititz Pike, Box 5093
Lancaster, PA 17606-5093

evzieg▮@gmail.com

Copyright © 2012
All rights reserved.

Although this is a semi auto-biographical work,
some of the names have been changed.

Scripture quotations marked (KJV) are from the King James Version of the Bible. Scripture quotations marked (TLB) are from *The Living Bible* © 1971 by Tyndale House Publishers, Wheaton, IL 60189. Scripture quotations marked (NIV) are from *The New International Version* of the Bible ©International Bible Society1973,1978, 1984.

Library of Congress Number: 2012915773
International Standard Book Number: 978-1-60126-352-0

Printed 2012 by

Masthof Press
219 Mill Road
Morgantown, PA 19543-9516

DEDICATION

We lovingly dedicate this book to
our six children and their spouses:

Karen Louise (Ziegler) and George Ungemach
Randall Earl and Linda (Neese) Ziegler
Doreen Kay (Ziegler) and Ken Creighton
Michael Wayne and Mary (Conahan) Ziegler
Konnae Lee (Ziegler) Berces
SuLien Marie (Nicodemus) and Grant Markley
plus
Our Korean exchange student daughter,
Audrey (Hyun Joo Yun)
and John (Youngsuk) Choi
Our "Baltimore Sun," Avon McCree

CONTENTS

Preface vii

1. Who We Are 1
2. Two Becoming One 23
3. To Chicago and Beyond 41
4. A "Normal" Pastorate—Times Three, 1954-1960 54
5. Young—and Still Learning 68
6. Scared Out of Our "Mitts" 82
7. When We Had Red Faces! 100
8. Shepherding the Black Rock Flock, 1960-1970 113
9. We Need More Boards in the Table! 146
10. "A Heap o' Livin'" 162
Photos 181
11. Bitten by the Travel Bug 192
12. Circling the Globe 219
13. Living in "Rufus P. Bucher Country" 1970-1983 238
14. God-Moments 268
15. Serving as the Atlantic Northeast District Executive, 1983-1989 298
16. Returning to the Lampeter Church, 1989-1999 316
17. At the Helm of the 1994 Wichita, Kansas, Annual Conference 324
18. In Joy and in Sorrow 335
19. Enjoying "Retirement" 363
20. Life Goes On 383

When It All Happened! 389
Index 399

Earl and Vivian Ziegler in costume for singing "I Remember It Well."

PREFACE

Music always has been an important part of our lives, whether it was playing the piano and/or organ, directing choruses, singing in a male quartet, singing in a women's trio, singing solos or duets; we enjoyed it all. We started singing "Anything You Can Do I Can Do Better" (from Irving Berlin's musical, *Annie, Get Your Gun*) at a public school parent-teacher program in York County, Pennsylvania, in the 1960's while we were pastoring the Black Rock Church of the Brethren.

Somehow, the word crossed the Susquehanna River that we occasionally dressed in costume and performed this song, and in the 1970's we were frequently requested to do it for people in the Quarryville community. After Edna McComsey and her daughter, Ethel, witnessed our performance, they gifted Vivian with a matching sun bonnet and long apron they had made. When Vivian added a black shawl that belonged to her grandmother, Kate Eshelman Zug, and some yarn and knitting needles, we included another costumed song to our repertoire, "I Remember It Well" from the musical, *Gigi*.

Around that same time, we attended a "white elephant" sale at the Wenger Implement Shop at the Buck. One of the items auctioned was a pair of new, denim overalls—about size 50! The bids were slow, so Earl bid fifty cents, and got the overalls. When he stuffed them with a pillow and added old eyeglasses plus an antique cane he got from his dad, they were just what we needed to complete the costumes for our little act. Regardless of what other numbers we did, the two songs when we "dressed up" were always the hits of the evening.

This book, initially a compilation of stories to be shared with our children and grandchildren, grew into a much larger treatise through the encouragement of many friends and parishioners who traveled with us on segments of our journey. We acknowledge the loving support of our six children, Karen Louise Ziegler Ungemach, Randall Earl Ziegler, Doreen Kay Ziegler Creighton, Michael Wayne Ziegler, Konnae Lee Ziegler Berces, and SuLien Marie Nicodemus Markley and their respective spouses. We also thank Betty Vasco, a faculty member with Vivian at the Swift Middle School for many years, who critiqued and proofread several chapters for us.

Although this book is somewhat autobiographical, it is not really an autobiography, but rather a collection of stories. Thus, they are not written in consecutive order, and do not include all (or even close to all) the memorable events and people in our lives. Amazingly, our sixty-one-year marriage has survived our working jointly on this project, although you can imagine the interesting discussions we had in choosing what to include (and exclude) and in resolving our differences in remembering how certain events happened.

However, we each claim to "remember it well," whether it is in singing the duet by that title or in recalling the events recorded here. Several of our children suggested that our title would be literally more honest if we added the word, "Enough!" After thinking about that, we almost agreed with them! However, after further contemplation and discussion, we decided to omit the "Enough!", realizing that although others may differ with us on some details, this is the way we remember them.

The incubation of our life's journey together began at Elizabethtown College where we met as students in the fall of 1949 and began dating in 1950. Although Vivian had declared there were two career people she would never marry—an undertaker and a minister—and Earl had been licensed to the ministry in 1948, we were married anyway in 1951. "I married the man, not the profession," Vivian insisted.

Thus began a sixty-plus year adventure that included a fifty-five year ministry for Earl, twenty-five years as an English teacher and middle school librarian for Vivian, directing travel groups all over the world, leading numerous workshops and retreats, serving as Moderator of the Church of the Brethren denomination, and parenting six children who then added eighteen grandchildren and four great-grandchildren.

Why did we decide to collect our stories and put them into a book? About four years ago, Rick Warren wrote an article entitled, "Three Ways God Wants to Use Your Experiences." He suggested that anyone's experiences could be used to minister to others, to motivate others, and to model for others.

In other words, they can be used to comfort people who are going through similar trials (2 Corinthians 1:6,7 TLB). Readers can receive hope and encouragement as we fulfill the admonition given by the Apostle Paul in 1 Thessalonians 5:11 (TLB): "Encourage each other to build each other up." It is our hope that this book, with its true stories from our lives, will inspire each reader to walk a little closer to the Lord in his or her journey through life. Blessings to all.

> Earl and Vivian Ziegler
> 3001 Lititz Pike
> Lancaster, PA 17606
> October 2012

WHO WE ARE
Chapter One

*"Be who you is, for if you ain't who you is,
than you is who you ain't."*
*(Author unknown but quoted
by Chuck Swindoll in a radio sermon)*

Earl –

I was almost named Herbert! Since I was born in a farmhouse in Sheridan, Pennsylvania, on March 4, 1929, the day that Herbert Clark Hoover was inaugurated as President of the United States of America, my parents considered giving me his name. However, after more thought, my parents, Abraham Hoffman Ziegler and Rhoda (Bucher) Keller Ziegler decided to name me Earl Keller Ziegler. In a family of eight children, I was number three, the first boy. A brother, Lee, who was number five, died from meningitis at the age of two.

With two older sisters and my sister, Verna (now Kline), seventeen months younger than me, I was sandwiched between girls who tend to grow taller than boys in their early teens. People always teased me, "When are you going to grow up? Verna is going to beat you." And she did . . . for a while. Those years were very competitive as I struggled in vain to outgrow and outdo her.

Living on a farm meant there was always work to be done, from early morning until dusk. We were early risers because we had to help with the milking, eat breakfast, and share in family devotions before we walked to school. As most families, we had our sibling arguments, but I discovered one amazing thing quite early in life: *you can't pray for someone and still remain angry with him or her.* One morning, after Verna and I had had a squabble in the milk house, Dad called on me to pray in our devotions. How could I pray and be angry at the same time? After our devotions were over, the squabbles and irritations were forgiven and forgotten . . . for a while.

In those days, we came in from milking and working with the cows, washed our faces and hands and changed into school clothes without showering. Today I shudder to think how we must have smelled, but we were never teased about it because other kids came to school from farms also and we all smelled the same!

In addition to raising crops and running a dairy farm, my parents had a milk route for a number of years as a retail outlet for selling our own milk. This meant that we had to bottle and deliver the raw milk every morning to customers in the town of Richland. Mom mixed some of the milk into chocolate milk which we also bottled and delivered to our regular clients. Any leftover milk and cream was hand-cranked into delicious homemade ice cream.

As an infant, when I was given my first taste of chocolate milk, I *loved* it! I preferred it so much that I refused to drink white milk from my baby bottles, so my mother wrapped a cloth around the bottle so I wouldn't see what color the milk was. In that way I was fooled into drinking the white milk.

In addition to my six siblings, two of my first cousins, Alice and Harold Keller, were also frequently at our farm. Their father, (my uncle Chris) had died in a tragic accident when Harold was three years old. As a widow, my aunt Ethel went to work to support her two children, and during the summer they stayed with us. In many ways, they were like two more siblings in our family. My uncle Samuel and aunt Bessie Ziegler lived in a house at the end of our lane and we also often played and worked together with their two children, Arlene (now Arlene Crouse) and her brother, Carlos.

My father invested in a threshing rig for the gleaning of barley, wheat or oats. To recoup some of his investment, he would thresh for the neighboring farmers. As a boy of nine, ten, and eleven years of age, I would sit on top of the blower cap (a dirty job) and guide the straw as it was blown into the mow in the barn. I later graduated to feeding the machine by hand, forking each wheat sheaf into the thresher during July and August, one of the toughest jobs I ever had to do. It was understood, that even though I was hired out to work for others, I always gave my pay to my dad. When I turned eighteen, I had two dollars to my name but was allowed to keep all that I earned from that time forward. While growing up around farm animals, I observed their reproduction and the births of calves and kittens, and do not recall that my parents ever explained anything to me about "the facts of life." One day in school I heard some boys quoting a dirty rhyme. That evening, as Mom was shoveling corn and I was holding the bag to receive it, I repeated the rhyme and asked her what it meant. (I thought I knew what it meant, but I wondered if she knew!) At first, she didn't answer me, but I did notice that she began shoveling a little faster. Then she said, "You ask your Dad what that means." I was left holding the bag.

And I never did ask my Dad.

* * * * *

My parents were very faithful churchgoers, and in spite of having the milking and barn work to do, we all worked together and were very seldom, if ever, late for Sunday School at the Richland, Pennsylvania, Church of the Brethren where we attended. Being on time was a top priority.

A life of integrity and hard work was also modeled by each of my parents. One crop we grew was tomatoes. Picking them was a back-breaking job, which I never enjoyed. The weather was usually hot, and the baskets got heavier as they got filled. One day, neighbor John approached dad while he was pumping gas into our Farmall tractor and I was standing beside him listening. John

Rhoda Bucher Keller Ziegler and Abraham Hoffman Ziegler, parents of Earl Keller Ziegler, on their Fiftieth Wedding Anniversary in 1974.

asked him, "Abe, why do you grow tomatoes instead of tobacco which would give you more cash for less work?"

His answer was one I never forgot. *"If I don't want my sons to smoke it, then I have no business raising tobacco!"*

I have always remembered that lesson.

I also remember a salesman who came to the farm wearing a beard and the garb of a strict Mennonite or Amish man. My dad asked him what church he attended and he grinned and said, "I don't really go to any church. I just dress this way because it's good for my business."

I never forgot that either. How deceitful he was!

* * * * *

My oldest sister, Ada, and I both loved books and studying. The other sisters were more interested in farm life than they were in books and all three married farmers. I would have loved having piano lessons, but dad wanted to treat each of his children equally, and said since he couldn't afford them for all, he wouldn't give piano lessons to any of them. Only my youngest brother, Glen, and I were interested in music lessons. When Glen got old enough, I persuaded dad to let me drive him to take piano lessons, and I studied piano in college.

Music was always a vital part of my life. I was the wolf in the musical, "Little Red Riding Hood" in grade school and always sang in the choruses throughout my school life. At the Richland Church, I was invited by Lydia Royer to sing in a boy's quartet and when I was sixteen, she trained me in congregational song leading with the use of a pitch pipe. In my junior and senior years of high school, I sang first tenor in a male quartet that received numerous invitations to sing at revival meetings in the Lebanon/

Lancaster area. The other members of the quartet were Harvey Weik, Melvin Krall and John Kegarise. In college, I tried out for the Acappella Choir and Men's Chorus, and was accepted into both of them.

My brother, Victor, used to love saying that one time he overheard my parents commenting, "We believe five of our children are going to turn out all right in life, but two are questionable, so we sent those two (Ada and me) to college!" Victor always loved to make people laugh.

I accepted Christ as my Savior as a twelve-year-old boy when evangelist John Fidler from Ohio was preaching at the Richland Church, and I was baptized in a creek on the Donough farm near Richland on January 25th, 1941, a day when the

Abraham and Rhoda Ziegler family about 1943. Back row, left to right: Earl, Mae, Ada, Verna, Victor. Front row: Rhoda, Lena, Glen, Abram.

ground was covered with snow. I still remember my baptism as a very meaningful moment. I really felt a sense of forgiveness for my sins. I also remember my mother carefully stuffing my clothes with newspapers to insulate me against the frigid stream water.

After I got my driver's license at the age of sixteen, I would sometimes ask my dad if I could use the family car. Usually he would say, "Yes," and add advice such as, "Behave yourself," or "Remember who you are."

* * * * *

One of my strictest high school teachers, which I now consider one of my best, was my English teacher, Miss Becker. She would write quotations and poems on the blackboard and make us memorize them. At the time, I thought this was a foolish exercise, but upon reaching adulthood began to realize that she had filled the banks of our minds with resources that we could draw from the rest of our lives. One that I have used many times in sermons and in counseling was:

"If you're tempted to reveal
A tale someone to you has told
About another, let it pass,
Before you speak, three gates of gold.
These narrow gates: First, is it true?
Then, is it needful? In your mind
Give truthful answer; and the next
Is last and narrowest, is it kind?
And if to reach your lips at last,
It passes through these gateways, three,

> *Then you may tell the tale, nor fear*
> *What the result of speech may be."*
> - Poet Unidentified

When directing tours on a rainy day, I have often quoted this one:

> *"It ain't no use to grumble and complain*
> *It's just as easy to rejoice.*
> *When God sorts out the weather*
> *And sends rain . . . why, rain's my choice!"*
> - Poet Unknown

* * * * *

My family moved from Richland during my junior year in high school into a different school district. Because my parents could not afford the tuition required for me to continue at Richland High School now three miles away, I spent my senior year at Newmanstown High School from which I graduated. I was told that since I was a transplant, I would not be considered for any awards nor be recognized for academic achievements at graduation. Consequently, I determined that if I ever had children, I would not pull them out of high school, . . . and I didn't!

* * * * *

After Ada graduated from high school, she went on to Millersville College. By my junior year in high school, I was oscillating between medicine and ministry as my future vocation. The influence and support that I received from my home congregation is what tipped the scale.

My parents were deacons in the Richland congregation before we moved to the nearby Heidelberg Church when I was seventeen. The practice there was that a young man was to be "called" into ministry by the church and was not to volunteer. With the encouragement of several older people in the congregation, the call became increasingly clear so I approached the elder in charge, Henry King. He became my advocate and led me through the process of volunteering. On August 2, 1948, at the age of nineteen, and having completed my freshman year at Elizabethtown College, I was licensed to the ministry. Consequently, I call the Heidelberg Church my home church because I was both licensed and ordained there, but my formative, nurturing time was at Richland.

Shortly after that, when it was my first turn to preach as part of the rotating schedule at Heidelberg, I chose as my text the words of Peter, "Silver and gold have I none, but such as I have, I give thee." (Acts 3:6)

* * * * *

The day I left home to begin college is another day etched in my memory.

During our family devotions that morning, my mom led us in prayer and mentioned me by name and that God would be with me during my college years, keeping me safe and pure. This made such an impression on me that I have recommended it many times to others: *Pray for your children by name in their hearing.* They will never forget it.

During my freshman year at college, in a class on public speaking taught by Dr. Ralph Schlosser, I was assigned

Abraham and Rhoda Ziegler family about 1960. Standing, left to right: Lena (Kreider), Earl, Victor, Glen, Verna (Kline). Seated: Mae (Patches), Rhoda, Abram, Ada (Good).

to make a speech. Because I was teased frequently about my broad Lebanon County Dutch accent, on the day of my presentation I introduced my speech with an apology, "Now, I want you to realize that I am from Lebanon County, so I hope you can understand me with my Pennsylvania Dutch accent."

After the speech, Dr. Schlosser encouraged me greatly with this bit of advice: "Earl, *never apologize for something that is a part of you.*"

How freeing and encouraging that was!

* * * * *

Vivian –

After my birth on June 29, 1930, in the St. Joseph's Hospital in Lancaster, Pennsylvania, my dad, Elmer Rupp Snyder, came to the maternity ward to see me for the first time. He asked his sister, Emma, a nurse who worked there, to show him his baby. She went into the nursery and came out holding a black baby. It was said that he turned really white and was speechless . . . until she confessed she was playing a trick on him. Then she returned to the nursery and brought me out. I don't know what color he turned when he first caught sight of me!

Until I was six and one-half years old, I was an only child, obsessed with wanting to learn. Having taught eight years in one-room schools, my mother, Kathryn (Eshelman) Zug Snyder, still had some elementary school books and with them, I basically taught myself to read. I also enjoyed "playing school" with her while she would iron or do other household chores. I would sit at the kitchen table and she would drill me with questions. Sometimes she would put a page of math problems on a sheet of paper and I would fill in the answers. We had spell-

Elmer Rupp Snyder and Kathryn Eshelman Zug Snyder after their wedding on August 15, 1929, parents of Vivian Snyder Ziegler.

ing and geography bees. (One says the name of a town, country, continent, river or mountain, etc. and the other must choose one that begins with its last letter). I loved it . . . and still do! Occasionally, she would give me a big word, like "Halloween," or a short phrase, and I had to see how many words I could find in it. I enjoyed that also . . . and still do!

I couldn't wait to go to school, and attended the Florin Grammar School, a two-story school with four grades in one room on each floor. In my first grade class, there were twelve students, and of those there were five named "Bobby": Bobby Williams, Bradfield, Gantz, Brown, and Gebhart. Our teacher was Anna Garber and at some point between my first and fourth grades, she got married and became Mrs. Hollinger. Because mother had taught me many things at home, I was more advanced than the others, but for socialization reasons, was kept in first grade to finish the year. I was only in second grade a couple weeks and then was moved to third, skipping second grade. Consequently, from then on through high school, I was always the youngest person in my class. (From my experience, I wouldn't recommend this practice.)

After I had been in school six weeks or so, I came home one day especially happy. Mother asked me why I was so joyful, and I answered, "The teacher smiled at me today."

As a former teacher, she felt that was sad that it had taken so long.

* * * * *

We lived between Florin and Mount Joy at an orchard of apple, peach, apricot, cherry, and plum trees and we had several fields where we planted produce like beans, beets, celery, cabbage, asparagus, and even gladiolus for cutting for market. When I would dig out dandelion or pick bunches of spearmint tea to sell, I was allowed to keep that money.

My parents practiced hospitality to the hilt. Very often, when missionaries or evangelists spoke at church, they would stay at our house. Some were spiritual giants in their day, such as Albert Helser, Donald Gray Barnhouse, Harry Ironside, William J. Pettingill, George Mundell, Albert Hughes, W.S. Hottel, Roland V. Bingham, and lots more. In retrospect, I can see why they enjoyed staying there. Our house, situated on a hill, had porches on three sides of it with great views, and mother kept the lawns and gardens always looking beautiful. If you didn't have to do the work, it was a lovely place to be.

We attended the Florin Church of the Brethren until I was eight years old. My parents were opposed to the Church of the Brethren's decision to join the National Council of Churches and the World Council of Churches, and so we left the church and joined the Elizabethtown Gospel Tabernacle which evolved in time into what is now the Mt. Calvary Church.

My father's sister, Emma R. Snyder, was a nurse and lived with us. In the mid-1930's she felt the call of God and in 1938 began her career as a single missionary nurse with the Sudan Interior Mission in Nigeria.

One night in the fall of 1937 she took me up to her bedroom after supper and explained that all of us are sinners and Christ died on the cross, taking the punishment of sin for us. That night, at age seven, I accepted Him as my Savior and experienced the exuberant joy of a newborn in Christ. Immediately, I wanted the *whole world* to know Him, so I took a small tablet and wrote out the words of John 3:16 on each page, making many handwritten copies. The next day I carefully placed a homemade, handwritten "tract" on the desk of each student at my school.

*****

I wouldn't describe my childhood as a happy one. When I was ten years old, on May 11, 1941, my father died within twenty-four hours after experiencing a cerebral hemorrhage, leaving my mother a widow with four children, ages almost 11, 4½, 2¾, and 5½ months old. For the next twelve years, Mother managed the orchard, totally dependent on the hired men who worked for her. We were always poor, but we were never needy. With all the fruit, produce, and chickens around, we always had enough to eat. In addition, she took cut flowers, vegetables, and fruits from our orchard plus dressed chickens and eggs to farmer's markets in Harrisburg, Elizabethtown, and Mt. Gretna. On market days, I would care for the young children, plus cook meals, and clean the house for the weekend. Mother made a list of jobs I should do, but I liked to do extra things to "surprise" her.

Snyder siblings shortly after their father, Elmer Snyder, died at age 44 on May 11, 1941. Left to right: Fanny Ruth (4 ½), Charles (almost 2), Vivian (almost 11) holding Paul (6 ½ months).

Some Saturdays I would attempt to bake a cake from "scratch." If they turned out okay, it would be a nice surprise dessert for Saturday evening or Sunday noon. If they were a disaster, I simply took them to the field behind our house and dumped the contents of the cake pan on the ground, figuring nobody knew. I don't think my mother ever did find out about those aborted and discarded "surprises." When I became a teenager, we reversed our roles, and mother stayed home and I went to market on Saturdays with a friend of mother's, Mrs. Roy (Maria) Forney.

Life like this would have been tolerable, but when I reached puberty, I was frequently harassed by inappropriate actions and stories told to me by several of our hired men, that today would be considered sexual abuse. That was the toughest part and the part that left the most scars on my psyche. I never told my mother what they said and did, as I knew she absolutely needed them to work for her.

* * * * *

My parents took their faith very seriously and were very strict. I was never allowed to wear slacks or even snow pants, because of Deuteronomy 22:5 which says *"A woman must not wear men's clothing, nor a man wear women's clothing, for the Lord your God detests anyone who does this."* (NIV) Although we had a pond on which the people from town would come and ice skate in winter, I never learned that skill. With the poor sense of balance which I have always had, I *felt sure* I would fall, and without wearing snow pants, as all the other girls did, I was too modest to risk falling wearing a skirt. My bedroom window faced the pond and on many a frosty night with the lights off in my room, I would crouch at my window opened about a half inch to hear, watch and listen to the skaters having a great time and wishing so much I could join them.

In fifth grade, I was a victim of bullying. A gang of kids, headed by a girl in my class who had flunked a grade and was bigger than the rest of us, would often follow me home, pushing me, calling me names and pulling my pigtails. My parents and teacher were aware of it, and sometimes the teacher would drive me home. Other times I would walk a long, circuitous route to avoid going past the homes of these students. The worst of these experiences occurred one evening when they threatened to throw me into our pond which I had to pass on my way home. They pulled my arms and hair, pushed and dragged me while I yelled and cried in fear because the pond was deep and dirty, and I didn't know how to swim. I don't recall what stopped them. Summer vacation halted the bullying, and everything was calm in sixth grade.

It also didn't help my self-esteem that I was overweight. As a young child, people would exclaim, "How cute! What a nice chubby girl you are!" I actually began to think it was an asset!

In third grade, another girl and I had an argument at recess about weight. She said, "You're FAT!"

I retaliated, "I am NOT fat. I'm just chubby."

She persisted, "No, you're not chubby; you're fat, and fat is ugly!"

I heard what she was saying and never forgot it. I think I also felt somewhat betrayed—that my parents hadn't told me the truth.

When I was eleven, we had a large cold storage building where in August, the hired men would bring the peaches they had picked. We sorted them and put them in half bushel, peck, and half peck baskets and had them displayed in rows on the cement porch for customers to see and buy.

One day I sold a basket of peaches to a customer and needed change. For security reasons, we kept the money in the house, so I said, "Excuse me for a minute while I run into the house and get your change." Then I took off running.

I thought I was being very polite and efficient until I heard the customer call after me, "Run fast, now, and perhaps you'll get some of that skinny off."

That remark, which in retrospect doesn't even make sense, cut me to the core. I felt it was a rebuke about my weight, about me as a person, and seventy years later, it still hurts me to think about it. It is a good example of *the hurt that a thoughtless remark can cause.*

The accumulation of negative experiences resulted in a low self-esteem that no amount of scholastic honors, later reassurances from a loving husband, successes, or accomplishments of our children could ever completely cure.

* * * * *

During my high school years, all types of extracurricular activities such as membership in the National Honor Society, playing the part of a black cook in the musical, *Rio Rico,* being in the play, *Tish,* serving on the staffs of the school paper and our class yearbook, singing in chorus, playing basketball, and attending musicals accompanied by Eugene Saylor, my music teacher, were all highlights and fun activities. I used to enjoy saying, *"I don't want books and homework to interfere with my education."*

* * * * *

In 2003, Earl and I attended a "Golden Alumni" dinner at Elizabethtown College. Among the attendees was my high school Problems of Democracy (P.O.D.) and physics teacher, Charles Arthur Shearer Hollinger (better known as "CASH" Hollinger because of the initials in his name). Amazingly, although he was in his 90's, he still knew me and after the dinner, he came and asked me if I remember where I lost my high school ring. I was dumbfounded. I knew I had lost it long ago, but had no memory at all of where and when it happened, so I was eager to hear what he would say.

"Do you remember when you were in a carload of students that I drove to Philadelphia to attend a citizenship seminar?" he asked.

I nodded, "Yes." (How well I remembered because we all laughed quietly *at HIM* on that trip as he drove up a one-way street going the wrong way!)

"Do you remember that while we were there, it began snowing, and as we returned to Lancaster, the snow was already eight to ten inches deep?"

"Yes, I remember that snow storm." My best friend in high school, Nancy Swope (Fitzkee), was along. She lived between Maytown and Bainbridge, and because of the snow, the roads became impassable, so she stayed overnight at my house in Florin. Mr. Hollinger was afraid to drive us to my home at the orchard, so he let us out on Main Street (Route 30) and we had to walk to my home in knee-deep snow.

When we got there, our feet were so cold they were all colors of red, blue and purple. We took off our wet, snow-encrusted socks and stuck our feet in the oven of the old coal range that we had in our kitchen. How wonderful that heat felt! I remember that night well.

Mr. Hollinger continued. "Do you remember that we were behind some snow plows as we entered Lancaster on Route 30 and we got stalled in traffic near the area of what is now the Host Resort?"

Actually, I didn't remember that.

Seated: Kathryn Zug Snyder surrounded by her children, left to right, Fanny Ruth (Snyder) Reider, Paul Zug Snyder, Charles Bertram Snyder, and Vivian (Snyder) Ziegler.

"Several of you students got out of the car and began throwing snowballs at one another. As you grabbed a handful of snow, shaped it quickly into a ball shape, and threw it, your ring got caught up in the snowball and when you threw it, the ring went with it." His dark eyes twinkled as he recalled the incident. I did not remember that at all, and I appreciated his solving that "mystery of the lost class ring" for me. I was so glad he shared that—approximately fifty-seven years after it had happened! What an amazing memory that man had!

* * * * *

My first assignment as a college freshman in English class at The King's College, New Castle, Delaware, was to write a one-page single-spaced essay on "Who Am I?" Professor Robert Davies received all the manuscripts and at our next class said that one of them, in his view, was outstanding. To my surprise, he called *me* to the front of the class to read my essay to everyone. Here is what I had written in September, 1947:

WHO AM I?

Who am I? I am first and foremost a child of God. Even before the foundation of the world I was chosen to be one of the select few who should be born again and able to share the glories of God throughout eternity. Since I am saved, my duty is to tell others of the saving grace of my Lord and Savior. I am nothing without the guidance, care, love, and wisdom of my Father. With Him, I can do all things. Nothing can separate me from His love, for I am His.

Again you ask who I am. Being an American citizen by birth, I am a niece of Uncle Sam in this greatest of all nations, the United States. Our country is the most noted for its abundance of natural re-

sources, its democratic way of government and its progressiveness. God has placed the secret of the world's most powerful force, atomic power, in the hands of this country. I feel that God has granted us these innumerable blessings because of the faith of our fathers and forefathers. I do not realize all that this means to me because my finite mind cannot fathom the meaning of these facts.

What is my background, you ask? I am of German, Swiss and Irish descent. My ancestors were hard-working people and were very religious. Eighteen years ago Kathryn Zug, a schoolteacher, consented to marry Elmer Snyder, an orchardist. They started their home at a seventy-eight acre apple and peach orchard that was named "Fairview Orchards." Here it was that I was born.

How was my family life? My parents were very happily married until Daddy had a sudden stroke and died. I, the oldest child, was ten years old and my brother, Paul, the youngest was five and one-half months old. Between us there were one girl and one boy living and another boy who had gone on to Glory. Mother now had to fill three capacities: that of executive of the business, father and mother. It has been hard, yes, but we have never been in want. Even though our earthly father is dead, our Heavenly Father supplies all our needs.

What are my interests? I am interested in many things and have several hobbies. I like to travel, and I collect old and foreign coins. Reading, playing the piano, experimenting in cooking, and sports are some of my favorite pastimes. I like flowers but don't enjoy weeding them, and above all, I like to have lots of friends.

What of the future, you ask? To me, the future is somewhat hazy. I want to be in the Lord's will. I expect to major in English with the idea of probably becoming an English teacher some day. I do not know if this is what He has in store for me or not, but I shall be willing to change my plans for Him. Who am I? At present, I am a freshman at The King's College planning to make the best of my college career, so in the not-too-distant future my ambitions will be realized.

TWO BECOMING ONE
Chapter Two

*"There are three things too wonderful
for me to understand—no four!
How an eagle glides through the sky.
How a serpent crawls upon a rock.
How a ship finds its way across the heaving ocean.
The growth of love between a man and a girl."*
Proverbs 30:18,19 (TLB)

Vivian –

Both of us graduated from high school in 1947. I got my diploma from East Donegal High School (Maytown) in Lancaster County, Pennsylvania, and Earl got his from Newmanstown High School in Lebanon County, Pennsylvania. That September Earl began attending Elizabethtown College, while I became a freshman at The King's College, New Castle, Delaware. (Today it is located at 52 Broadway in the heart of New York City.)

At King's, the women's dorm, "Lexington," was styled like the stereotype Southern plantation mansion, complete with pillars on the front porch. I lived in a second floor room with three other girls. Four girls lived in an adjoining room, and the eight of us shared a single bathroom. The men's dorm, chapel and classes were held in barracks-type buildings.

Since my finances were limited, I worked at whatever jobs I could get, such as cleaning classrooms and certain areas of the women's dorm and typing catalog cards for the library. Every class began with prayer, and I loved the Christian atmosphere that prevailed. Chapel services were superb, as they often featured wonderful musicians and great speakers from across the nation, including the very young Billy Graham and Cliff Barrows.

My fondest college memories involved the choir under the direction of Dr. Gordon Curtis, and I felt honored to sing with them both years that I attended King's. The choir had a very active concert touring schedule both years, including many weekends and at least one long trip each year that had us going through Pennsylvania, upper New York state and New England. We even sang on the stage of Carnegie Hall in New York City. Because we practiced, sang, prayed and traveled together so much, we became like one big family.

I will never forget one Easter sunrise service with the college choir in the pier auditorium at the beach in Ocean City, New Jersey. Seeing the sun emerging from the horizon, rising up from the ocean waves that seemed to go on and on to infinity, and then, at the same time, singing great anthems such as, "O Thou Eternal One," made the resurrection of Jesus Christ seem so present and real to me. We also sang several anthems on the sidewalk bordering Niagara Falls as a crowd of people gathered around us listening to our vocal witness. I felt so privileged to experience moments like those.

After discovering that courses in Pennsylvania history, education and teaching methods were required in order to teach in Pennsylvania, and that none of these were offered at The King's College, I decided to transfer between my sophomore and junior years to Elizabethtown College, my mother's alma mater (1923). Because of limited funds, and the fact that my home was only six miles from the college, I commuted as a day student. Near the end of my junior

Vivian Zug Snyder and Earl Keller Ziegler, our Senior Photos at Elizabethtown College, 1951.

year at Elizabethtown, I was honored to be elected by the student body to be the editor of the *Conestogan*, the 1951 yearbook.

* * * * *

Earl –

During my four years at Elizabethtown College, I lived in the men's dorm which had been formerly a military barracks. We fellows enjoyed very much playing funny pranks such as when one group put a tractor on the roof of Alpha Hall, one of the girl's dorms. Another time, several fellows carried my bed out to a nearby field.

At first, I roomed with Irvin Wenger, but during my sophomore and junior years, my roommate was Dale Hylton who came from Virginia. It was funny because he had a broad, Southern drawl and I had a Lebanon County Pennsylvania Dutch accent, and both of us got teased about how we spoke. Before our senior year, Dale married Gladys Stehman, so I lived alone my senior year. I often teased Dale that he kicked me out because he preferred having Gladys as his roommate rather than me! I then became close friends with Don "Buckets" Reid, a black basketball star, who lived next door.

Since my funds were low, I worked in the college kitchen as a dishwasher and cleaned the offices across the street at Continental Press. My first car was a '36 Ford coupe with a rumble seat in it but during the spring semester of my sophomore year, I sold it to my sister, Verna. From Keller Brothers (my mother was the only sister of the Keller Brothers!), I purchased a new 1950 sea-green Ford Fairlane in my college junior year. While I was still a student, on December 30, 1950, I performed my first wedding, for fellow student, Arlene Weidman, and Paul Witman. On that occasion, I was probably far more nervous than they were! My first baptism was for a fellow college student, Bill Kell, whom I baptized with the guidance of the college pastor, Nevin Zuck.

I was a sophomore, in the spring of 1949 when the Elizabethtown College Choir, in which I sang tenor, was on a weekend tour in the Montgomery County, Pennsylvania, area. Following a Saturday evening concert at the Indian Creek Church of the Brethren, members of the Springfield Church of the Brethren, hoping to secure a student summer pastor, approached Professor David Albright, the choir director, inquiring about pre-ministerial students in the choir.

Prof. Albright challenged me to consider the invitation to go with them to their church the next morning and share devotions with the Springfield congregation. He excused me from the choir concert on Sunday morning with the promise I would return for the Sunday evening concert. The result was that the Springfield Church called me to be their student pastor for June,

Springfield Church of the Brethren, Coopersburg, Pennsylvania, 1950-51.

July and August, 1949, living with Elmer and Susan Bachman and their son, Roland.

Because of my desire to be engaged fully in college life through such extracurricular activities as the mixed and male choirs, being a member of both the Student Senate and the Sock and Buskin Drama Club, vice-president of my college class, and president of the Student Christian Movement, I declined the call to continue serving part-time at the church during my junior year. However, I served the Springfield Church again the following summer and then continued throughout my senior year, traveling every weekend to Coopersburg to live with Leroy and Nina Kramer, my "adoptive parents" for the next year and one-half. I supplanted my one hundred dollar salary from the church by pumping gas at Leroy's gas station part-time, assisting farmers in gathering hay and putting corn in silos.

While at Springfield that year and one-half, I experienced many firsts. I was privileged to baptize five persons, facilitated the

Earl conducting the mixed chorus at the Springfield Church of the Brethren, 1950-1951.

reunion and consecration of a divorced couple, experienced deacons who didn't "deak" and several females whose parents thought I should marry their daughters.

Another trendsetter for us happened at a funeral I had while at Springfield. Jacob Ankeny, an immigrant from Germany with a heavy German accent and a member of the church, died, and his family requested special music as part of the memorial service which was being held at 10 a.m. on a Wednesday. Unable to find anyone, I asked Vivian to duet with me, and we sang, "Wonderful Peace." That was the first of hundreds of duets, some serious and some lighthearted, that we sang throughout our ministry.

As a young twenty-two-year-old pastoral student, I was confronted with the death of Sam and Larue Yohn's one-day-old infant daughter. Although they had three older sons, I still remember the trauma connected with that infant death, possibly because I felt so inadequate to minister to that grieving family.

All these experiences were a wonderful preparation for my seminary training. I made some life-long friends with couples my age like Paul and Anna Jacoby and Gerald and Grace Kramer, among others. For many years, I was invited back to speak at their annual homecoming services.

*****

Vivian –

I was an English major, minoring in Social Studies and Spanish, while Earl was a Social Studies major minoring in English, and both of us took all the teacher education preparatory courses. Consequently, we were in many of the same classes. I do not recall many conversations with Earl during my junior year. One reason may have been that I was overweight. During that year I began taking medications to help me lose weight and they worked! The change was so slow that people who saw me frequently didn't notice the difference.

During that summer, our paths never crossed. When our senior year began, I had lost a total of about thirty-five pounds. Since my family's funds were still quite limited, I helped out by tending a stand every Friday evening at a farmer's market in Elizabethtown called "The Market Basket." I sold apples and other fruits from our orchard, eggs, produce, dressed chickens and things like that. I noticed that Earl had a part-time job at a nearby stand selling books for Dr. Henry Bucher.

One Friday evening when the customers were few, Earl walked over and said, "Hi, didn't I see you on the Etown College campus earlier today?"

"Yes, you could have," I answered with a smile. "I'm in some of your classes."

We introduced ourselves, exchanged pleasantries and that was that.

*****

Earl –

My version of how we met is that in our junior year, I always thought Vivian was kinda cute. However, in the fall beginning our senior year, when I saw that Vivian was so much thinner, I thought to myself, "Wow!" Many of our teachers had the practice of seating students alphabetically in their classrooms. Since her name was "Snyder" and my last name was "Ziegler," I was always in the last row, assigned to a seat in back of hers. I got tired of looking at her back and wanted to see what the front looked like!

* * * * *

Vivian –

The first two times Earl asked me for a date, I had conflicts and had to refuse, but he persisted and asked a third time. We went to a basketball game in the Elizabethtown College gym. We only wanted to see the varsity game, so we didn't arrive until the junior varsity game was over. The bleachers were almost full, and we had to walk in front of rows of people, our fellow students, to get to an area where there were two seats still available. As we climbed up the bleachers to our seats, one of Earl's friends, Dave Wilson yelled with a LOUD voice, (which was an asset several years later when he became a minister!), "YEAH, ZIG!" Other friends joined in and applauded. I'm sure both of our faces were red when we finally got seated.

Memories of our dating days are rather hazy after over sixty years! However, I remember good times of singing around the piano, especially as a duo on a song that was popular then, "It Is No Secret What God Can Do," and thinking it was amazing how He had brought us together. I also remember double dating with Don and Arlene Campbell on several occasions and stopping at the Clearview Diner for dessert. I was so shocked to see Earl order chocolate ice cream on lemon meringue pie! I quickly learned that he was a "chocoholic" and enjoyed eating chocolate with *anything*, any time!

It was obvious that Earl loved music. If I wasn't quite ready when Earl arrived for a date, or if I was being otherwise occupied, Earl would entertain himself at playing the piano. He had his own unconventional, somewhat jerky style, and my sister, Fanny Ruth, age 14, who was becoming a very good pianist herself, would sit at the top of the stairs, out of his sight, and crack up laughing. She had to put her hand over her mouth so he wouldn't hear her, but then he usually was playing so loud, he wouldn't have heard her anyway.

* * * * *

Earl –

Springtime at Fairview Orchards was a great olfactory experience. A row of lilac bushes lined the road and the fragrance and beauty of the apple orchard in bloom was just heavenly. Vivian and I were in the same college class called "The Romantic Movement of Poetry," taught by Dr. Ralph Schlosser, and we enjoyed taking a blanket and laying it under an apple tree among the blooming violets and studying together. Through the years we have often laughed about the irony of that course title and our growing love for one another. Others would say, "I'll bet you studied each other more than you did poetry!" We actually did do both!

* * * * *

Vivian —

On one of our first dates, Earl arrived at the Snyder farmhouse and was met at the door by my ten-year-old brother, Paul. Upon seeing Earl, Paul "greeted" him by asking, "What do you want here?"

Earl's first meal at my home was a multitude of disasters. To "entertain" him in the living room while Mother, Fanny Ruth and I prepared dinner, Paul showed Earl a box of old photographs of my growing-up years.

Just moments before we sat to eat, a food mixer was being used to mash potatoes. Apparently, whoever was responsible for the potatoes was distracted by other duties, and the vibrations of the beaters caused the mixer to "walk" over the edge of the table. The mixer and the bowl of potatoes fell on the floor. Naturally, the bowl broke, and the potatoes and glass were splattered everywhere. Fanny Ruth's quick solution was to call in the dog—who promptly did a good job of cleaning up the worst part of it.

When that was over, and we finally sat down to eat, Paul asked Earl, "Who do you love the most?" (He was hoping to hear Earl say, "Vivian.") However, Earl did some quick thinking and diplomatically answered, "The person I love the most is Jesus."

Then Mother asked him if he would have our blessing.

* * * * *

Two weeks before that memorable meal was March 4th, Earl's 22nd birthday, and I wanted to surprise him. I had baked a cake which I wanted to be just perfect. To ease getting the cake layers out of the round pans, I had traced around the pan bottoms on waxed paper, cut out the circles and placed them in the pans before pouring in the batter. After baking, I put the two layers together and iced the cake. It looked beautiful.

After our date, I invited Earl to come into the house for some dessert. For our little "party," Mother dished some ice cream and I brought out the cake. Earl was impressed. Then, as I attempted to cut the first piece to serve to him, the knife caught on something. To my horror and embarrassment, I realized I had forgotten to remove the waxed paper under the top layer, so there was a layer of waxed paper all through the center of the cake!

* * * * *

In the next four months, we both graduated from Elizabethtown College and Earl moved to Center Valley so he could better serve as pastor for the Springfield Church of the Brethren during the summer. The third week of June he carpooled with four other ministers, (Milton Hershey, Peter Heisey, Hiram Gingrich and Monroe Good), to San Jose, California, to attend the Church of the Brethren Annual Conference.

After applying for a summer job at twenty-one places, I finally found employment as a short order cook at the Clearview Diner at Rheems, working from 4:00 p.m. until midnight. One night when I came home from work about 12:30 a.m., Earl was waiting for me, having just returned from his trip to California. What a great reunion that was! In the wee hours of that morning, while sitting together on a wooden bench (made by my grandfather, Nathan Shelly Zug), on the front porch of our house at Fairview Orchards, he proposed to me, and I accepted. It was June 29th, 1951, my 21st birthday.

* * * * *

Earl –

During my senior year of college, I continued serving as part-time pastor for the Springfield Church of the Brethren at Coopersburg, Pennsylvania. When Vivian and I started dating midway through the year, it became the "talk of the congregation."

One Sunday I invited Vivian to go along with me for the day. Because the church was having a special emphasis weekend with an outside evangelist, Rev. Alvin Alderfer, I didn't have to preach.

During the evening worship service, as their custom was, everyone knelt while the visiting preacher led in prayer. After praying "around the world," he prayed for this particular church and for their "young, enthusiastic pastor and his capable wife." Snickers could be heard all through the church, and some people laughed so hard (silently) that the benches shook. After the service, some of the members and I set the preacher straight on our relationship, as Vivian and I weren't even engaged at that point.

Through the years, whenever I would meet Rev. Alderfer, we always had a good laugh about his "prophetic" prayer.

* * * * *

On another Sunday, May 6, 1951, I took Vivian along to the Springfield Church again to attend Sunday School and worship where I taught a class that morning and preached. Immediately after the service, we headed toward Annville where Ernest Shenk and Marian Stauffer were to be married that afternoon. Since Ernest and I had been good friends since boyhood and Marian was my second cousin, they had asked me to be an usher. Although I wore a suit and tie in the morning worship service, I needed to change into a black suit, white shirt and different tie for the wedding. Because of heavy traffic, the trip did not proceed as fast as we had expected. When we were still about a half hour from Annville, I asked Vivian if she would mind driving while I changed my clothes in the back seat area. She agreed, so we stopped and changed places. When we arrived at the Annville Church of the Brethren, I was all dressed and ready to usher.

(I have always had fun accusing Vivian of sneaking peaks at me in the rearview mirror that afternoon as I was undressing and she was driving!)

* * * * *

During her college years, Vivian was a member of the Calvary Bible Church in Elizabethtown. Although she became a Christian at age seven, she wasn't baptized until she was thirteen years old. Rev. Roy S. Forney, pastor of the Mount Joy Gospel Tabernacle, where her family then attended, baptized her by immersing her one time backwards in the stream at the Cove, east of Mount Joy.

After our engagement, in planning for our future life and ministry, we agreed that Vivian would change her church membership to the Church of the Brethren. Since I was already an ordained minister and she had family roots in that denomination, it wasn't a hard decision for her.

The Church of the Brethren baptizes by immersing three times forward, so we thought it would be wise for her, as a future minister's wife, to be rebaptized. She had no problem with that either as she regarded baptism as an "outward witness to an inward faith." She was not ashamed of her belief in Christ so was glad to "witness" again publicly—to a different group of people—about her faith.

So, about three weeks before our wedding, I planned for a baptism service at a creek near the Springfield Church and added Vivian to the group of applicants. Interestingly enough, that baptism service was well attended by the congregation as all were eager to see their young pastor baptizing his future bride.

* * * * *

Vivian –

Although neither of us attended the Elizabethtown Church of the Brethren on Washington Street, we decided to be married there. We felt it would be most appropriate for a Church of the Brethren minister to be married in a church of that denomination. Since the Elizabethtown Church was understood to be the "College Church," and we both had just graduated a couple months earlier, we chose that one.

Money was scarce, so the three attendants' white cotton organdy gowns were homemade. Even though my sewing abilities leave much to be desired, I began making my own wedding gown from white nylon lace but soon realized I needed help. Fortunately, our neighbor, Mrs. Henry (Sadie) Becker, was a skilled seamstress who finished it beautifully. (Our daughter, Doreen, wore it for her own wedding in June 1980, when she married Ken Creighton.)

Wearing a tiara borrowed from my matron of honor, my best friend in high school, Nancy (Swope) Fitzkee, I attached netting to it to form my wedding veil. Our two attendants were our fifteen-year-old sisters, Lena Ziegler (now Mrs. Irvin Kreider), and Fanny Ruth Snyder (now Mrs. Paul Reider). I carried a small white Bible topped with a corsage of tiny white pompons while the three other girls each carried a bouquet of green ivy.

Our brother-in-law, Monroe C. Good, husband of Earl's oldest sister, Ada, married us. Gertrude (Mrs. Ephraim) Meyer was organist, and Bob Ziegler, one of Earl's over one hundred first cousins, was soloist. We changed the wording slightly of a familiar hymn written by Frances Havergal to personalize it, and Bob sang:

> *"Take our lives and let them be*
> *Consecrated Lord to Thee.*
> *Take our moments and our days*
> *Let them flow in ceaseless praise,*
> *Let them flow in ceaseless praise.*
>
> *Take our love, our Lord, we pour*
> *At Thy feet its treasure store.*
> *Take ourselves, and we will be*
> *Ever, only, all for Thee,*
> *Ever, only, all for Thee.*

And that has continued to be our prayer during our first sixty years of marriage . . . and more.

* * * * *

Earl –

My brother, who was four years younger than I, Victor K. Ziegler, served as my best man. Our ushers were Lloyd Gingrich, a close college friend, Dale Hylton, my former roommate, Roy Forney, Jr., Vivian's third cousin and family friend, and John M. Drescher, a college friend of mine and Vivian's high school classmate.

On the day before my wedding, my dad gave me a one sentence sex education. He simply said, "You know, Earl, *with added privileges come added responsibilities.*"

When you think about it, that one sentence said a lot!

* * * * *

Facing the future together as Mr. and Mrs. Earl Ziegler! (August 12, 1951)

Vivian –

Sunshine interrupted by intermittent spotty showers marked our wedding day, August 12, 1951. Although it was clear when guests arrived, during the ceremony rain hit the church roof in torrents. We exited the church through the traditional shower of rice in clear weather conditions.

Our reception was held outdoors in the backyard of Fairview Orchards with a self-serving table consisting of several folding tables topped with a white tablecloth. People sat around on folding chairs in groups. I don't remember our menu except that our "punch" was simply Kool-Aid. Halfway through the reception, we experienced another downpour, and everyone grabbed a chair and their plate and hurried to get indoors. Fortunately, our house had a large open area in it, so as Earl and I opened our gifts on our dining room table, everyone could still see and hear. Relatives and friends knew that we planned to leave in two weeks for seminary in Chicago, so we were not given the traditional small appliances, lamps, cookware, crystal or china as gifts. Instead, we received twenty-four sets of pillow cases, fourteen table cloths, and a sprinkling of other gifts.

* * * * *

Earl –

After opening our gifts, Vivian changed into her "going away suit," pinned on her pompon corsage, and we drove away in my green Ford Fairlane. Our first night was to be at Kline's Motel in Reading, Pennsylvania, but on the way, we decided to make a brief stop at the home of Vivian's aunt and uncle, Henry and Fannie Shearer, where her grandmother, Kate E. Zug, also lived. Grandma Zug was in ill health and could not attend our wedding, so we stopped in to give her a first-hand report.

After resuming our drive toward Reading, I noticed a familiar-looking car following us through the back country roads, so I stopped. When they also stopped, I recognized my older sister, Mae, and her husband, Wayne Patches. "Why are you following us?" I asked. They laughed and said they really weren't following us but were simply on their way home to their farm. In fact, because we had left the reception about an hour ahead of them, they assumed we'd be well on our way. I explained that we had visited Vivian's Grandma, and because of that, we coincidentally met on the back roads at the same time.

* * * * *

Our tight money situation was also reflected in our honeymoon plans. After our night in Reading, we headed to a little row of cottages in the Pocono Mountains where I had made reservations for one of them for Monday through Thursday night. We made our own breakfasts by buying a box of cereal and some milk. Since our cottage had no refrigerator, we kept our milk in the home of the landlord. Friday night was spent in the Long Run Church of the Brethren parsonage with Rev. Curtis and Anna Mary Dubble and Saturday night we stayed with Calvin Koch's, members of the Springfield Church. I was scheduled to preach for that congregation the next day.

* * * * *

My services at Springfield ended the last Sunday of August 1951, following which Paul and Anna Jacoby immediately began driving Vivian and me eight hundred miles to attend Bethany Theological Seminary on West Van Buren Street on the west side of Chicago, Illinois. As a newly-married couple, we lived in Chicago for the next three years.

* * * * *

By working during my college years at on-campus and off-campus jobs and taking a part-time pastorate, when I graduated, I had paid off my entire college debt and owned my car. Vivian also had worked, but still had a small debt to pay, so during the week before we left for seminary, I sold my car to finish paying her debt. Consequently, we began seminary with virtually no money, but we had no debts . . . and no car . . . but we had each other . . . and we were happy.

TO CHICAGO AND BEYOND
Chapter Three

*"I'll go with you anywhere,
as long as you go forward."*
(David Livingstone, pioneer missionary to Africa, to his aides)

Vivian –

Two weeks after we were married, Paul and Anna Jacoby, a young couple from the Springfield Church, volunteered to drive us to Bethany Seminary in Chicago. Earl had applied and been accepted as a student there very early, before he knew he was getting married! Consequently, when he informed Bethany that he would be arriving with a wife, he was told that all the apartments for couples were filled. What were we going to do? Neither of us wanted him to postpone his studies for a year or more.

After numerous discussions of the pros and cons, Monroe and Ada Good, Earl's sister and husband, and their two young sons invited us to share their four-room and bath Bethany apartment with them until another accommodation would be available. Thinking it would be just a matter of weeks, we accepted their offer. Even though it would be tight quarters, dividing the rental costs would help both couples. So, off we went.

In some ways, this experience was a great training ground for me. Ada and I took turns by weeks at buying groceries, planning and preparing the meals for all six of us. From her experience, she taught me many short cuts and disciplines in cooking and housekeeping. As a young bride, there was so much I didn't know. The only privacy that Earl and I had was in our small bedroom.

Earl took classes full-time, and we both agreed that I should take advantage of some seminary education during the three years that we would be there. Consequently, I took one or two classes each semester and worked part-time to provide some income for us. The first job I found was at a company called Media Records, located in the heart of the "Loop" in downtown Chicago. My job there was to tally on a comptometer the amount of square inches that select store chains had purchased for their advertising in stacks of newspapers from all over the United States. We measured how many inches of space their ads devoted to furniture, to linens, to clothing, etc. After a morning seminary class, I boarded a street car each weekday and took a twenty-minute ride to work. I returned home on the "L" train which came to within four blocks of our apartment on Van Buren Street. On winter evenings, it was almost dark when I walked that long road home through the city streets alone, but that was a different time, and it wasn't as dangerous then.

In our first week, there was a seminary-sponsored, get-acquainted event. We joined in playing a game in which everyone stood in a large circle. A person in the circle's center would suddenly point at a person and say either "Zip, Zap," or "Zoom" and quickly count to ten. If he pointed at you, and said, "Zip," you had to quickly give the name of the person on your left before the center person counted to ten. If he said, "Zap," you had to give the name of the person on your right, and if he said "Zoom," you were to give your own name. If you failed to say the correct name fast enough, you had to exchange places with the person in the center. If the circle was very large, several persons could be in the center at once with each working a different segment of the circle. Anyway, I remember that a couple times that evening, when someone said "Zoom" to me, in my attempt to respond quickly, I automatically gave my *maiden name.* Almost instantly, I realized my mistake and burst out laughing. After all, I had had that name for twenty-one years and had only had my married name for two weeks!

* * * * *

One of the first seminary courses I took was "Basic Doctrines of the Christian Faith" taught by William Beahm. Although I felt I had a good faith foundation by growing up in an active Christian family, having taken Bible courses at The King's College, and even having served occasionally as an adult Sunday School teacher at Calvary Bible Church, the content of this class caused me to rethink my values and beliefs. It was tough, but the result was that I developed a faith that was firmer and stronger than before.

Dr. Beahm, who was short in stature but a giant in brainpower had the unusual hobby or quirk of genealogy. When he first met someone, he would ask who his parents were and even his grandparents. After that, whenever he would pass him on campus, he would include all his genealogical data in his greeting. For example, he would say as he passed me, "Hello, Vivian Zug Snyder Ziegler."

His sister, Anna Beahm Mow, was also on the Bethany faculty and I took a course she taught on creative writing. With a delightful hearty cackle of a laugh, Anna was a captivating storyteller and a woman of great insight and spiritual depth. She shared how her greatest unfulfilled desire as an adolescent girl was to be beautiful. She felt that she was so homely, and it took many years before she could accept the truth and significance of the statement in 1st Samuel 16:7b—*"The Lord does not look at the things man looks at. Man looks at the outward appearance, but the Lord looks at the heart."* (NIV) Years later, Andrew Murray wrote a song about her entitled, "Sister Anna, Beauty Queen."

* * * * *

Earl –

In addition to our formal classes, the seminary required us to do some form of "practical work" in the field of ministry. During my freshman year, Owen Stultz and I chose to provide a morning worship service each Sunday for the teenage boys in a reform school, and Vivian went along to play the piano.

One Sunday in a sermon on the love of God, I made the statement, "God loves you like a father." After the service, one boy came to me and said, "If God is like MY father, I don't want anything to do with Him."

This taught me a lesson that I never forgot. *People see things from different perspectives because of the background from which they come.*

* * * * *

Living in Chicago afforded us many cultural opportunities. The Sunday Evening Club, held downtown in the Forum each week, offered presentations by top-notch theologians and philosophers from around the world. During his 1952 campaign for President, we even got to see and hear Dwight D. Eisenhower in person.

One evening Vivian and I attended a vocal concert given by the great contralto, Marian Anderson. The only tickets we could afford were for seats high in the "peanut gallery" and Ms. Anderson just appeared to be a tiny speck on the stage. However, from our high perch, I spied some empty seats in the second row of the main floor of the auditorium. During the intermission, Vivian and I scurried down innumerable flights of stairs and claimed those seats. Seated among the fur-coated rich and the media critics, we had a never-to-be-forgotten close-up view of the famed soloist when we could literally see the whites of her eyes and watch her breathing. What a thrill that was!

* * * * *

In mid-December of my freshman year at Bethany, when my sister, Ada Good, was five months pregnant, Vivian and I were finally able to move out of the Good apartment into a nice-sized room on the second floor of Wieand-Hoff Hall, which also housed the administrative offices on the first floor and the library in the basement. About six or eight young couples lived on that hall in similar rooms, all sharing the men's and women's separate bathrooms and showers at the end of the hall, and a community kitchen and laundry. In the kitchen were several refrigerators and each couple was assigned a shelf or two. On a schedule chart, we signed up if we planned to eat early or late so that we wouldn't all be cooking at once. We each had a bit of cupboard space for our dishes, spices and a few staples, and although it sounds complicated, for those who were flexible, it really wasn't that bad an arrangement.

* * * * *

Vivian –

During our first year of seminary, and our first year of marriage, Earl was invited to have special weekend services in a church in Indiana. Since this was his first speaking engagement outside of the state of Pennsylvania, he was very excited and looking forward to this experience with great anticipation.

I had already discovered that Earl was (and still is!) a very hard person to surprise or fool, so I wanted to do something special on April Fool's Day that would *really* surprise him. I carefully wrote and typed a letter supposedly from the church in Indiana saying that they had second thoughts and had changed their plans. They were withdrawing their invitation and regretted any inconvenience this may cause him, etc. I even "forged" the name of the person who had been corresponding with Earl. As an added touch of authenticity, I took a used stamp off an old letter and pasted it on the envelope so it would look like it had come through the mail. The only hint of it being a joke was that just above the return address, in letters so tiny that they were scarcely readable, I printed "April Fool." Then on April 1, I placed the letter in the pile of our incoming mail.

Earl opened the envelope eagerly, and was crestfallen when he read the message. He said, "I just can't understand this. Why would a church change its mind like this?"

I could hardly keep a straight face. After allowing him to stew a bit, I asked what return address was used, trying to call his attention to my tiny "clue." At first, he only saw the obvious one. When he finally saw it, I had to actually convince him that it was an April Fool joke. His speaking engagement was still ON. Even after the explanation, he could hardly believe he had been so fooled!

* * * * *

Earl —

During the summer between my freshman and middler Bethany years, Vivian and I moved back to Pennsylvania and lived in a bedroom on the second floor in the rear part of a large mansion next to my parents' home. The owner, an eccentric old woman, Mrs. Dunlap, lived in the mansion, and allowed us to rent a bedroom and an adjoining bathroom and have cooking privileges in her kitchen. Along with Monroe Good and several other men, I worked that summer putting pitch on roofs, a hot and difficult job but one that paid well. Meanwhile, Vivian worked at a ladies' underwear manufacturing plant in Lebanon.

During that summer, I had several opportunities to preach here and there. For one occasion, I chose the subject of "Joy"—the Joy we can experience in having Christ as our Savior, the Joy which is a fruit of the Spirit, and the Joy resulting from sharing with and serving others. When I finished speaking, the elder of that church stood up and said, "Although what Earl said this morning may be true, we should all remember that Jesus wept!" On that somber note, the service on "Joy" was dismissed. What a discouraging way to end a worship service!

* * * * *

For my middler year at Bethany, Vivian and I got a second floor three-room apartment in the rear of 408 Homan Street. We shared a bathroom with Maurice and Jean Strausbaugh, who lived with their two children, Dennis and Connie, in a larger apartment in the front. In addition to our classes, I did painting jobs on campus and got a part-time job sorting mail at the Chicago post office, and Vivian worked at a desk job at Sears.

Excitement was building in our home because Vivian was expecting our first child early in December. Since this was a new experience for both of us, we were disappointed when the due date came and went without the arrival of our little one.

About 1:00 a.m. on December 19th, 1952, Vivian began feeling pains. About an hour later she wakened me and said she thought this might be THE day. Was I ever excited! She had her little overnight bag packed for weeks already, but when she called me, I got up and took a shower.

"Why are you doing that?" she asked.

"Because I am soon going to meet my little son or daughter, and I want to be clean the first time they see me to make a good first impression," I explained as she laughed. I was also taking a class on "Preaching" at that time, and that day happened to be my scheduled turn to preach a sermon before the class and have them critique my content and presentation.

Vivian's pains intensified, so about 4 a.m. we decided to take the walk across the street to the Bethany Hospital, stopping on the way a couple times for a spasm of pain to come and go. In those days, husbands were unwelcome in delivery rooms, so Vivian was relieved to discover that her nurse would be Estella Horning, a doctor's wife, with whom she had some seminary classes. After waiting until Dr. Wieand arrived, Karen Louise Ziegler was born at 7:07 a.m., weighing in at five pounds, ten ounces.

As soon as I heard the news, I had to rush off to my class which began at 7:30. Of course, before I began my sermon, I had to share the wonderful news that I had just become a father. The class was probably somewhat lenient with me in their criticisms as they took into account that I had been up most of the night!

Because of Vivian's pregnancy and Karen's birth, we planned on spending Christmas in Chicago that year. It was one of our cheapest, simplest but most happy Christmases of all! The gifts for our family were simply handkerchiefs on which Vivian made a crocheted edging. I gave Vivian a couple combs and she gave me six nice Christmas balls for the tiny tree we had. The week before Karen was born, Vivian made popcorn which she colored red and white, strung together and draped around our tree. Of course, most special of all was having a newborn baby in the house reminding us in an unforgettable way of the greatest Christmas gift of all, when God gave His Son to us as a baby in a manger.

*****

Earl –

Another segment of practical experience which was required at Bethany was to take a summer pastorate. Between my middler and senior years, we traveled to Montana, where we served the Milk River Valley Church of the Brethren. To make the trip, we bought an old 1936 Dodge sedan from Rev. Henry King, the elder of the Heidelberg Church of the Brethren. Because he had taken good care of it, it ran like a top. (In fact, we have often regretted that we ever sold it!)

Living in the wide, open spaces of northern Montana, fifteen miles from the nearest town of Kremlin, was fascinating for us Easterners. With our six-month-old daughter, Karen, we lived in what resembled a chicken house with no electricity and no running water. It was one of several out-buildings on a farm owned by one of the leading members of the church. For cooking we had a Coleman 2-burner camp stove and when Vivian wanted to bake, we had an old wood or coal-burning kitchen range. Our toilet was an outdoor privy and a high shelf nailed to the house outside our front door served as our "refrigerator." On our first night there, our bed broke down because they had not put in the slats correctly to support the mattress!

Since the people were so isolated, any visit was an event that called for coffee, cookies and a nice, long visit. Everybody kept a pot of coffee on the back of their stove, so they were always ready for unexpected guests. Since our church was the only church in the community, it was attended by Christians from all denominations.

Rain was very scarce that summer, and when we did get a thundershower, the farmer, his wife and children ran out with all sorts of dishpans and buckets to collect the water. They actually scooped it up from puddles so that they could use it to water their garden.

Between shepherding the church that summer, we took a couple days to sightsee in beautiful Glacier National Park, attend a Cree Indian Rain Dance, and see a real Western rodeo.

The last weekend at the Milk River Valley Church was an unforgettable, frightening experience. The plan was to have a big celebration our last Sunday there climaxed with a Love Feast service in the evening. On Saturday night at 10 p.m., Geraldine Good came to our "chicken house abode" (we lived on their farm next to the house) and excitedly announced that she can't find her husband, Roy. "Where could he be? He's not come for supper. Perhaps he had a stroke in the field. Would we help find him?"

Clearly, Geraldine was upset and concerned, and so were we.

Soon his daughters, sisters and community friends were hunting him, but there was not a sight of him all night long. We moved a heavy bureau inside our cabin door in case a crazed and mentally distraught man would attempt to come in, and we got very little sleep.

On Sunday morning, we had no church service as the community and church folks joined together in calling, walking through the grain fields, checking the barn, and poking in the hay. Blood hounds were brought to hunt, and a small plane was chartered to fly overhead, searching for Roy in the vast wheat and corn fields, but he was nowhere to be found.

With no success, by early Sunday evening it was decided that all would leave, so it would be very quiet around the farm and house. And that did it!

After everyone had returned home, around 9:30 p.m. Roy appeared from nowhere and entered the farmhouse kitchen. His explanation was that he had been disorientated for a while, having possibly experienced a heat stroke. When he discovered people were looking for him, he got scared and hid in the barn, burying himself in the hay.

We were scheduled to leave on Monday morning. As Roy was pumping gas into his tractor that morning, I approached Roy and asked, "Roy, why did you do this to your family and us?"

He mumbled, and without looking at me, he said, "Some people drink their problems away. I chose to do it this way."

We left in our '36 Dodge, headed east over the Big Horn Mountains, bewildered, confused, failing to comprehend the significance of such bizarre behavior. How sad that the great summer we had among those warm, supportive people had such a tragic ending just before our departure.

On our way home, we stopped at Yellowstone National Park and our little old Dodge climbed over the Tetons effortlessly while we passed numerous newer cars stalled at the roadside with steaming radiators!

While driving through Indiana, we were stopped by a policeman for going 38 miles per hour in a 25-mile per hour speed zone. On the ticket, it said we had to go to the police station to pay a fine.

When we arrived there, we were told that they had received a very unusual phone call. Some anonymous person had been following us for a number of miles and saw us get stopped and receive the ticket. He took the unusual step of calling the police station and telling them that he had been observing my driving for many miles and had been so impressed by what a safe driver I was. Because of that call, the local authorities waived the fee, and we continued on our way to Pennsylvania. Praise the Lord!

* * * * *

Vivian –

The third-floor apartment above ours on Homan Avenue had a piano in it that was so old and heavy that it just stayed with the apartment. It would have been too much trouble to move it out! That was an attraction for us, so we applied for that apartment for our senior year at Bethany, and got it.

The layout of the apartment was exactly like the one we had on second floor, and for this year, we shared a bathroom with Wayne and Gwen Miller and their three children. Many nights, after the children were all in bed, Wayne and Gwen, and Earl and I would visit in one kitchen or the other taste-testing a new recipe and enjoying one another's fellowship. Gwen, Wilma Ford (the wife of another Bethany student, Don Ford), and I sang as a trio at several social functions.

During the three years that we attended Bethany, I was able to acquire almost one and one-half year's credits by taking part-time classes. Earl's class of 1954 had the distinction of having had three different seminary presidents: Dr. Rufus Bowman, who served in 1951-52 and died during the summer; Dr. Warren Slaybaugh, interim in 1952-53, and Dr. Paul M. Robinson, who became president in 1953.

From about February until graduation, the chatter on the campus was all about which church each student would be serving. After a "trial sermon" weekend, meeting with church officials, and much prayer, Earl and I agreed to begin our ministry in the Woodbury congregation in Middle Pennsylvania.

Sole occupants of the third floor at 408 South Homan Streeth in Chicago. Front, left to right: Chris, Wayne, Kevin, and Gwen Miller holding Terrie. In back: Earl Ziegler holding his daughter Karen. March 7, 1954.

In mid-June, after graduation, we loaded our possessions into our old Dodge, which wasn't too difficult as we only had two items of furniture: a folding crib and a combination 10-inch TV, radio and record player. Being three months pregnant, we had little cash but lots of ideas, hope and enthusiasm as Earl, Karen and I moved into the Woodbury parsonage on July 1, 1954, to begin the next chapter in our lives.

A "NORMAL" PASTORATE —TIMES THREE, 1954-1960
Chapter Four

"This isn't nearly as bad as I thought it would be."
(Annie Hoover, Member of the Woodbury Church of the Brethren)

Vivian –

In the best of circumstances, "trial sermon" weekends can be very harried times for ministers and their families. To buoy our spirits, someone at seminary advised us, "Don't think of it as the church officials judging you; think of it as your opportunity to judge *them*!"

During our "trial sermon weekend" with the Woodbury congregation in Middle Pennsylvania, we met with the committee composed of representatives from all three churches in the congregation after the Sunday morning service and enjoyed a delicious meal at the Lester and Sarah Sell home. Strange things were happening during the meal and we were very puzzled. As the table grace was spoken by Earl, we heard a funny but soft mimicking sound like, "Mum, mum, mum, mum, mum." We thought perhaps a child was out in the kitchen.

As the table conversation progressed, and someone would laugh, we heard a loud laugh that was almost like a cackle. I thought perhaps this family had a mentally disturbed person in the next room. The Sells carried on the conversation as though they didn't hear it. Unknown to us, the Sells had a pet parrot that loved to mimic the sounds it heard.

We moved into the living room to answer serious questions about our beliefs, doctrines, goals, values, special interests, etc. and interspersed among our responses was this loud, shrill sound of laughter. "Ha, ha, ha, ha, ha, ha, ha!"

The more we laughed, the more the parrot laughed. Even after the Sells explained what it was, it was hard to conduct an interview and be serious with the comical parrot responses in the background.

Obviously, they hired us in spite of all those distractions!

* * * * *

Earl –

My first full-time pastorate was with the Woodbury congregation, immediately following my graduation from Bethany Theological Seminary in Chicago in 1954 until 1960. At age twenty-five, I came to the 700-member congregation (composed of three churches—Woodbury, Curryville, and Holsinger), having negotiated a whopping salary of $2,400 per year plus the parsonage. For medical coverage, the congregation paid two-thirds and I paid one-third, and the congregation also agreed to a pension contribution of 10% of my cash salary.

Each of the three churches had its *own* Board of Administration and Deacons, Youth Group, Women's Fellowship (which Vivian attended), summer Vacation Bible School, and Fall or Spring Revival Meeting (two weeks each). With a multiple pastorate like this, I had lots of experience condensed in the six years we served there. I not only delivered three sermons every Sunday morning, but also had three of everything else: choirs, special music, bulletins, Christian education programs, new member orientation classes, baptismal services, and a host of Sunday School classes. I also had triple the baby dedications, weddings and funerals that most pastors have with one congregation. It was good I was young ... and energetic. We sometimes marveled that a congregation this size had such faith to hire someone so young to be their spiritual shepherd. And I had no assistants ... except a part-time secretary!

* * * * *

Vivian –

The parsonage for the three churches in the Woodbury congregation was on the main street of the little town of Woodbury, in Bedford County, Pennsylvania, in the heart of the valley called "Morrison's Cove." The Woodbury and Curryville Churches were named for the towns in which they were located, and the Holsinger Church of the Brethren was in Baker's Summit. Although the preaching schedules shifted each week, a typical Sunday schedule was for worship to begin at Curryville with an early service at 9 a.m. Then Earl drove three miles to the Woodbury Church for a sermon there at 10 a.m. Finally, after a very fast drive over seven miles of curvy and hilly roads, he preached at the Holsinger Church at 11:15 a.m. In the month of December each year, our schedule would be downright crazy.

At that time, it was popular for every adult Sunday School class to have a Christmas party, and every class expected their pastor and his wife to attend. So, every December, in addition to the "usual" monthly meetings in each church, preaching, teaching, and occasional weddings and funerals, we attended as many of the parties as we could fit in our calendar and got various church members to baby-sit.

* * * * *

Earl –

During the first week that we were at Woodbury, I was driving home from making hospital calls in Altoona and Roaring Spring. Ever the optimist, I had ignored the gas-indicator gauge on our old Dodge until midway between Roaring Spring and Woodbury when my car sputtered and died. Looking around, I realized I was quite close to a farm owned by one of the Woodbury deacons, Paul Stayer, a member of the search committee. With confidence, I walked up the lane to the house and knocked on the door. No answer. Apparently, the Stayers were not at home.

With my farm background, I knew that most farms have their own gas tank, so I looked around, found it, discovered it to be unlocked, and also located an empty gas can. I proceeded to put a gallon or so of gas in the can and then started carrying it down the lane toward my car. Just when I had almost reached it, the Stayers came driving toward me, slowing down to turn into their lane.

Vivian and I have had many laughs through the years as we speculated about what they must have thought as they arrived

The Church of the Brethren in Curryville, Pennsylvania, 1954-1960.

home and caught their new pastor red-handed while "stealing" their gas during the first week he was there!

* * * * *

I was still twenty-five when I had my first funeral at Woodbury, that of a six-year-old girl who had attended our Vacation Bible School and who was simply walking on the sidewalk. As a drunk driver approached her, he lost control of his car and drove up on the sidewalk, killing her. Some tactless person who probably meant well said to the grieving mother, "It was God's will."

I have always felt that explanation was 100% wrong and would prefer to think it was a result of a wrong human choice.

* * * * *

My first wedding in the Woodbury parsonage occurred in December 1954, when a young couple from the Holsinger Church requested that I marry them. The groom, Elmer Lamborn, was in the military service and was only able to get a short three-day pass, so he and his bride, Mary Alice, decided against a church wedding, preferring to be married in the parsonage.

"We ought to make it really special for them," Vivian declared.

We tried to decide what to do. After much thought and discussion, we decided to buy a small throw-rug, and during the ceremony, the couple would stand and then kneel on that rug. Afterwards, we planned to give them the rug as a wedding gift.

On the day of the wedding, it was hard to tell who was most nervous—the couple or the pastor and his wife! They knocked on the door, and we invited them in. I directed them to our "altar area" and they stood on the little throw-rug. I went through the ceremony and all went well. They knelt on the rug for the wedding prayer and gave each other their

The Holsinger Church of the Brethren in Baker's Summit, Pennsylvania, 1954-1960.

first kiss as a married couple. Suddenly, I had an alarming thought. As nonchalantly as I could, I calmly asked Elmer, "Oh, by the way, did you bring your marriage license with you?"

Fortunately, they did and I was able to breathe easier. We gave them the rug and wished them well. (In 2004, they celebrated their fiftieth wedding anniversary, and they still have that rug!)

We often wondered what we would have done if they had not had their marriage license and the ceremony had already been completed!

* * * * *

Vivian –

In January 1955, the Woodbury Church of the Brethren was in the midst of a week of evangelistic meetings, and I was expecting our second baby any day. Rev. Hiram Gingrich from Annville, our guest evangelist, was staying all week in our parsonage guest room. Hosting him was easy because, except for breakfast, he was invited into congregational homes for his meals. Usually, Earl, as pastor and chauffeur, was included at lunch, and for the evening dinners, Karen, age 2, and I were also invited.

Although the week passed relatively uneventfully, two crises developing within the wider congregation were that a woman in the Curryville Church, Susie Sollenberger, was dying of throat cancer, and a Holsinger Church member, Dora Lamborn, was also dying of cancer.

About 3 a.m. Sunday morning I awakened feeling labor pains but they were somewhat sporadic. When it was about 4 a.m., the phone rang. It was the Sollenberger family requesting that Earl come immediately because Susie was close to death. Earl was torn as to what to do. However, he reasoned aloud, "The pains are far apart and you are not alone. If things start moving quickly, ask Hiram to take you to the Nason Hospital (in Roaring Spring—about five miles away).

He woke Hiram and warned him of the circumstances. Needless to say, Hiram got up immediately and got dressed . . . just in case. He paced nervously through our living room area, and I was sure he was praying and hoping with all his might that Earl would return soon. For his sake and for mine, I was doing the same!

About 6 a.m. Earl did return, for Susie had died. My pains were getting stronger, but I have always had a fear of going to the hospital too soon and being told to go home because what I was experiencing was "false" labor. This had happened to friends of mine, and I was determined that it would *not* happen to me.

Sunday School was scheduled to start at 9 a.m. About 7:30 we received another phone call. The Lamborn family called to say Dora was sinking fast and could Earl please come. Although my labor pains were intensifying, we decided that Earl would go and come back as soon as he could. Hiram would go to church by himself. Some neighbors, who were members of our church, offered to take Karen to Sunday School.

Earl came home in time to transport me to the hospital, but when we got there, I didn't want to go in. My pains were about five minutes apart, but I was still afraid of being sent home. We decided to walk around the hospital several times, hoping that this would induce the birth process. Since at that time fathers were not allowed in the delivery room anyway, Earl felt he wanted to return to the Woodbury Church for the morning worship service at 10:15. Just before 10 a.m., I agreed to be admitted.

Randall Earl was born at 12:55 p.m. with two inches of black hair all over his head. (By the time he was nine months old, his hair had become blond and remained so until it turned gray!) Earl came running in as soon as he could after the services at Woodbury and Curryville. I had news to share that he was a father for the second time, and this time it was a six-pound, five-ounce boy. Later, when he left the hospital and visited the Lamborn family, he discovered that Dora had died around the same time that Randy was born. That day was a vivid example of how God takes home His saints and brings new lives into the world.

* * * * *

Randy and I came home from the hospital and things went well . . . at first. When he was about a week old, he began to get diarrhea. I was nursing him, but he began spitting up everything he drank. We took him to Dr. Heaton, our family doctor, who said we should take him to the hospital immediately because he was dangerously dehydrated. Because of the seriousness of his illness, the doctor ordered me to stop nursing him. (Today they probably would *not* recommend that!)

The nurses told me that because he was used to being nursed, he refused the bottle at first. Consequently, they fed him intravenously. I stayed with him much of the time, and my aunt Mary, whose husband, Roy Forney, was pastor of the nearby Martinsburg Church of the Brethren, helped us by caring for Karen during that week. Randy slowly improved, and after about six days, we were able to bring him home. (Within the first ten days after Randy's birth, Earl had had two funerals, preached once at each of our three churches on the following Sunday, and we both had attended the wedding of Byron and Delma Over, at which Earl officiated.)

Randy now seemed like a different baby. When I had brought him home from the hospital the first time, he was a relaxed baby. After this hospital experience, he was tense. We counted 37 needle marks on his tiny body where he had received needles to be fed. I always felt he was tense because he was expecting us to "hurt" him, and that just made us want to cuddle and love him more!

* * * * *

As the pastor's wife and a busy young mother, I never accepted an office in the women's fellowship groups of either of the three churches we were serving. However, I did play an active role, attending and helping them plan their meetings. We would meet as a committee and make plans for the year ahead and assemble those plans into a little, attractive, purse-sized booklet.

Women's fellowship meetings were usually held in homes, but I would encourage them to meet at the church where there was more space. One woman countered, "But we don't *want* more women to come to our meetings. Then we couldn't meet in homes anymore!"

I could hardly believe my ears—that a Christian woman would say something like that!

* * * * *

Earl –

The Woodbury congregation was my guinea pig for trying new things. The first year went great, as they were eager for new leadership. The three-church parish was growing, with giving and attendance both up from the previous year. But we had one problem: as a family with two children, we were going farther and farther into debt. Our expenses exceeded our income each month. Because Vivian would write all our expenses in a record book, we could account for every nickel spent. She could not go to work outside the home because of our two small children and her role as a pastor's wife. That would have been totally unacceptable in 1954. Besides, we wanted to raise our own children. In addition, we tithed faithfully, and that was a conviction that would not be compromised.

Totally embarrassed and too proud to admit our financial situation, we stewed over it for several months. Clair Goodman, (not his real name), a progressive dairy farmer in Morrison's Cove, Bedford County, Pennsylvania, had been elected chair of the Ministry Commission and thus was my official boss to whom I was reportable. One day I finally swallowed my pride and stopped by farmer Clair's barn when he was milking and blurted out the reason for my coming. I concluded my story by saying, "I need a raise now, or I will have to look somewhere else for a church."

Clair looked me straight in the eye and with a contemplative but kind tone of voice, said, "Earl, maybe you and Vivian don't know how to manage."

I left that conversation in the barn boiling mad, hurt and humiliated.

The Lord dealt with my anger and chided me. "Have you ever heard of humility?" *Pride goeth before destruction, and a haughty spirit before a fall.* (Proverbs 16:18—KJV)

After a few days of stewing over my hurt and my blood pressure had become normal again, I took our record book of the year's income and expenses and dropped it off at Clair's house for him to peruse. One day later he called me and invited me to lunch at his house. He redeemed my spirit with these words: "Earl, I have checked your figures, and I want to tell you, you and Vivian are better financial managers than I am!"

After that, he promptly called a meeting of his board and they gave me $400 which amounted to a 17% raise.

God is good when we share our burdens in an open, honest way. Didn't Jesus advise us to "Ask and it will be given to you; seek and you will find; knock and the door will be opened to you. For everyone who asks receives; he who seeks finds; and to him who knocks, the door will be opened." (Matthew 7:7,8) *It is so hard at times to humble ourselves!* What a lesson to learn!

* * * * *

Vivian –

We began the family tradition of sending Christmas letters to our friends and relatives in 1956 and have been doing it every year since.

In December 1956, we wrote: "We are enjoying our work here at Woodbury very much. We've been here almost 2½ years so far. Earl preaches three times every Sunday, once in each of our three churches. I teach a Sunday School class of fifteen young couples, all married within the last two years. Meeting with the women's groups, youth groups, various Sunday School classes, committee meetings, and then practicing with the various music groups keeps us rather busy."

* * * * *

Earl –

At Woodbury, I was invited to write and teach a two-week sex education course to all tenth graders in the Northern Bedford School District. Two years later, when one of those tenth graders became the class valedictorian in his senior year and spoke at his commencement, he mentioned that one of his most helpful courses had been the one on sex education that I taught. It confirmed again the need for healthy, honest information for our youth.

* * * * *

Jesse Shoemaker was an old man with crippling arthritis. His gnarled hands and bent back spoke louder than words about the pain he endured almost constantly. Every Sunday he slowly made his way down the aisle of the Woodbury Church to his regular seat along the center aisle in the second pew from the front. During the sermon, he would watch me and listen attentively.

He was not wealthy, healthy or outstandingly gifted, but he was faithful in attending church and loved the Lord. He and his wife had worked hard and raised their family well. As a result, many of their children and grandchildren were also members of the church.

Often at the end of a morning worship service, he would approach me to shake hands with him as he left the sanctuary, and with tears in his eyes would say, "I wish I could have given a bigger offering this morning." Or, "I wish I could go and help that poor family." Then he would add, "But I am old, and now all I can do anymore is pray. Pastor, I am sitting in my pew praying for you from the beginning of the service until you say the benediction."

What a gift of encouragement for any pastor! Often as I was preaching, I would search for a word or feel uncertain, but when I would look down into Jesse's eyes, I would feel a surge of strength as a result of his prayers.

If we would make a gallery of the faithful as listed in Hebrews chapter eleven, of Christians we have known, Jesse's name would be near the top of the list!

* * * * *

In the 1950's, people still frequently invited guests to their home for dinner. Many times the pastor and his family were included. At that stage of our lives, we had several young children which sometimes complicated things as we had to contend with high chairs and booster seats.

Bob and Annie Hoover were members of the Woodbury Church and close to our age. Bob served as one of the church's volunteer organists, and they had one son, James.

One Sunday noon they invited us to dinner, and they served boiled potatoes, cooked dandelion, and a wonderful oyster casserole. Everything was delicious. When we were halfway through the meal, Annie sat back in her chair, heaved a great sigh while declaring, "You know, this is the first time I've ever had a preacher and his family in my home for a meal, and do you know what? *This isn't nearly as bad as I thought it would be!*"

YOUNG—AND STILL LEARNING
Chapter Five

> "Daddy, you still have an awful lot to learn about little children."
> *(Our daughter, Karen, age 5)*

Earl —

(From a personal letter I wrote in December 1957, while we were serving the Woodbury, Curryville, and Holsinger Churches):

"We've had about seven calls from other churches and every call becomes more attractive. The last delegation really made our people talk. One of my pastoral board members said to the board, 'If Earl is worth $5,000 to someone else, he is worth that much to us!'

"Things are going real well for us. Not to brag, but I believe I accomplish about as much in each of my three churches as some slow pastors do in a one-church situation. We have the highest Brotherhood Fund giving in the district, highest giving to the district fund. Last Sunday we had five hundred in Sunday School. All three churches are now remodeled. Still lots of work to do. I'm having a wedding Saturday and a baby dedication on Sunday. In one year I dedicated forty-three babies!

"I am trying to develop strong lay leadership in each of my churches. Sometimes I am almost exhausted at thinking of the responsibility. But the strange thing is that Vivian and I both enjoy it very much. We both feel so much in God's will and that's why we are really happy."

* * * * *

A quote from our December 1957, family Christmas letter:

"As many of you know, much of the compensation received in this profession is in the form of joy in seeing people grow in their spiritual lives. A few weeks ago we had such an experience. In 1951, the Curryville Church burned down, and in its place, they now have erected an $85,000 building. On November 24, they had a mortgage burning service. Prior to that, there was a remaining debt of $800. We announced that sum as our goal for an offering which was to be received November 17.

"A deacon's wife derided me saying, 'You think our church is made of money. Someone will have a red face on the 24th, and it will be you! We'll never get $800.'

"I simply asked them to give 'as the Lord directed.'

"The offering went above all expectations reaching $2,100. To us that was a *real thrill*—and to the church as well."

* * * * *

Vivian –
In seminary, we were warned to *not* make close friends in the congregations we would serve. Our goal was to have people

want to worship and serve *the Lord*, not to become followers of *us*! Examples were cited of congregations which had grown under the ministry of a popular pastor, but when he left, the church fell apart. Most of the time we did a good job of this, being open and friendly, but not close.

However, we had one exception at Woodbury. Bob and Ruth Guyer lived about a block from us and had two children, Rodney and Ryan, the same ages, within weeks, of our Karen and Randy. Bob was an electrician, energetic, fun-loving, and a sincere Christian worker in the church. Earl and Bob would love to get together and banter about church work, politics, pastors' salaries, and almost any subject. As young mothers, Ruth and I had similar interests and frustrations, and we enjoyed sharing with one another. When the four of us were together, there was always lots of laughter.

In March 1957, Ruth and I were both pregnant and expecting our third babies at about the same time. On a Friday night, a church committee met in our parsonage living room and Bob was one of the members. Before the meeting started, I was in the kitchen ironing. Bob came out to heckle me.

"Why are you doing that ironing tonight?" he asked with a twinkle in his eye.

"Because I might not be able to do it tomorrow! I might be in the hospital," I answered.

"Aw, there's nothing the matter with you," he retorted. "You aren't going to have that baby for a week or two yet."

And we both laughed. He knew full well that when a woman's due date was approaching, what she *didn't* want to hear were words hinting that she would be pregnant two weeks *longer*!

That same night I did go to the hospital, and just before midnight on March 15, 1957, Doreen Kay was born, weighing in at 8 lbs. 14 oz. At that time, maternity wards had up to four beds in them, and Ruth and I had joked that wouldn't it be great if we would end up in the same room.

The next evening, Ruth came into the hospital and just after midnight, her daughter, Risa, was born on March 17. Although our daughters were born only about 25 hours apart, their birthdays are two days apart! But we *did* get to share the same hospital room.

(Two years later the Guyers' son, Robert or "Bobby" was born, and on September 30, 1959, we had our son, Michael Wayne—so each couple had four children, all close to the same ages. Unfortunately, when she was in her late 30's, Ruth died very suddenly of an aneurysm in the brain.)

* * * * *

Vivian –

From the beginning, we decided that Karen and I and any future children would attend Sunday School and morning worship at the Woodbury Church which was the closest of our three churches to our home. Although I would go to the other two congregations for special services, class parties and various programs, we felt the children needed the stability of being in the same class every Sunday. This plan also gave me the opportunity to teach my own age group, the young married class, at Woodbury. Since we owned only one car, our kind neighbors, Ed and Roxy Over, provided transportation for the children and me to and from church.

By the time Doreen was born in March 1957, I had Karen, 4, Randy, 2, and a newborn to get ready by myself every Sunday morning so we would be ready to go out the door when Ed and Roxy arrived. Earl usually left an hour earlier.

Sometimes, when he was almost ready to go out the door, Earl would say, "I feel like my sermon this morning needs another 'window' in it. Can you think of an illustration about forgiveness (or whatever his theme was that day)?"

"If you would have asked me earlier, say on Thursday or Friday, I might have had time to look for one, but I don't have stories stored in my head, ready for telling at a moment's notice," I would say. Then I would feel bad because I couldn't help him.

One day I got an idea. In my reading, whether it was from a newspaper, magazine, book, or whatever, if I came across a good sermon illustration, quote or poem, I would clip it. Then I pasted it on a 4x6 card and on the upper left corner wrote the single word that it illustrated, such as "FORGIVENESS," "MONEY," "MARRIAGE," "FAITH," "LIGHT," "DOORS," "PEACE," etc. If I found a second or third item about that same subject, I would clip it and continue pasting it on that card until the card was filled.

At first, I did this when Earl was not around, and that next Christmas, my gift to him was about one hundred or more cards on numerous subjects wrapped in a rubber band. He *loved* that gift!

So, each year since then, I've given him another pack of cards and interfiled them alphabetically with the ones he already had. In the beginning, we kept them in a shoe box, but like Topsy, the collection grew, and we put the cards in 4x6 file drawers. Today we have nine drawers *full* and will soon need our tenth! Both of us have found this to be an invaluable resource and neither of us ever preaches a sermon or teaches a class without perusing those drawers. We would heartily recommend this simple practice of clipping and pasting to other pastors and teachers, as we know how helpful it has been to us.

* * * * *

Earl –

Melvin and Lucille Brumbaugh, an average couple in their early thirties, and members of the Woodbury Church, had been blessed with seven children, ages two through twelve. At their invitation, I shared a meal with them around the supper table. What a happy family they seemed to be!

However, I noted that the conversation around the table was lively among the children and their mother, but father Melvin was always very quiet. He never had much to say outside the home either.

One September Saturday, late in the evening, I got a phone call from Lucille. "Pastor Earl, I'm worried about Melvin. He hasn't come in for supper. I don't know where he is. What should I do?"

After a few minutes on the phone with her and clarifying some facts, I responded, "Please don't do anything out of the ordinary or you may frighten him." I was thinking that Melvin may be feeling ill and be somewhere close by.

I immediately drove to the Brumbaugh home and stayed with Lucille while she called two of her sisters to come and stay with her and the children all night.

Early on Sunday morning, it was evident that something was drastically wrong as Melvin still had not returned. He had simply disappeared. After a quick consultation with the deacon board, the Woodbury Church services were cancelled, and many of the members gathered at the church to pray and then go on search parties in the Woodbury Barrons, a small mountainous area behind the town in which the Brumbaughs lived. Search parties spread out in every direction. As word spread, the people in this small central Pennsylvania town came walking and driving to volunteer to search for one of their own, a neighbor and friend. All day was spent searching, but no trace of Melvin was found.

That next week, church and community search parties combed a wider area looking for Melvin. Could he have gotten confused and lost? Might he have had a mental breakdown? Or did he simply desert his family, choosing to be an absent father? None of these possibilities fit the character of Melvin.

For one month, people in groups or as individuals, went looking in out-of-the-way places for the missing father. Meanwhile, some protection was provided around the clock for Lucille and her children by family and church members.

About two months later, early in the deer hunting season, a member of the Holsinger Church of the Brethren was out hunting on a cold, snowy morning on the other side of the mountain and came upon a human figure resting against a tree with a hunting rifle lying beside him. He called the game warden who then contacted the state police. Upon investigation and identification, we knew that Melvin had been finally found. Apparently, in a moment of despondent, distraught or deranged thinking, he had ended his life.

The church rallied around his widow and children and supported them in every way for the next year or two. It was my first brush with suicide as a young twenty-six-year-old pastor. Although the climax of this missing person's case was tragic and difficult, it gave closure and peace to the family for they now knew where Melvin was.

Some mysteries are never solved but seem locked up with the key thrown away.

This was one of them.

* * * * *

Vivian –

While we were at Woodbury, we learned to know Rev. Ordo and Peg Pletcher who were pastoring the Leamersville Church of the Brethren. The Pletchers had three boys, Randy, Trent and Reid, all of whom later became very active in education as teachers and principals, but who, at that time, were in elementary and junior high school. Our daughter, Karen, was about eighteen months old when we came to Woodbury and we had three more children born during our six-year tenure there, so they were all quite young.

Once in a while, Earl and I would have business or want to do some shopping in Altoona, the closest "big" city. To get there, we passed through Leamersville. When Peg discovered this, she offered to baby-sit for us, and occasionally we accepted her offer.

When we came back to pick up the children, she almost always had her table set and a meal ready to eat. What a help that was to a young, busy, and tired mother! In addition to our verbal thanks, Earl sometimes surreptitiously would place a monetary "tip" under his water glass or plate. Peg, who had a great sense of humor, would always enjoy a big laugh about that.

One summer, probably about 1957, Earl and Ordo were co-directors of a week-long junior high camp at Camp Harmony in Western Pennsylvania. The camp manager was Peg's brother, so Peg went along as camp nurse, and the Pletcher boys were campers. Our three children (at that time) and I also went to camp that week so they could be close to their daddy and have the experience of living in the woods. Sometimes, Randy, at two and one-half years old would be placed in our portable playpen to corral his activities and at other times I would place our five-month-old Doreen, in it to keep her safe. We ate our meals in the dining room with the campers.

Both Ordo and Earl were creative, "out-of-the-box" thinkers, so their camp was full of unusual happenings. On one occasion, they planned to teach the story of Elijah confronting the prophets of Baal (1 Kings 18:16-40). In the dining room, the largest indoor gathering place at the camp, they created a small stone "altar" and placed a few dry twigs on top of it. Ordo ran a wire from the ceiling to the altar and somehow planned to run a flame of fire along that wire so it would appear that the fire had descended from "heaven" to ignite the offering on the altar. However, his plan went askew, and in their attempt, they almost set fire to the dining hall!

Although it was a serious scare at the time, we have had many laughs with the Pletchers since then when recalling that incident.

* * * * *

From our 1958 Christmas letter:

"Other happenings in 1958 included: Earl learned to water ski this summer . . . Vivian played the organ for a wedding for the first time . . . We ate our first "smorgasbord" meal . . . Earl was elected Middle Pennsylvania District Moderator for 1959 and also elected to serve on Standing Committee . . . Vivian's Christmas gift was a Maytag dryer, and how she loved that, especially on zero degree days . . . Karen started first grade . . . and Earl moved his study out of the parsonage on New Year's Day, 1959, into the new $55,000 education wing of the Woodbury Church."

* * * * *

Our next door neighbors at Woodbury were a quiet Mennonite couple, Mark and Mary Stauffer and their little daughter,

Gail. Mechanically, Mark was a genius, and he had his own welding shop on the other side of his house. Mary was sickly, and in about our second year there, she died.

As a widower, Mark was extremely lonely, and often called late at night asking Earl to come over just to talk. Gail was a gifted child, an excellent pianist, and a girl who needed a mother.

Mark met Dorothy Hershey, a Mennonite from Paradise, Lancaster County, and one winter weekend decided he would go east to visit her. He asked Earl if he would check his house and furnace while he was gone, and Earl was glad to do it for him.

To everyone's surprise, Pennsylvania was hit with a huge snowstorm that weekend. Travel was virtually impossible for several days so Mark called to tell Earl he would not be back when he had anticipated. He asked, "Would you please continue checking my house and furnace for several more days?"

Earl answered, "Sure, that will be no trouble at all, but I have one bit of advice for you, Mark. *Be sure you make hay while the sun shines!*"

Mark's answer was just a hearty laugh.

He must have done it, too, because on November 15, 1958, they were married in the Paradise Mennonite Church, and Earl served as Mark's best man at the wedding.

We soon discovered that Dorothy and I shared many similar interests in crafts, music, gardening and reading and that she was an excellent cook with one of her specialties being cinnamon buns. Often late at night we would get together with them and enjoy fresh-from-the-oven cinnamon buns, coffee, and interesting discussions. They always knew when the visit was over because Earl fell asleep promptly at 11 p.m. no matter where he was!

* * * * *

Earl –

The Woodbury parsonage was a two-story, solid brick structure with four bedrooms, one of which was a guest room, and one bathroom. In the basement was the original coal furnace which had a mind of its own and was very inefficient at heating the house. On the coldest winter nights, I'd have to get up in the wee hours of the morning to put in more coal or the fire would go out before morning. We were sure the congregation wasn't aware of this problem, but we didn't want to complain.

One winter, the Woodbury Church had a two-week revival with Rev. Wilmer Petry from Ohio as the evangelist. It was expected that visiting speakers would always stay in the parsonage guest room. Rev. Petry, who was probably in his late 50's or early 60's, had a crippled leg, walked with a cane, and had a very outgoing personality. We discovered quickly that he was *not* shy!

When he came down for breakfast on the second morning of his stay, he began asking me questions about the heating system of our house. He had heard me get up in the middle of the night to tend the furnace and asked what was being done about this situation.

"Well, nothing," I admitted red-facedly, adding this weak explanation, "we don't want the church to think we're complainers."

"Complainers?" he practically shouted. "With your young children, this is a health issue! With your busy schedule, you should not be plagued with waking up and tending your furnace at night! My crippled leg has been aching because of the cold these last two nights, and I am going to talk to someone at church tonight about this. This can't go on this way!"

And he did!

Within a matter of weeks, a new oil furnace was installed.

When Rev. Petry returned to Ohio, he left behind one very grateful parsonage family.

* * * * *

Vivian –

Karen, 5, and Randy, 3, shared the same bedroom, sleeping in bunk beds. One night Karen frightened the household by waking up from a nightmare screaming . . . and then she had to go to the bathroom. Because of her loud outburst, Randy also was awakened and became quite frightened.

While Earl was supervising her climb as she returned to her top bunk, he calmly suggested she should try to not holler so loud next time. Settling down again under her covers, she lifted her head and gave these words of advice: *"Daddy, you still have an awful lot to learn about little children."*

* * * * *

Earl –

The climate and unity in all three churches in the Woodbury congregation was at an all-time high. Preaching three times on a Sunday morning had been a heavy schedule and so, by age 32, I was exhausted, . . . but not too exhausted . . . because three children were born during those same six years!

Without my knowledge, one Sunday in August 1959, a search committee from the Black Rock Church of the Brethren in York County, Pennsylvania, had attended the worship service at the Curryville Church to hear me preach. The three men, Stanley Baugher, John Runk, and Russell Royer, came into the church at three different times and sat in three different locations to be as unnoticed as possible. I never suspected a thing, and neither did the Curryville folk. After lunch that same day, a knock at the parsonage door unveiled the mystery of their purpose for being in the community. When the Woodbury congregation later received my resignation notice, one of the deacon's wives approached and asked if I had been in cahoots with those men. When I said I was oblivious to their purpose, she responded angrily, "I would like to wring their necks!"

I had proposed that the Woodbury Church and the Curryville Church become a two-church yoked parish since the members lived among each other and the church buildings were only three miles apart. The Holsinger Church could have yoked with the Claysburg congregation nearby. As discussions pursued these suggestions, I quickly realized that the focus narrowed to "who will get to keep Earl," and so, for the sake of unity and harmony, we tendered our resignation.

After some heart-rending and difficult decisions, Vivian and I chose to accept the invitation from the Black Rock Church of about 450 members to become their pastor. We moved into their brand new parsonage ten miles south of Hanover and began our ministry as their first full-time pastor on April 1, 1960.

* * * * *

Vivian –

The night before we moved from Woodbury, a group of people from Curryville (Warren and Hazel Bush, Warren and Mary Frederick, Vernon and Estella Stayer, Glenn and Tina Bechtel, Wilmer and Martha Harnish, and Ben and Florence Blattenberger) came to our parsonage bringing food for a farewell party. We had a bittersweet time together, enjoying each other but knowing that after the next morning, our relationship would never be the same again.

On the day of our move, Iola Russell from the Woodbury Church stopped by with a delicious chocolate cake to take with us. Charles and Dolores Hershberger, also from Woodbury, came with a gift of a milk glass vase and candlestick set "just so we would remember them," so typical of the many wonderful friends we were leaving behind in Morrison's Cove.

We had arranged with our neighbors, Mark and Dorothy Stauffer, that they would keep the three older children on the day of our move and bring them down to us on the weekend. Mike at six months was still being nursed, so we took him with us.

On the evening of moving day we got a phone call from Dorothy. As she was keeping the children that day, Randy had found a paper punch and put it in his mouth. Soon he called her because he couldn't get it out! Frantically, she tried and tried to help him, and when she finally got it out, two teeth came along with it! She was so apologetic. Since they were baby teeth, it wasn't a big deal to us, but she felt bad about it for years afterward.

*****

Earl –

Living between the mountains in Morrison's Cove had been a wonderful place to live for six years and begin raising a family. In fact, Bedford County boasted more Church of the Brethren members than attended any other protestant denomination. When we left there on March 31, 1960, we took much of Morrison's Cove with us in our hearts and memories. A new chapter in our lives was about to unfold.

SCARED OUT OF OUR "MITTS"
Chapter Six

"Memories and mistakes should be guideposts, not hitching posts."
(Paul Powers)

How would *you* answer this question: "What were the most frightening moments of your lifetime? Here are a few of the incidents that would be on *our* list:

Vivian –

In my senior year at Elizabethtown College, I was elected to be editor of the 1951 *Conestogan*, the college yearbook. This required much after-hours work, and sometimes my assistant editor, John Dean, and I worked at layout, captions and such until very late. Since I didn't live on campus, when we finished working, I walked to the end of College Avenue to catch the last bus going to Lancaster at 11 p.m., get off at Florin, and walk about three-fourth mile to my home at Fairview Orchards.

One night I walked to the bus stop suspecting that I might be a bit late. However, I optimistically thought that the bus must be at the west end of Elizabethtown turning around, and then would soon be coming for its final run to Lancaster. I was so sure it would come that I had no "plan B."

After waiting at least a half hour, I was beginning to realize that I actually had missed the bus. What was I going to do?

Just then, a car pulled up in front of me. In it were two young guys. The one I could see, the one sitting on the passenger side, resembled a fellow who was in some of my college classes. I didn't know him well, but I knew his name. He started talking to me and asked why I was waiting there along the street. I explained that I was waiting for the bus and I bluffed, "I'm sure it is just at the other end of town and will be coming soon."

"We just came through that area, and the bus is not there. You've missed it. How are you going to get home?"

"Well, I don't know," I confessed honestly.

"Come on, hop in our car, and we'll take you home," he suggested as he got out of the car and held the door open.

What was I going to do? I slid into the center of the front seat and immediately smelled a combination of alcohol and tobacco emanating from the driver, whom I did not know, and as I did that, I also realized that the man to whom I had been talking was also a total stranger. He was not the college student that I thought he was. He just looked like him.

Now I realized I was in a real dilemma. My mind flashed to a prominent story in the news that year. A man named Edward Gibbs had picked up a young woman on the Franklin and Marshall College campus in Lancaster, Pennsylvania, and taken her to some remote cabin and murdered her. From all appearances, it seemed that she had voluntarily accepted a ride with him. With those thoughts, I breathed a silent prayer for my safety.

These guys said they were working in Marietta and they asked if I knew other girls who might be interested in dating them.

I fed them a line, some truth and some fiction, and hoped we would soon get to my home. As we got closer, I realized that I had put my whole family in a vulnerable position. If these men realized that there was no "man of the house" in my home, they might attempt to rob us or even return at another time to burglarize our house.

They pulled up to the front of the house which was darkened, except for the porch light, which Mother always left on as long as someone was still not home. I was afraid they wouldn't let me out because I was sitting between them. However, when I promised I would bring another girl the next night and we would meet them at the same spot where they had picked me up, they allowed me to go into the house, and drove away. Of course, I had no intention of meeting them again.

The next day I was a troubled girl. My worry was, if I didn't show up, they could come looking for me because they knew where I lived. So, I confided in Glenn Forney, another college student, whose parents were friends of my mother's, and who was like a brother to me. We decided to park on College Avenue about a half block from the bus stop and watch to see if two guys ever came and stopped there. The time came when I was to meet them, and time moved on. Thankfully, they never showed up. To my knowledge, they never came back to my house either. I still shudder to think of all that *could* have happened.

Once again, after I had done something really stupid, God had answered my prayers and rescued me. Praise His Name!

* * * * *

At Woodbury, in our upstairs bedroom, Earl and I slept on an old double bed. I have always enjoyed reading in bed, so we had a clip-on bed lamp fastened on the top of our oval headboard.

If the lamp got off-center, occasionally it would slide down the side of the metal headboard to the bed.

In late morning one day when Earl was at his office at the church and I was home with the children, I went upstairs and smelled smoke. I followed the scent to our bedroom, and to my horror, the smoke and even flames were coming from our bed. The lamp was still on and had slid down to the bed. The lighted bulb created enough heat to actually start a fire in our bedding and mattress.

In my panic, I did an admittedly stupid thing. I ran to the bathroom next door, filled a cup with water, and brought it to the bed and threw the water on the fire. This small amount of water had virtually no effect, so I got a second cupful of water and threw it on the fire. Again, it had no effect.

Suddenly, I realized how futile and inadequate my actions were and I needed to do something more. I opened the window, threw out the burning bed clothes and then, powered by adrenaline, folded up the mattress and managed to throw it out the window onto our side yard. All the smoke and flames were then gone from the house. Even though I doused it thoroughly in the yard with water from a hose, the fire was deep in the mattress and smoldered for a long time before it finally was extinguished. (By the way, we were so poor at that time that we couldn't afford to buy a new mattress, so when the mattress finally dried out, we stuffed the hole with lots of rags and an old coat or two and continued to sleep on it.)

I felt that was quite a close call, and our house, the church's parsonage, could so easily have been destroyed by fire. In spite of our mistakes, God is gracious and comes through every time!

* * * * *

Earl –

A teenaged boy, whom I will call Calvin, (not his real name), came from an unchurched home and began attending the Black Rock Church of the Brethren's youth activities. Although we knew little about him, we were pleased to see his interest and we welcomed him.

About 3 a.m. the morning after an Easter Sunday, our phone rang and I answered, still groggy from sleep. I awakened quickly when I heard Calvin's frightened voice say, "Pastor Ziegler, someone just shot my dad. Can you come over to our house?"

"I'll be there," I promised.

Out of fear, I promptly dialed Dr. Wilbur Foard, our family doctor, who agreed to meet me at the end of the lane leading to the farmhouse where Calvin lived as soon as we could get dressed and drive there. He, in turn, also alerted the police.

The doctor and I met as planned and approached the house on foot. Calvin met us at the door, and pointed to his father, lying unconscious on the floor. "Who shot him?" we asked.

"I don't know," the distraught boy sobbed, adding, "I didn't see anyone. The shot woke me up, and when I came down to the kitchen, he was lying here like this."

When the doctor examined him, he determined that the shot was not fatal, but an ambulance took the injured dad and Dr. Foard to the hospital, letting me alone with the four children. I stayed in the kitchen with Calvin and his three younger siblings who also had been awakened by the commotion. All the doors were locked, and we huddled together in the safety of the kitchen because there was a possibility that the shooter, whoever he was, could return or even still be nearby.

After what seemed like a long, long time, the state police arrived. After questioning Calvin, the police began a thorough search of the barn and surrounding sheds. Dawn was breaking when the police returned after an unsuccessful search. "Did you check the house?" they asked. Calvin and I looked at each other questioningly and I responded, "No, we've just been right here in the kitchen." "Perhaps, before we leave, we should just look around in here," the police decided. "After all, it appears that the shooting happened in here."

So, they began going around, looking in closets, opening doors, and searching everywhere. One of them opened a door from the kitchen that led to a stairway to the basement. He went down the steps and yelled excitedly, "I found him."

Lying on the floor down there was a man, asleep in a drunken stupor. Further investigation proved that he *was* the shooter, and during the whole time that the police had searched the premises outside, the children, Calvin, and I had been locked in the house with him!

* * * * *

Vivian –

At Black Rock a mouse was caught in a trap in our attic. When Karen, 9, and Randy, 7, brought it downstairs to throw it out, they first came running toward me holding it by its tail and waving it in the air. Naturally, I screamed!

Later, Doreen, 5, observed, "Mommie, when you saw that mouse, you were nearly scared out of your *mitts*, weren't you?"

* * * * *

Earl –

One winter night in the 1960's, while we lived in the Black Rock parsonage, we were awakened by a knock on the door about 2 a.m. I quickly put on a robe to answer it, and there was a woman dressed in a coat. She explained that she had been riding in a car with her boyfriend who had been drinking. A fight had ensued, and he stopped the car momentarily, pushed her out the door, and then drove on. Would I please take her home?

Not thinking of any other alternative, I went back to our bedroom and quickly got dressed.

As I helped the woman get in my car, I noticed that she was wearing nothing underneath her coat. All the way to her home, I prayed that nothing would happen, because I could imagine the headlines if we would get in an accident or be stopped by the police: "Local Pastor Discovered with Naked Woman!"

When we got there safely, she got out, thanked me, and I returned home.

We never saw or heard from her again.

* * * * *

Vivian –

In July 1965, Earl was invited by the National Headquarters of the Church of the Brethren at Elgin, Illinois, to host a tour group to visit the mission work in Ecuador. Before that, members of the national denominational staff had always been chosen to be tour group leaders. Someone had questioned: Why not send a pastor so he could see missions at work first-hand and come home and share his enthusiasm with his local congregation? Others agreed, and Earl was fortunate to be the first pastor selected.

When he asked the Black Rock congregation for permission to go, they not only gave their permission, but they said such an experience should be shared, so they offered to send me with Earl. Since our four children were ages 6, 8, 10, and 12 at that time, we were living on a very tight budget. We felt that the offer from Elgin and the generosity of the Black Rock Church were a clear direction from God for us to take the "trip of our lifetime."

For each of us, going to Ecuador was our first commercial airplane flight. Fortunately, it was a fairly smooth one, and my greatest anxiety was experienced at our landing in Quito. As the plane approached the runway, we literally flew between the mountains. For a first-time flyer, looking out of the windows and seeing mountains close to us on *both* sides, combined with the usual "bumpiness" of descending through the clouds and encountering air pockets, made our landing rather frightening.

After visiting the various mission projects, enjoying a potluck meal with John and Theresa Herr, Merle and Jean Crouse, Dr. John and Estella Horning and others, our tour group visited mountainous Indian villages including a Quechua Indian market, experiencing the uneasiness of being the only Caucasians among several hundred natives. We rode a train to the tropical city of Guayaquil, where we saw our first banana trees and coffee bushes, and where a tour member who had propped his elbow on an open bus window, had a passing-by thief grab his watch from his arm and run away with it.

In a remote jungle area, we crossed a river on a crude pulley apparatus and climbed a muddy bank to visit the village of a very primitive Indian tribe and its witch doctor. I had trouble climbing the steep and slippery slope until a male indigenous tribe member, wearing only a loin cloth, saw my difficulty and offered a helping brown hand which I gladly accepted.

We stayed in a hotel on the square in Quito and had a front-row window view of the "Cinco de Mayo" procession of masses of people singing, waving tree branches and carrying a statue of the Virgin Mary from a suburban village into a church which was almost next door to us. On this, our first overseas trip, we saw breathtaking scenery, were awed by cultural and economic differences, rejoiced and were inspired by the progress of missionary efforts, and accumulated precious memories.

One unforgettable moment occurred in the lobby of our hotel where we met Mrs. Marjorie Saint and Mrs. Yudarin, two of the widows of the five martyred missionaries to Ecuador about ten years earlier. They had just returned three weeks before from witnessing the baptism of Kathy Saint, sixteen, and her fourteen-year-old brother, Steve, by the same Auca Indian who had killed their father. The baptizer had become a Christian and was a leader in the Auca community. Steve and Kathy wanted to be baptized in the Cururai River where their father had been killed. What a testimony and gripping story they told!

We will never forget Marjorie Saint's words when she said that sometimes people summarized the aborted mission of the five missionaries by saying that they had failed. She disagreed with that appraisal, and affirmed convincingly, "These men *succeeded*—not in reaching the Auca Indians for Christ, but in doing God's will."

While flying home, we were aboard an Ecuadorian Airline four-engine plane from Quito to Miami, with a short stop in Cali, Columbia. The flight was uneventful until we approached Cuba. As many passengers were finishing dinner and the stewardesses were serving coffee, we suddenly hit violent turbulence. The plane was shaken and tossed about like a cork on the ocean, and at one point, it dropped about 4,000 feet or 2/3 of a mile. (We were told this later.) In the ensuing chaos, people were screaming, children were crying, food trays were thrown into the aisles, and hot coffee was spilled everywhere. One person had a heart attack and several people were scalded by their coffee. The stewardesses were overwhelmed. One woman, several rows back from us, got up to help, explaining that she was a stewardess on another airline.

When we reached Miami a short time later, passengers were asked to remain in their seats until they were able to transport the heart attack victim and the scalded persons to waiting ambulances. During this lull, the "volunteer" stewardess told us she thought at first that we had lost a wing since we had dropped so far so suddenly. Fortunately, she had been wrong, but we thanked God that He brought us back on solid ground safely.

From that time on, I have never enjoyed flying, and turbulence terrifies me . . . but Earl can sleep through it all!

* * * * *

Earl –

"Biggy" was an appropriate nickname for this strapping big six-foot-one-inch broad-shouldered, 285-pound hunk of a man. A gem when he was sober, after he had a few drinks, he was a bear! And he was drinking most of the time.

His wife, at her wit's end from unpaid bills, six children, and being emotionally abused, came to my office to talk. During his rampages, she often found refuge at her parents' place. Occasionally, in his sober moments, he would stop by and talk with me also. He always said, "You are one person with whom I can talk. I need help!" His visits with me always gave her yet another false hope. In spite of everything, she loved him, but the countdown of a successful relationship with him was close to zero.

One evening he came home drunk. In fear, all the children scattered, leaving only his wife to soak up the brunt of his drunken brawl. "Biggy," she yelled, "I can't take it anymore. You've *got* to get help, or I'm leaving!"

He cursed, invoking my name, and threatened to kill me, according to his wife's report. Indeed, he left the house, went to a bar, and called me on the telephone, angrily declaring, "I'm going to kill you," and hung up.

At noon the next day I was sitting in my church office when I saw Biggy drive up and knock on the door of the parsonage located across the parking lot. Fortunately, that day the children were all in school, and Vivian was substitute teaching.

He wheeled around and headed for the church office. Instantly, my blood pressure rose because there was only one door to the office, and I knew when he got there, I'd be trapped. I could have run and hid, but instead I prayed as Biggy approached. If he had a gun, it was not visible. I prayed again, "Lord, save me from this man. Please, Lord, perform a miracle."

Biggy knocked on my office door. Slowly, I went to the door, prayed again and opened it and there he stood. It was a rendezvous between Goliath and David. I looked him in the eye, and he started to cry. I invited him in and offered to pray with him. We both got on our knees together in prayer. He was asking for help, and I was thanking God for a sober Biggy.

After an hour and one-half, he went home to his family. For several months, he brought his family to church, but the power of the drinking habit eventually overcame him. The tragic result of his lifestyle was that this father of six died young.

* * * * *

Alberta Mauer was a lady in her seventies who loved to travel. When she heard we were planning a trip to Africa in 1974, she sent in her reservation immediately with a note saying that a lifetime goal for her had always been to see Victoria Falls, named by the Scottish explorer and missionary, David Livingstone. She was so excited.

When we got to Zambia, we went to view the Zambezi River and its world-famous mile-wide Falls with heights varying from 250 to 360 feet, over 100 feet higher than Niagara Falls. Noticeably absent were any guardrails or fences at the top of the cliff-like walls that lined the deep gorge where the Zambezi River flowed. The constant high splashing of the Falls resulted in a fine mist falling constantly in the area, almost like rain in reverse. Because of this, we were given rubber raincoats to wear and were warned to watch our step because the ground tended to be slightly slippery. We gathered around our attractive female Zambian guide, nattily dressed in a bright red suit, as she stood facing us with her back to the Falls and made her explanations about the Fall's history and features.

Alberta was almost deaf, and between that fact and the guide's accent, couldn't understand anything that was being said. She wandered over to the very edge of the chasm to look and listen. A nurse in our group, Florence List, watched her and called, "Alberta, aren't you getting too close?"

Alberta didn't hear the question but she did hear her name and turned around to have the question repeated. However, she was so close to the edge that when she turned around, one foot got off the edge, and she fell down, head first and backwards.

I was nearby and was the first to make a move. I had noticed a small stunted-looking tree near the spot and quickly put one arm around the tree and grabbed Alberta's foot with the other. A big, husky stranger came over, surveyed the situation with a glance and exclaimed loudly, "Oh, my God! Oh, my God!" But he didn't lift a finger to help! However, others in the group quickly came to her rescue and together we managed to pull Alberta back up.

After she was safely on solid ground, I looked down from the spot where she had fallen and noticed a small cactus plant growing out of a crevice in the cliff. Although it was small, it was precisely located and just big enough to stop her fall momentarily until others could help her. Although she was disheveled and understandably shook up, we were even able to retrieve her glasses and wig!

That evening, the whole group returned to that spot while colored lights enhanced the beauty of the Falls. After the sobering events of the day and the realization of what *could* have happened, we sang together *"How Great Thou Art"* with voices full of emotion. There were few dry eyes. I held Alberta's hand tightly, and she retired early after her nearly fatal fall.

The next morning I took her by the arm and together she and I went to see Victoria Falls in the daylight, fulfilling her lifelong dream.

About a month after our return home from that trip, Alberta sent the Mechanic Grove Church a note and a gift of $100 in appreciation for their pastor having saved her life.

This experience has helped me to understand and believe the story of Jonah in the Bible. If God could provide a small cactus, just big enough and in the precise spot to break Alberta's fall long enough for someone to rescue her, it is also very believable that God could provide a fish, big enough, and in the very spot in the sea where Jonah fell, so that ultimately he could be saved from death.

* * * * *

In the Quarryville community in the 1970's, there were three brothers who were bullies and discipline problems in the schools. Consequently, they dropped out of school, either by expulsion or by their own decision.

The oldest, Jerry, (not his real name), was very intelligent, very tough, and about six feet tall. He began dating seriously one of the girls who attended the Mechanic Grove Church. Knowing his reputation, her parents consulted with me and asked me to have a talk with their daughter. A meeting was arranged, and in our discussion I pointed out the hazards of dating a troubled youth, with a different background and values. The result was that the girl decided to break up with him.

Jerry was furious. He blamed me for the break-up. On a Saturday night after doing some drinking, he phoned the parsonage at 2 a.m. and told me in no uncertain terms what he thought. He ended his tirade with a threat: "The next time I see you, I will kill you." Then he hung up, and I locked every door in our house.

The next morning, when I went to place my sermon notes on the pulpit before the service began, I discovered a note which said, "Preach the Word. I'm listening!" It was unsigned, and I was puzzled. I looked up and there sat Jerry in the sixth pew. A chill went through me as I recalled his threat from earlier that morning. It suddenly occurred to me that Jerry was probably the one who had written the note and placed it on the pulpit so that I would see it.

Quickly, during the hymn, I breathed a prayer for Jerry and for my own protection, and then stood up to preach the sermon I had prepared. At the end I gave an altar call, and to my amazement, Jerry came forward. At first, the thought that went through my head was—"Is Jerry coming forward to stab me here in front of the whole congregation?" However, I dispelled that thought quickly and approached Jerry with open arms, giving him a big hug, and welcoming him into the family of God as a brother. It was a scary experience for me, but out of it, God performed a miracle.

Jerry's conversion was genuine. He continued to attend church and even taught youth Sunday School classes sometimes. His Christian journey was a bumpy ride with an occasional backslide to his old habits.

On one occasion, he was arrested for a drinking violation and placed in the psychiatric ward. I went to visit him, and when I was about to leave, I gave him a big hug. Jerry started to cry. I asked him what was wrong, and he said, "You are the only person who has ever hugged me."

In amazement, I asked, "Didn't your dad ever hug you when you were little?"

"No," Jerry sobbed. "He never had time for me and my brothers. We seldom saw him. He only came around now and then and made our mom pregnant, and then he was gone again."

What an illustration of how *a parent's neglect often results in delinquent sons.*

* * * * *

Vivian –

On July 17, 1979, when faced with a free afternoon in Anchorage, Alaska, I decided to go shopping in a mini-mall which had been built over a train station. While browsing in a small gift shop, I suddenly felt the floor vibrate. I thought that probably a train had come into the station below. However, another potential customer asked the clerk, "Was that an earthquake?"

She looked at the wall where a number of art works were hanging and said, "Yes, it was. We can tell when we get one by those pictures on the wall. If they shake and then hang crooked, it was an earthquake."

"Does that happen often?" asked the tourist.

"Yeah, we probably feel that every few weeks," the Alaskan native replied nonchalantly. "We hardly even notice it."

At that same time, Earl was using his free time by taking a nap in our 4th floor hotel room. He woke up feeling the bed shake and sat up at the side of the bed. It seemed to him that the hotel next door was swaying slightly and he thought, "I'm really feeling dizzy. I'd better lie down again until this feeling passes."

When I came home, I told him that we had experienced an earthquake. He found that hard to believe until the next day when the local paper reported that Anchorage had experienced a 4.7 earthquake at 11:44 a.m. the day before.

* * * * *

On that same Alaska trip in 1979, we took the narrow gauge White Pass and Yukon Railroad trip from Whitehorse to Skagway. After riding a while, the train developed a mechanical problem and couldn't go on. As luck would have it, we were stopped just short of crossing a railroad bridge over a very deep chasm. Another train came to pick us up, but we had to walk across the "see-through" railroad-track bridge to reach the second train on the other side. With no handrail, this required agility similar to that of a tight-rope walker at a circus, and I was paralyzed with fear. Earl was busy helping some of the older ladies on our tour to get across, but I was on my own. Knowing that my sense of balance was so terrible that I never could roller skate or even ride a bicycle, I just couldn't force myself to step out and walk on the slats between the rails while looking down between them at the rocks that lay so far below. Most of our group had already crossed, but I stood paralyzed, afraid to move forward.

Just then, Barry Nyman, one of our tour members, came to me and offered to help me get across. By taking it "slow and easy," we did it! We managed to reach the safety of the other side. How thankful I was for Barry's helping hand that day!

* * * * *

In thinking of terrifying moments, I must include the time when Black Rock Church members, Dean and Frances Wentz, Curry and Lucy Beckner, and Annabelle Werner visited us at Mechanic Grove. We decided to go out for supper at the Robert Fulton Tea House which was just about three miles down the road. Since it was so short a ride, we decided that rather than going in two cars, all seven of us would ride in the Wentz car.

None of us were small people, but we put three on the front seat and four squeezed in back. Together, we enjoyed a leisurely and delicious meal. Then we packed into the car again and headed for the short distance to our parsonage home.

Just as we pulled out of the Tea House parking lot, a white car sped by us, sideswiping the side of Dean's car. Never hesitating for a moment to check the damage or apologize, the car forged ahead.

Dean, a World War II veteran, felt his anger instantly ignite, and in a moment, we began the ride of our lives. He accelerated, keeping the culprit car in sight, and we raced over curvy and narrow southern Lancaster County roads which were well-known to the hit-run driver ahead, but unfamiliar to Dean. Our back seat seemed packed even tighter than before, as we had all just eaten a big meal!

Finally, the white car pulled into the driveway of a home, and we pulled in right behind it. Now we were afraid there would be a fight, as Dean was really steaming. It didn't help matters when the driver denied hitting our car even when shown the scrapes in the paint. However, we got his license number, and he did give Dean his name and address.

From his home in York County, Dean contacted his lawyer and brought a suit against the driver who had tried to hit and run. We don't know how it all was resolved, but we never forgot that harrowing and dangerous ride while packed in the car like sardines!

* * * * *

The one thing that each of these frightening incidents had in common was that God protected us, and no one was hurt—even though we were "scared out of our mitts!"

WHEN WE HAD RED FACES!
Chapter Seven

"If you're never scared or embarrassed or hurt,
it means you never take any chances."
(Julia Sorel)

Vivian –

When I was eleven, a dessert called "Angel Delight" as made by my aunt Mary Forney was my favorite food of all. A concoction of whipped strawberry jello, sweetened crushed strawberries and whipped cream, I thought it tasted heavenly and was so appropriately named.

One Sunday the Forneys visited their widowed sister-in-law and her family for dinner, and Aunt Mary brought a large crystal bowl full of Angel Delight for dessert. Aunt Mary carried it proudly into the kitchen from their car and set it on the kitchen table. The dining room table was set, and most of the company moved in that direction in anticipation of a delicious meal.

"Vivian, will you please put the Angel Delight in the refrigerator?" my mother asked as she poured browned butter on top of her fluffy mashed potatoes.

I hastened to perform the task. In trying to open the refrigerator door and also hold the heavy crystal bowl filled with the tantalizing pink dessert, I lost my grip on the bowl and it fell to the floor exploding into thousands of tiny glass fragments with globs of pink goo everywhere. The guests came running to see what had happened, and I was totally embarrassed, humiliated, and *so sorry* that the valuable and beautiful dish was irreparably broken . . . and also that no one (including myself) would be having Angel Delight that day! Aunt Mary was very gracious about it all, more so than my mother who shared in my embarrassment.

I then had the tricky job of cleaning up the mess I had created, and have always remembered the incident as one of my most embarrassing moments.

* * * * *

One of the most embarrassing moments that I experienced in high school occurred when I was in a dramatic play entitled, *Tish*. It involved the antics of three women: Tish, who was normal-sized and the smartest (Jeannine Roth Stoner), one tall and skinny woman named Aggie (Gladys Blessing Ney), and Lizzie who was short and fat. Guess which one I was!

Anyway, we sometimes had rehearsals at night. On the evening of my embarrassing episode, a classmate, Warren Mueller, was driving. Warren's dad owned a flower business and greenhouse at the edge of Mount Joy and had a closed truck that he used to deliver flowers. Because room was needed to accommodate large sprays of flowers, the truck had no seats in it except the driver's seat. To haul passengers for play practice, Warren had placed some half-bushel peach baskets upside down in the truck bed and we were to sit on them.

Warren picked me up at my home first, and I sat on a peach basket placed on the passenger side. Then we went to pick up J. Omar Brubaker, another classmate and member of the play cast, who lived on a farm near the present site of the Donegal High School. Warren drove down the Brubaker's inclined lane, turned around, and parked at the end of the walk leading to the house with the truck now facing uphill. Omar climbed in past me and got situated on a basket in the center area behind us. Warren started the truck with a jerk, and my basket-seat and I promptly fell over backwards. All three of us were surprised, but I was probably the most surprised of all . . . and embarrassed. To compound my chagrin, during the late 1940's few girls wore slacks, and I was wearing a skirt at the time. Fortunately, however, it was dark!

Years later, Warren seldom met me without teasing me about falling backwards in his truck that night.

* * * * *

Earl –

During the summer of 1949 while I was student pastor at Springfield and living with church members, Elmer and Susan Bachman, I was dating a niece of the Bachmans, a nursing student at the Lehigh Valley Hospital in Bethlehem, Pennsylvania. One Saturday evening, I came in a bit later than I should have, and to dim the lighting, I placed my jacket over the lamp shade and prepared for the night. Quickly, I smelled smoke and discovered a hole was burned through my jacket. How embarrassing it was to have to explain to the Bachmans!

* * * * *

During our pastorate at Woodbury, the youth of one of the churches sponsored a "Backwards" party. Those attending were to put on all their clothes backwards and even walk backwards, etc.

With difficulty and lots of help from Vivian, I got dressed to go to the party. My shirt was buttoned up my back, my fly zipper in the back, my cap on backwards, and I was all ready to leave when the doorbell rang. A couple I had never met before had come to request that I officiate at their wedding!

We often wondered what in the world they must have thought when the door was answered by a pastor wearing his clothes backwards!

* * * * *

One of our Black Rock Church members, whom I'll call Jim (not his real name), experienced an accident at work when a sliver of metal flew up from what he was working on and went directly into his eye. He required surgery to have it removed.

While he was in the hospital, I visited him and discovered he was in a 4-bed room with three other men. When I entered the room, I greeted all of them, introduced myself as Jim's pastor, and turned to talk to him. He was feeling pretty well and was excited about the success of the operation. He began to give me a graphic description of what had happened to him and what the doctors did during his surgery. As he progressed in telling the gruesome and gory details, I felt myself getting light-headed.

The next thing I knew I was lying *under* Jim's bed, and a nurse was hovering over me with smelling salts. One of the other patients who had witnessed the whole thing had rung immediately for a nurse.

Imagine the scene. When the nurse arrived, the excited patients explained, "Jim's pastor needs help."

"Where is he?" she asked quickly looking around the room.

"He's over there, under Jim's bed!"

About that time I began "coming to." As I began to grasp the situation, I was very embarrassed, but that scenario has produced kidding from the nurses and laughter ever since, whenever we think of it. In a few moments I was fine again. I just could not absorb all those blood-curdling details!

* * * * *

Vivian –

On our trip to Ecuador Earl and I visited an open air market attended by Quechua Indians. It was somewhat scary to be the *only* Caucasians among so many Indians and unable to speak their language. At the same time, it was fascinating to see most of them wearing ponchos to keep warm, the long black-braided hair worn by the men, and the way certain woven materials, vegetables and nuts were lined up or arranged in neat little piles waiting to be sold.

We passed a street vendor who was making and selling a pastry product that looked like doughnut holes. We had been warned to *not* buy or eat *anything* that had been touched by human hands. However, these looked and smelled so delicious that we bought a couple "just to taste them." We discovered that they really *were* as good as they looked.

On the way back to our hotel in Quito, we rode on a rickety bus over bumpy, rutted, dirt roads. The ride took us through wilderness areas, only occasionally passing a small family hut or two. The terrain was mostly barren ground with very few trees or bushes.

Suddenly, I had the urgent feeling that I needed to go to a bathroom NOW, and I told Earl about my dilemma. To complicate matters even more, we were seated near the back of the crowded bus. Judging by the time it had taken to get to the market in the morning, we had not traveled even halfway back to our hotel. What in the world would I do?

Meanwhile, the bus bounced on and with each mile and each bump, the urgency increased. Soon I became frantic. When I felt I could hold it no longer, Earl made his way up to the driver and asked if he would please stop somewhere where there were a few bushes (for privacy). Even so, it took a little while before we came upon any, and when he did stop, there was a bush right beside the bus and another scrawny bush about twenty feet away. Although it was small, I chose the second one and rushed off the bus to that spot to quickly get relief. It was obvious that that bush had been used for similar purposes in the past.

How embarrassing it was to have to ask the whole bus to stop for one person, and to have to relieve myself with so little privacy. However, it was better than any alternative that we could think of!

As our lives went on, we were blessed to be able to do much more traveling all over the world, but both of us never forgot the consequences of eating native-cooked and handled foods. We never repeated that mistake again!

*****

Earl –

One Sunday during the morning worship service at Mechanic Grove I was making the announcements, including welcoming any visitors. Jesse and Ruth Ann Wood had several female exchange students from South America with them. Before the service, I had been introduced to them and remembered they had difficult-to-pronounce names. I desperately wanted to say them correctly so as not to embarrass the girls, the Woods or myself.

I asked the girls to stand and told the congregation that "we want to welcome to our service today Rosita from Peru, and Margela from *Brassiere* and . . . Immediately I knew I had said something wrong. All over the audience, people were snickering. In my attempt to be so correct, I had wanted to say "Brazil," but the wrong word came out of my mouth!

In almost sixty years of ministry, that was my *most* embarrassing moment!

* * * * *

Vivian –

One of the lessons of social etiquette that I was taught as a young person was that when you were with someone—at a meeting or at a restaurant or wherever—and they spilled gravy on their necktie or had spinach on their teeth, the kind thing to do was to tactfully tell them. I always felt I would want to know. In fact, recently I was at a dinner and afterward was greeting people and a woman whispered to me, "Do you know that you still have your napkin tucked into your belt?" Immediately I pulled it out and thanked her, really appreciating that she cared enough to tell me about it.

Some years ago an open-air tent meeting was being held about fifteen miles from the Mechanic Grove parsonage. Some long-time friends invited me to ride along with them. When I got into the back seat, the wife moved from the passenger seat into the back seat with me so that we could chat more easily. In making the move, I noticed that she had a very large egg-sized hole in her nylon stocking. Feeling that if it were me, I would want to be aware of it, I told my friend about the hole and she thanked me.

At the tent meeting, my friend asked me to walk on that side of her so the hole would not be so noticeable. After the service, when we walked to the car to go home, it was dark, so there was no problem. However, our little exchange must have grated on her husband all evening.

Back at the parsonage, the husband politely opened the door for me. When we were outside the car and away from the hearing of his wife, he firmly told me, "Vivian, that was a very unkind thing you did this evening."

I was dumbfounded. What had I done? I looked at him quizzically.

"You should never point out a flaw or fault in someone when they have no opportunity to correct it," he advised. "My wife worried about that all evening. Actually, I noticed it just as we were leaving home, but I knew we'd be late if I told her about it and she changed her stockings. So I didn't tell her. You told her, and she was disturbed about it all evening."

I felt reprimanded at the time, but have been grateful ever since to know that he cared enough to set me straight. After all, that's what true friends are for, and he proved, in that instance, to be a true friend to me. It was a lesson I never forgot!

* * * * *

At one of Mechanic Grove's annual Mother-Daughter banquets, the men of the church had served a delicious meal ending with what looked like a fried egg for dessert.

In reality, it was a slice of angel food cake topped with a circle of cool whip with a half apricot, cut-side down, placed strategically in the center. On that creative note, the women left the basement and went upstairs to the sanctuary for their program.

A three-generational vocal quartet, composed of my mother, Kathryn Zug Snyder, my two daughters, Karen and Doreen, and myself, was scheduled to sing two numbers. One of the songs we chose was entitled, "I Love to Whistle." After blowing a pitch pipe for the key, we planned to sing acappella. As a novel beginning, we planned to whistle the first line and then join in singing. My mother declared she could no longer whistle, so my daughters and I said, "That's okay, you just come in when we start to sing."

The church was full, as the banquet had been well-attended. When it was time for our number, we simply stood up from our seats on the front row, turned around and prepared to sing. I gave the pitch, and we started to whistle. That is, we *tried* to start to whistle. I don't know if the pitch pipe squeaked, as it sometimes was prone to do, or if one of us was off-key, but someone started to laugh. We tried to become sober and begin again, and the same thing happened. My mother was embarrassed and getting irritated. We said to one another, "Now, let's stop this foolishness. We *must* get serious. We *must* control ourselves."

We tried once more, but failed again. In spite of being humiliated and embarrassed, we simply couldn't keep ourselves from laughing until tears were running down our cheeks. By this time, in empathy, the audience was laughing *with* us and even applauded. Concluding that it was a lost cause, we sat down, totally devastated and ashamed. We did sing a serious song later in the program but never, *ever*, attempted "I Love to Whistle" again.

* * * * *

Earl –

Another most embarrassing moment for me was the time I introduced a couple in which the husband had married for the second time. Several weeks after their wedding, they joined the church. As I introduced the bride to the congregation as a new member, I introduced her using his first wife's name! I heard the audience sigh, "aaaah," and I knew I had blown it!

Without saying a word, she came over to me, gave me a big hug in front of all the people as if to say, "I understand, and I forgive you." And she did. She ministered to me that day!

I am still embarrassed about that incident.

* * * * *

A somewhat similar incident occurred when Dan Hershberger married Gayle Brubaker. After the ceremony was finished, I had the couple turn toward the audience and introduced them as "Mr. and Mrs. Dan Brubaker."

When I saw smiles break out all across the audience, I knew instantly what I had done wrong and immediately corrected the introduction.

* * * * *

Vivian –

In 1994, we were in Branson and staying in a hotel unlike any I had ever seen before. Because it was built on a hill, the third floor was actually the ground floor. Although it did have a first and second floor, the registration desk and the front door were on the third floor.

One morning, Earl and I came from our fifth floor room down to third to board our bus along with other members of our tour group. Just then I realized I had forgotten my camera, so I told Earl that I was going back up to our room to get it. Meanwhile, everyone boarded the bus.

I got the camera, and when I got on the elevator to descend, I hit the button for first floor, as one would do in most other hotels. I got out and nothing looked familiar. At first I thought that perhaps I had just come down to another area of the hotel, so I walked down the hall a short distance. However, continuing to see nothing familiar, and realizing that the clock was ticking and that probably the whole group was waiting for me, I asked a cleaning lady for directions. Then I ran back to the elevator, pressed the button for the third floor, and rushed out the front door. There, to my dismay, I saw the bus headed toward me, *entering* the parking lot of the hotel, and it came and stopped right beside me. I was very puzzled.

When I boarded the bus, everyone was applauding and laughing. Then I was told that Earl had counted heads and said, "If I counted right, it seems like one is missing. Is your seatmate here?"

Everyone said, "Yes."

(I had been sitting alone in the back much of the time as Earl needed an extra front seat for those occasions when we had a guide with us, and also, back there I could more easily move from side to side to take pictures.)

Earl then told the bus driver, "Well, I guess everyone's here. Let's go." So the bus headed out the exit.

Then some alert person in the back, who remembered that I had been sitting back there the day before, called out, "Where's Vivian?" Everyone looked around, and of course, I was nowhere to be seen.

Then a very chagrined Earl had to tell the driver to go back as the one person missing was his own wife! Members of that tour group enjoyed ribbing Earl about that gaffe for years afterward, and you can believe, he has been more careful ever since with his seat count!

* * * * *

On February 14, 1997, Earl accompanied me to an Amish farm where we picked out the only male Pomeranian puppy out of a litter of five as my Valentine gift. We named him Sparky, and he was so cuddly, intelligent, beautiful and clean that he became a treasured family member for the next nine years. When we moved to the Brethren Village on January 1, 2003, we brought Sparky with us. By this time, Sparky knew a dozen or more tricks and loved to perform them for guests at our cottage.

Vivian and her Pomeranian friend, Sparky.

On New Year's Eve, 2005, we were asked to provide twenty minutes of entertainment at one of the parties being held in our village. I got a brilliant idea: Why not have Sparky do his tricks?

At the program I read a few jokes, then imitated Ed McMahon's introduction of Johnny Carson by saying, "We have a special guest with us tonight. He is a resident of our village and some of you may have seen him as he took his walks. He loves to perform, so it gives me great pleasure to say Heresssssssssssssss's Sparky!"

At that point, Earl came in carrying Sparky. He set him on the platform beside me, and we made the big mistake of *not* having him on a leash.

I commanded him, "Sparky, sit," to begin his routine. He ignored me and instead looked at the audience. He sniffed around on the stage, then stepped off and started greeting and sniffing the people in the front rows. It was quickly apparent that he had no intentions of taking orders from me or of doing tricks. We were totally embarrassed, and Earl promptly attempted to catch him before he caused someone in the audience to have a heart attack. It was impossible for us to recover graciously from our misjudgment of our pet dog's public performance abilities.

After an apology, all three of us hurriedly exited from the assembly hall in embarrassment.

SHEPHERDING THE BLACK ROCK FLOCK, 1960-1970
Chapter Eight

"Earl, stick to your preaching!"
(Ida Stambaugh, Black Rock Church Member)

Earl -

After the invitation to consider an "on site" visit to Black Rock had been extended, in November 1959, our entire family was introduced to the Black Rock congregation, and I preached a sermon. Later I was told that the call was extended, not because of the preaching or the question and answer period that followed, but because of our children's antics. When Vivian was introduced to the 300+ people in the congregation, she had cute little two-month-old, red-headed Mike peering over her shoulder smiling at the congregation. Also, during my sermon, four-year-old Randy got bored, so he proceeded to go up front and changed the hymn numbers on the board. The folks said they "fell in love with the children, and we happened to come along." Teasingly, they would later remind us of this reason for our 94% call.

Two factors that weighed substantially were: (1) The Black Rock Church (Upper Codorus congregation) was moving from the free ministry to a full-time pastoral program. Since I had grown up under a free ministry arrangement, I understood the strategies and pains of such a transition and felt that would be a plus factor. (2) Geographically, we would be moving our children to a rural area closer to their grandparents and cousins. Our oldest child, Karen, was seven and in second grade. On that November weekend, she was introduced to Linda Beckner, (the beginning of a life-long friendship), who attended Black Rock and was also a second grader in the Manheim Elementary School, where Karen would be attending.

Consequently, we accepted the call to the Black Rock Church of the Brethren, beginning our pastoral ministry there on April 1, 1960. An added bonus was that a new parsonage was being built next to the church by Henry Miller, a contractor and one of the free ministers of the congregation. They hung the doors the day we moved, amidst all the mud resulting from a week of heavy rains.

* * * * *

At Woodbury, Karen had walked to her school across the street, so on the day after our move, we all watched her board a school bus for the first time and continued watching it until it drove out of sight.

About a week later, the contractor, Henry Miller, came to our front door holding five-year-old Randy by the hand and asked how long we had been missing him. Rather sheepishly, we admitted we'd been so busy we hadn't really missed him. Henry lived about two miles away, between our home and the school. As he was on his way to work on our house that morning, he met this little boy wandering alone, and Henry recognized him. When we asked Randy where he was going, he explained, "I wanted to find out where Karen's school was, so I followed the road the bus took." We then asked him, "How did you think we could find you?"

Shepherding the Black Rock Flock, 1960-1970   115

"My shoes were all muddy and you could have tracked me by following my foot prints," was his reply.

Within that same first week, at 11:00 p.m. and before we had located a medical doctor in this new community, Doreen, our two and one-half-year-old, suddenly began to have convulsions. Since we didn't have a telephone installed yet, I quickly dressed and drove to the Henry Miller residence and woke them out of their sleep and pleaded for them to call a doctor. Henry called Dr. Wilbur Foard in Maryland, and he came directly to our house around midnight. After that, Dr. Foard became our family doctor, and what a great man he was!

For the record, Doreen has never convulsed since. What a scare!

* * * * *

Our mixed quartet in 1961: Left to right: Karen, Randy, Doreen, Mike. (Photo by Leon Kopp)

About the year 1912, a young man was riding the train but his guilty conscience made his trip miserable. He had purchased a ticket early in the day and traveled from Hokes, Pennsylvania, to Sinseim, Pennsylvania, en route to see a young lady he much admired. However, by some omission, his ticket had not been collected or punched.

Being a resourceful and frugal person, he had decided to use the same ticket over again on his way home. Now the conductor was asking him why his ticket said it was for use from Hokes TO Sinseim when he was traveling the opposite direction. The young man shrugged his shoulders and pointed out quite logically that "the distance is the same both ways—so couldn't the tickets be used interchangeably?"

The conductor walked on, but the persistent pangs of conscience tormented the youth. Later, his mind was eased only after he had purchased another train ticket and, to the amazement of the ticket seller, immediately tore it in pieces. "I cheated the railroad company out of the price of this ticket and now I have repaid them," he explained.

This incident from the early life of Noah S. Sellers reveals the character traits of a man who was to serve the Church of the Brethren for over forty-two years as a minister and his community for forty-eight years as a public schoolteacher. He was my predecessor as the leader of the free ministers of the Black Rock Church before my coming there.

His integrity and spirit of graciousness were also evident in these excerpts from a letter he sent to the congregation just before I came:

"Let us not think that now because we have a pastor there remains little for us to do. A good pastor will make us work harder than ever. Unless we are willing to assume the added responsibilities the pastor may request of us, the effectiveness of his ministry will be greatly lessened.

"When Brother Ziegler arrives, he will be our pastor. The functions formerly performed by us such as funerals, anointings, and weddings should then be his. If all of us will give the Zieglers our love, our loyalty, our cooperation, our support, and our prayers, it will make their stay while among us not only a pleasure for them and for us, but it may well mark the beginning of a new era of spiritual growth and development in the history of this, the oldest congregation of the Church of the Brethren west of the Susquehanna River—the Upper Codorus congregation."

And Noah was always a valuable advisor and supporter of my ministry there.

* * * * *

Vivian –

We were in our tenth year of marriage when we moved from the three-church parish in Woodbury to the one-church of Black Rock. I naively thought that one result of our move would be that Earl would have more time at home to spend with the family. However, I quickly discovered that the number of churches served made no difference. Earl continued to work sixty hours and more per week, and thought nothing of it.

Through the fifty plus years since, I have discovered that it is not the job but the man himself requiring him to be constantly doing things and planning for even more, and I've learned to accept that.

* * * * *

Ground breaking in 1964 for the new sanctuary at the Black Rock Church of the Brethren: Left to right: William Lucabaugh, Jr., Joel Baugher, Earl Ziegler, Henry Miller, Noah Sellers, Cathy Breneman, Gladys Werner, Glenn Miller.

In 1962, we invited Dr. Paul Hoover and his wife, M.E., to the Black Rock parsonage for dinner. While Earl was saying grace, 7-year-old Randy spoke out loud. When the prayer was finished, we reprimanded him, and he acted surprised and said he didn't know that his dad was praying.

Dr. Hoover asked us if we had ever had Randy's ears checked.

About four years earlier, when we lived in middle Pennsylvania, I had asked our family doctor if there might be a problem with Randy's hearing. He just laughed and said, "When you call him for meals or tell him you have candy for him, I'll bet he comes quickly."

I smiled and agreed that he *did* do that.

"Well, he's in a stage when he just hears what he wants to hear. You have no cause to worry," the doctor assured me. Being a part of a generation that respected the opinions of a doctor, we accepted that and didn't check any further.

So, when Dr. Hoover asked if we'd ever had him checked, we had to say, "No."

"Well, I'd advise you to do that," he said and he gave us the name of an ear specialist in York.

This time we followed through, and upon examination, it was found that he had collapsed tubes causing him to have less than half-hearing in both ears. We then realized this blockage had been the cause of many of his behavior problems in his early childhood. In March 1962, after small tubes had been implanted surgically and he had a tonsillectomy, his hearing improved miraculously.

It was thrilling, and pathetic too, to observe his reactions those first weeks as he discovered that rubbing his arm across a table made a noise, that the refrigerator had a motor, and to have *him* telling *us* that we all talked too loud! (That was a real switch!)

Coming home from school one day, he said that his teacher had once said that her favorite sound was when everyone in the room was writing with their pencils. He was all smiles as he said, "Today I heard that sound that my teacher likes."

* * * * *

George and Martha Brant, April 1997.

George and Martha Brant became dear friends of ours in the Black Rock Church.

Martha was one of the church organists, and George served on various boards. With their five children close to the same ages of our four, when we would get together, each of the children had a playmate. Since they lived along the main highway between Glenville and Hanover, if Earl was driving that route and had something to discuss with either George or Martha, he would stop. The Brants had a picket fence around the front of their lawn with the gate near their house. Earl would park his car on the roadside and just jump over the fence rather than walk up to the house and open the gate. George and Martha got a huge kick out of their young and agile pastor doing this, and often kidded him about it.

One evening the Brants invited us for supper. Included in Martha's menu were barbeque sandwiches, baked beans and potato salad. After the prayer, George and Martha noticed that Earl wasn't eating much besides bread, and they asked why. Earl then explained that he was allergic to mustard, and Martha had put mustard in every dish she was serving us! She was so upset. Although we told her it was okay and not to worry about it, she stopped eating, got up from the table and quickly fried a hamburger and opened a can of green beans so Earl would have something to eat. Whenever we ate together after that, she *always* remembered not to include mustard!

* * * * *

Earl –

Sallie Wildasin was a great saint and deaconess in the church. At age 89, she became ill and could not recover. As she was getting weaker, the family was called to her bedside in her home to gain comfort and strength from each other. I was called at 11 p.m. to minister to Sallie and her family. While waiting for her homegoing, she suddenly aroused, looked around and said sadly, "He's on the wrong track." She later joyfully called out several names (of deceased persons) she saw as life was ebbing from her body.

Then, to everyone's surprise, Sallie suddenly sat up and raised her eyes and arms toward the ceiling and began singing the words of Charles Wesley, "Father, I stretch my hands to Thee, No other help I know; If Thou withdraw Thyself from me, Ah! Whither shall I go? Author of Faith, to Thee I lift my weary longing eyes; O let me now receive that gift! My soul, without it, dies."

And a few moments later, she was gone.

* * * * *

The Black Rock/Lineboro Community Chorus was forged out of a friendship between the Rev. Harvey Schlicter and myself. He was pastor of the Lineboro (Maryland) United Church of Christ and was a good baritone soloist. For several years the two churches sponsored joint Sunday evening Lenten Services. Because of our common musical interests, Passion Sunday and Palm Sunday evenings were dedicated to a musical cantata for about six years until I left the area. He supplied an excellent organist and I directed the chorus. We always sang to capacity crowds of 400-500 worshippers. In the year of 1966, one of the main Baltimore TV stations (WBAL) invited us as their guests to sing the Easter cantata. What a privilege and honor it was to sing over television!

* * * * *

Wayne (not his real name) hailed from Tennessee, bringing with him a southern drawl and an infectious personality. A beautiful young lassie, Sally (not her real name), in our church youth group caught his eye, and he was relentless in his pursuit of her. After several months of courtship, they were married in a private ceremony in the pastor's home. Things went quite well for about ten years. Although he never brought his family to church, Sally came faithfully with their four children.

In his home state, Wayne had grown up among moonshining relatives. Periodically, the family would return to Tennessee to visit with his family. Each visit made Sally more aware of his rugged background and his growing tendency to slide into drinking occasionally. Soon their marriage was in trouble. Wayne was a great guy when he wasn't drinking, but a bear when he drank. More and more he drank to cover his problems and feelings of failure. Consequently, fighting erupted frequently over his drinking away his paychecks and letting the family without basic necessities.

One Sunday noon, he came home shortly after the family had returned from church. Sally was busy preparing the noon meal, including mashed potatoes. Without warning, he exploded at her, took the bowl of mashed potatoes, threw it on the floor, and left, breaking the screen door on his way. Sally called me Sunday afternoon and explained her fright for herself and the children, and asked: "How do I handle this? I don't believe in divorce, but I can't continue taking this abuse. I love him. He is the father of my children. What shall I do?" Later that night, he returned, remorseful and begging for forgiveness.

Knowing Wayne as well as I did through my counseling with him, I risked an unpastoral answer. "Tell him you are filing for divorce, that you've had it." I knew he would be shocked and come running to me for help. And that is exactly what he did.

That next morning he called from work and asked for an appointment with me. He came, admitted his addiction to alcohol, and sincerely asked for God to change his life and to help him show love to his family. It sounded, oh, so good! So I said to him, "When will you drink again?"

"I'm finished drinking. I love my family."

"How many beers do you have in your car now?" I asked.

"One whole case plus two cans," he replied honestly.

"What will you do with them?" I queried.

Thinking quickly, he replied, "I'm going to give them to you."

"Okay, good!" I said, and invited him to bring them in and place them in the closet of my office in the church where we were meeting.

He did it and left feeling confident he could win the battle.

* * * * *

"What do *I* do with a case of beer plus two cans?" I mused. Then it hit me: what if the janitor or a deacon would come into my office and see this beer! I could sure be in trouble! Trying to explain the situation to a deacon who felt his calling was to keep the pastor and parishioners in line (and there are a few like that!) would be futile.

After a few days of mental gymnastics over this dilemma, I confided in a parishioner whom I trusted and told him the story.

To my knowledge, no one ever found out what evil lurked (temporarily) in my closet!

* * * * *

Vivian –

When our children were small, we wanted them to have interracial friendships and learn that *all human beings are precious in God's sight and experience the same feelings that we do.* Our way of doing this was to welcome inner-city fresh air children into our home. Beginning in the early 1960's, we got different black girls and boys through Pilot House in Baltimore and kept them for one or two weeks in the summer. Some interesting experiences resulted from this.

Randy and our "Baltimore Sun," Avon McCree.

We took one boy swimming with us. He was wearing sneakers, and we noticed he was having difficulty walking. When he was in the pool, we checked his shoes and discovered he had stashed about thirty band-aids (from our medicine closet) inside them—for future use after he got back home.

One twelve-year-old girl was a bed-wetter, something we hadn't expected. Most were very warm and polite while we had them, but we rarely heard from them after that.

However, Avon McCree, who began coming to our house when he was about nine, was different. His age was between Randy and Mike, and he "clicked" with our boys. Consequently, we requested him each year for five or six years. The age of twelve was supposed to be the final year that a child could be in the program. It seemed Avon was "twelve years old" for about three or so years! Isn't that amazing?

Actually, Pilot House was aware of his "real" age, but they made an exception because we requested him by name, and he was eager to come. His grandmother was a major influence in his life, and she was a devout Christian.

One year we got him for two weeks and sent him along to Camp Eder with Randy. Another year, we took Avon along to Bush River in Maryland for our annual day of picnicking, swimming, boating and water skiing with Jim and Marian Measley. We all packed into the Measley van, and with their boat hooked on the back, Jim drove us to the park and beach area where he had taken us many times before. The property owner came out to collect the entrance fee, and Jim was getting his wallet out to pay him. At first, the man greeted him with a broad smile, but then he happened to look into the van and saw all of us, including Avon.

His smile vanished. "I'm sorry, but you won't be able to enter our park and beach today," he said, and abruptly started to turn away.

Jim was shocked. He didn't understand, in fact, none of us did—at first. "Why? What's the matter?" he asked.

"Because you brought *him* along," the man answered, rolling his eyes toward Avon. Fortunately, Avon and Randy were busy chatting and didn't realize what was happening.

"If that is the way you *really are*, you are never going to see us here again," said Jim emphatically. He put his wallet away, and quickly drove us out of there. A few miles down the road we found another park with a beach where we were welcomed. Although the Measleys had gone to that first beach for years, they never did return there again after that incident.

What a clear and unforgettable lesson in prejudice for all of us!

* * * * *

An addendum to the story of Avon:

We kept in touch with Avon for years afterwards and used to call him our "Baltimore Sun," a play on the name of the city newspaper there. We would sign our Christmas and birthday cards to him as "Mother and Dad Ziegler," and he reciprocated with "Your Son, Avon." To this date, he has never married. He went to college and became a civil engineer, working for the city of Baltimore as a water tester for many years. He has visited us occasionally, and attended Doreen's wedding in 1980. One time he went along with us to New York City to visit Audrey (Hyun Joo Yun) and her family.

In the late 1970's we were talking to him on the phone and he told Earl he wants to make him a suit. At first, we were not sure what he meant, but as we talked more, he said he was doing tailoring "on the side," and in appreciation for what we had done for him as a boy, he wanted to make a suit for Earl. He asked for Earl's measurements, and Earl gave them to him over the phone. About three weeks later, we received a large package in the mail. In it was a black pin-striped suit, exquisitely made. For many years, that was Earl's very best suit, the one he wore for many weddings and funerals, and he loved it. It fit him perfectly, because it was "tailor-made" for him with love, by our "Baltimore Sun," Avon.

On Mother's Day Avon often phoned me, including 2011. In our conversation, I mentioned that Earl and I

Earl and Vivian with Avon, May 12, 2011.

were hosting a bus tour to the Inner Harbor and the National Aquarium in Baltimore on May 12. Avon, now 57, was able to adjust his work schedule and meet us. We had a wonderful day touring, reminiscing, and enjoying spending time with one another for the first time in twenty-five or more years. During that visit, he made an interesting observation. "From the day I first met you, the only time I could sense that I was different from the rest of your family was when I looked in the mirror!"

* * * * *

In 1965 we received a call from the International Christian Youth Exchange (ICYE) program at New Windsor, Maryland, asking if we knew of anyone who would consider hosting an international student for a year, or if we would consider doing it ourselves. They had a South Korean female student who had requested coming to a family who had musical interests. Because we enjoyed music and knew virtually nothing about South Korea, Earl and I became interested, discussed it, then conferred with our children, and decided *we* would offer to host her. We were then assigned a 17-year-old girl, Hyun Joo Yun, from Seoul, South Korea, and were told she was quite gifted musically.

But there was one little snag. The ICYE students arrived in the United States about a week before they went into the homes of their host families. During that time, they went through a period of orientation, explanations of American customs and expectations, and a general adjustment to our climate, foods, and ways of life. That summer it was to be held at Beaver College, Pennsylvania. The problem was that all hosts were to pick up their exchange students on the very day that Earl and I were returning from our trip to Ecuador. When we contacted the officials and explained our schedule, it was agreed that when our plane from Miami landed in Philadelphia, we would drive directly to Beaver College and pick her up.

So, that was what we did. When the ICYE official met us, he said Hyun Joo was the last student there, but that we were getting the "cream of the crop." We asked what he meant.

"Last night we had a talent show with all of the students. Although some others were very good at what they did, Hyun Joo far excelled any of them. She has a beautiful voice and also did a fantastic Korean dance number for us. I know you'll really enjoy having her," he explained.

Then she was brought out to meet us. She was wearing a light pink dress and came right over to me, and we hugged each other. I have a hereditary weakness, (my mother had it also and so do both my daughters), in that whenever any little emotional thing happens, tears flow down my cheeks. This happens at weddings, when a band marches by at a parade, when someone walks forward in church to accept Christ as his/her Savior, when I read a touching story, etc. On meeting Hyun Joo, the tears came. She immediately noticed this and brought a tissue from her pocket and wiped my eyes. That touched me all the more! The fact that this young Korean girl ministered to my need in the first five minutes that I met her touched my soul.

Hyun Joo Yun (Audrey)

As we drove home, she told us that she would like her "American name" to be Audrey since she was an admirer of Audrey Hepburn. In her biological family, she was the youngest of five children, and in our family, she would be the oldest of five children.

We soon discovered that she was not only an award-winning soprano soloist in Korean high school competitions but was also an accomplished pianist, violinist, dancer, artist, and an excellent student.

Audrey attended South Western High School in Hanover, Pennsylvania, as a member of the senior class and carried a full schedule. The community quickly learned about her abilities by word of mouth, and she was flooded with invitations to speak and/or perform for civic clubs, women's groups, church groups, and other local functions. When she accepted these invitations, (and she couldn't say "no" to them), she wore colorful Korean-style dresses and viewed her role as an ambassador for her country. Not only were her performances excellent, but her commentary was winsome and humorous. She always gave each group her best, and everyone grew to love her.

* * * * *

People would sometimes ask Audrey, "What surprised you most about America?"

Often she would answer, "The different colors of my family's hair: one child's hair is brunette, two are blondes, and one is a redhead. In Korea, everyone's hair is black!"

* * * * *

Although her command of the English language was very good, she did have trouble with certain American words and slang expressions. For example, George and Martha Brant's oldest daughter, Sue, was close to Audrey's age. We were all attending a picnic one Sunday and Martha came over and invited Audrey to come to a *surprise* birthday party for Sue to be held the following Sunday afternoon. Within minutes, Audrey went over to Sue and excitedly said, "Oh, thank you, Sue, for inviting me to your birthday party next Sunday."

Of course, Sue was surprised to hear that . . . and Audrey was surprised that Sue seemed surprised. She was very puzzled.

When I got her aside, I told her it was to be a *surprise* birthday party, that Sue wasn't supposed to know there was going to be a party. She was to keep the invitation as a secret . . . especially from Sue. Audrey still didn't understand.

The answer to our dilemma came when she asked the next question, "Mother, what does the word *surprise* mean?"

Later, we all had a good laugh about it.

* * * * *

Audrey had a friend, U Gene Lee, who was a student at Georgetown University. Audrey had been a member of an award-winning high school female quartet in Korea, and U Gene had been a member of an award-winning high school male quartet. Sometimes these quartets performed in the same concerts, and that's how these two met. During the year that Audrey was with us, U Gene came to visit us on several weekends. The two of them filled our house with musical solos and duets, and we felt such quality singing should be shared with the church. So, we arranged that U Gene would come one weekend, and announced in the bulletin that he and Audrey would be singing a duet. In the middle of that week, U Gene phoned us about his arrival time and Earl said to him, "Why don't you come a little earlier so we'll have time to run over the music?"

There was silence at U Gene's end of the line.

Thinking he hadn't heard him, Earl repeated the question: "Why don't you come a little earlier so we'll have time to run over the music?"

Hesitatingly, U Gene asked, "What do you mean by 'run over the music?'"

Can you imagine what he must have been thinking!

Actually, U Gene and Audrey sounded so good together that on one of the weekends that he came, they made a 33 1/3 record which was then sold as a fundraiser by the church youth group.

* * * * *

Earl –

Audrey returned to Korea in 1966 after completing her year as an exchange student and attended college there. In 1970, when we went on an Around the World Trip, we stopped in Seoul. Audrey and her friends had reserved and decorated a school bus for our transportation from the airport to our hotel. She had eight or ten of her college friends travel everywhere with us while we were in Korea and serve as our personal translators. What a win-win situation, as our tour members loved the personal attention and the explanations the students gave, and the students loved being able to practice their English with a group of Americans! Vivian and I got to meet Audrey's parents and stayed in the home of her married sister and husband. On our last night there, the students prepared a buffet meal and musical concert for us in an open pavilion, complete with a piano they had moved in just for that occasion. How many American college students would voluntarily make the effort of moving a piano across a city and presenting a musical program for a group of foreigners?

* * * * *

Vivian –

One August day in 1966 I received a totally unexpected phone call from Emory Markle, supervising principal of the South Western School District in Hanover.

"We have a problem. Our librarian, Ruth Lawler, is expecting a baby and has requested a year off from work. Could you help us out for one year by serving as librarian in our junior/senior high school?" he asked.

I was shocked! "Oh, my," I replied with mixed emotions. "I was an English major, and have never taken a library course in my life!" I admitted.

"I realize that, but I feel that with your English background and a little coaching, you could do a fine job for us. Ruth has already told me that she would be willing to teach you."

"Could I just think about it for a day or two, and discuss it with my husband?" I queried in what I am sure was a weak voice.

"Of course. I didn't really expect an answer immediately."

This offer seemed almost too good to be true, as we certainly needed the money. Since we were still struggling to make ends meet, I had done sporadic substitute teaching in the neighboring Susquehannock School District during the previous year. However, with four children in grades 9, 6, 4, and 2, I was kept busy being a homemaker, writing "Day by Day," a two-page devotional for the semimonthly Church of the Brethren *Messenger*, directing the church choir, and teaching an adult Sunday School class each Sunday. How could I take on a full-time job on top of all that? Plus, I knew *nothing* about running a library, and school would be beginning in just a couple weeks.

After much discussion with Earl and prayer, I called Mr. Markle and said I would accept his offer. He seemed very pleased, and gave me the phone number of Ruth Lawler, the librarian, whom I had never met. In telling this story, I usually remind people of the saying, *"Fools rush in where angels fear to tread."*

When I met Ruth, we became instant friends. In one afternoon, she gave me a complete course in library science and school librarianship! Fortunately, she was a very organized and disciplined person, and taught me effective and time-saving techniques that I continued to use during the next thirty years. Although the task ahead seemed almost overwhelming, Ruth said she was willing to be "on call" at any time if and when I ran into a problem. That was a great assurance, and fortunately, the year went really well without my having to call her very often. In fact, as the year drew to a close, I was sorry to see it end.

Then the school district surprised me again. Would I be willing to teach ninth grade English part-time and be Ruth's assistant in the library part-time? Since I had discovered that I really enjoyed working in the library, I agreed to this arrangement *and* began taking several graduate courses in library science one night a week at Shippensburg University.

I soon discovered that teaching English is very different from being a librarian. In addition to taking a college class, writing, and keeping up with my home and church duties, I now had test papers and essays to correct, lesson plans to prepare, and discipline decisions to make. It was a difficult year, and I felt as though I were running a race as fast as I could and yet falling behind a little bit every day. By March, I was on the verge of a nervous breakdown and realized it would be physically, mentally and emotionally impossible to continue to the end of the year. Consequently, I resigned as of April 1, 1968, feeling my public school career was finished.

However, amazingly, that summer the South Western school once again contacted me. I was asked to work half days as an assistant in the library, and I felt that was something I could handle. At least, I was willing to try. Again, Ruth and I worked together until she resigned and I then worked with her successor, Kate (Ruhl) Strawbridge. I continued as a half-day library assistant and taking classes at Shippensburg and Millersville Universities until we moved from York County in 1970.

* * * * *

The Black Rock Church and parsonage were built on a hill, above a macadam parking lot open to the road. One winter Sunday when Earl walked out of the parsonage carrying an armload of church bulletins, he noticed that freezing rain had formed an icy coating everywhere. When he got to the end of our sidewalk and attempted to cross the parking lot, he began sliding downhill. Without stopping, he continued sliding upright all the way down, crossed the road, and stopped near our mailbox on the other side. Later, whenever he told people about that experience, he usually concluded proudly . . . "And I never dropped a single bulletin!"

* * * * *

A nearby farmer came to the Black Rock parsonage one day to sell apples. I bought some, but as he was transferring them to a bag, he spilled them, and they all rolled down the hill. Disgusted, he filled the bag with others and said, "Let the children go and pick up those apples down there."

* * * * *

Bob Mock, a seminary friend and evangelist, held a week of meetings at the Black Rock Church. In his concluding service, he observed that he knows now why the church built the parsonage on a hill: "They built it there so Earl would have a runway to get his car flying down the road!" (Apparently, he had noticed Earl's heavy foot while driving!)

* * * * *

Earl –

Isaac Myers was an older member who was having difficulty swallowing. His family doctor called me and informed me nothing more could be done for him. Would I minister to him?

I visited Isaac and his daughter with whom he lived and suggested the anointing service. His family gathered round as he was anointed. That very night he ate his first meal in several weeks. This is only one of many miraculous healings I've seen as a result of anointing services.

* * * * *

Ida Stambaugh was a delightful old lady, a member of the Black Rock Church, and she had diabetes. The disease became so bad that she was hospitalized and had both legs amputated. I visited her one day, and she was propped up in her hospital bed. Her lunch of beef and noodles had just been served, and she was struggling to cut them. Wanting to be helpful, I offered to feed her, and she agreed. I put some beef and noddles on her spoon and she ate it. Then I repeated it. After the third spoonful, I made the mistake of asking her, "Ida, how am I doing?"

With a twinkle in her eye, her prompt and witty reply was, "Earl, stick to your preaching!"

* * * * *

Vivian –

Karen, Randy, Doreen and Mike all attended the Manheim Elementary School near Glenville, and Earl and I were active in the Parent-Teacher Association (PTA). In 1962 the PTA fundraiser was a talent show featuring local talent. In a weak moment, Earl and I agreed to sing a duet and chose the number, "Anything You Can Do I Can Do Better," from the Rogers and Hammerstein musical, *Annie, Get Your Gun!* I put on a handmade sunbonnet made by my Aunt Fanny Shearer, and Earl wore one of his dad's farmer straw hats. Amazingly, our song was a hit, and after that we were asked to perform it for various church and civic groups. When the Black Rock Church had a farewell program for us, Misty Green and Bill Sunday performed "Anything You Can Do I Can Do Better" and mimicked the way Earl and I did it. It was hilarious!

About twenty years later, in the 1990's, we added a different twist to the end of our song. When I sang the last phrase, "Any note you can hold I can hold longer . . . ," Earl disagreed, singing, "No, you can't!" at the same time that I sang, "Yes, I can," and we held that last note as long as we could. We still do that, but at the end, I poke Earl, dressed in his overalls, in his pillow-padded stomach with my elbow, and he falls over backwards. I step away triumphantly, brushing my hands and smiling broadly because I "won!"

Many times Earl and I entertained at retirement homes, church and civic groups. We told jokes, introduced games, and I played piano while Earl led singing. Sometimes we sang duets, often accompanied by my sister, Fanny Ruth Reider, Martha Brant from Black Rock, Carol Hoover from the Lampeter Church, or other pianists from our local churches.

In spring 2009, the Lititz Church of the Brethren held a talent show fund-raiser for their building fund, and Earl and I agreed to sing a duet. No one there knew that we sang or what we had planned. After singing just a few measures of "Anything You Can Do I Can Do Better," the audience was shocked to see these two people around 80 years old singing a song like this (or at least trying to)!

When I poked Earl at the end of our number and he fell, a doctor's wife in the audience was about to call 911, because she was so sure Earl had hurt himself. Then he suddenly jumped up laughing! Although we had many chuckles over that experience, we agree we're finished singing duets.

* * * *

In the same month in 1966 that Audrey returned to Korea, Frank and Esther Boldosser, members of the Black Rock

The Black Rock parsonage mortgage burning ceremony in 1963. Left to right: Henry Miller, Earl Ziegler, Gloria (Bortner) Myers, Stanley Baugher.

Church, began hosting John Willis, an International Christian Youth Exchange (ICYE) student from New Zealand. John joined the Boldosser's only child, Paul, as a member of the senior class at Susquehannock High School near Glen Rock. Since John had grown up on a sheep farm, he fit right into the Boldosser's farm routines and chores. The church youth group soon discovered he had a great sense of humor, and he was loved and well accepted by everyone.

Because a farmer's work is so daily and is never finished, the Boldossers were unable to take many days off to show John our country. We had taken Audrey to Washington, D.C., to the World's Fair in New York City, to Ocean City, to camping experiences and to symphony concerts, but John missed out on most of the little "extras" like that.

In the summer of 1967, the Church of the Brethren Annual Conference was held in Eugene, Oregon. We bought a Sears pop-up camper-trailer (because I don't like to sleep on the ground) and planned to take our whole family across America to the west coast. In discussing John's plight, we decided to ask seventeen-year-old, John, to join us. This meant that seven of us were packed in the car for the five-week, 8,800 mile, cross-country trip. It wasn't as tight as it sounds because our children were ages 14, 12, 10, and 8, but it was close living! In our family's annual Christmas letter for 1967, we listed some of our most outstanding experiences along the way:

- Showing Karen Bethany Hospital in Chicago where she was born
- Taking a "duck" ride in the Wisconsin Dells
- Experiencing the violence of the edge of a tornado in South Dakota while we tried to sleep in our camper

- Seeing the Passion Play in Spearfish, South Dakota, on a very cold evening and almost freezing in the process
- Being only ¼" car-window distance away from a brown bear in Yellowstone Park
- Visiting the Milk River Valley Church in Montana where Earl and I had a summer pastorate in seminary days (1953)
- Feeling the inspiration of Annual Conference and the fun the children had at the heated swimming pool at our motel
- Being reminded of the greatness of God as we viewed the beauties of nature in Glacier, Crater Lake, Sequoia, Yosemite and Grand Canyon National Parks
- Visiting Disneyland, Knott's Berry Farm, Hollywood, Los Angeles' Chinatown, the San Diego County Fair (where we saw Ricky Nelson in person), relatives and friends in California
- Seeing the Pacific Ocean for the first time (and freezing again as we tried to swim in it)
- Being the only Caucasians in a congregation of a thousand blacks during a Sunday morning worship in San Diego
- Attending a bull fight in Tijuana, Mexico
- Seeing the colorful costumes of various American Indian tribes at their Pow Wow Festival in Flagstaff, Arizona
- Attending a real, Western, all-Indian rodeo
- Driving through a violent electrical storm in New Mexico and watching in awe as a gorgeous Texas sunrise emerged the next morning

Needless to say, after experiencing all of this with John, it felt like he was another family member for we had grown to love him.

He returned to New Zealand and in time, had his own sheep farm, married Glenda and together they had four children. He returned to the United States for short trips since, and we have hosted his parents here as well as two of his daughters. We have also been to New Zealand several times, including spending about two months there during our sabbatical in 1982. When we took tour groups to New Zealand, we always included the South Island, where John lived, with a day or two in his local community of Invercargill. John and Glenda arranged for lodging for the group in the homes of members of their church, and did everything they could to make everyone feel welcomed.

We feel so blessed to have friends like these, and although they live "down under," on the other side of the world, with today's technology, they are just a click-of-the-mouse away via email.

* * * * *

Earl –

A popular education venue for pastors and leaders in the '50's and '60's was to hold week-long Family Life Institutes on college campuses. A memorable experience for Vivian and me was the privilege of attending the National Conference on Church and Family in Green Lake, Wisconsin, in April 1961 and hearing such well-known authors and educators as Evelyn Duvall, Paul Popenoe, Dr. Alan Guttmacher, and David and Vera Mace and others.

John and Glenda Willis in New Zealand with their family in 1982. Left to right: Jonathan, John holding Helena, Tony in front, Melanie, Glenda.

For my own professional growth, I also attended workshops at Notre Dame University, the Marriage Roundtable in Philadelphia and others. Vivian and I attended family life workshops in 1957 on the Bridgewater College campus, in 1959 at Manchester College, and then I hosted three similar ones for the Brethren in Pennsylvania in the 1960's, two on the Elizabethtown College campus and one at Juniata College.

* * * * *

One Sunday I was scheduled to speak at another church, so Vivian was asked to fill the pulpit at the Black Rock Church. The next evening, at a meeting of the church board, as the meeting began, the chairman, Curry Beckner, made this announcement:

"I make a motion that whenever Earl goes away on a Sunday morning, we ask Vivian to preach at our morning worship service, and furthermore, we request that he go away quite often!"

Apparently she had done a great job!

* * * * *

Vivian –
Leaving Black Rock was especially painful for Randy who had just completed ninth grade. On the day after the bulk of our things had been moved and the children had been delivered to the various homes where they would stay while we were gone on our Around-the-World trip, Earl returned briefly to his study to pick up some things. In the bushes outside his church-study window, he spied a piece of paper. Thinking it was litter, he went to pick

it up and discovered it was a note placed there the day before (on moving day) by Randy. On it was written: "To Whom it may Concern: I was FORCED to leave Black Rock, and anyway, I WILL be back! Randy Ziegler."

After we had been at Mechanic Grove several months, Randy insisted, "I predict it will take me a *few years* to adjust and to be able to call this area home."

* * * * *

In contrast, when we proposed moving from Black Rock across the river to Mechanic Grove, the reaction of our son, Mike, 10, was, "If we move, it's okay with me, because then I'll have *two* sets of friends—one group at Black Rock and one at Mechanic Grove."

* * * * *

This poem, written by Goldie (Wolf, Baugher) Sterner, was read at the Farewell Service when we left Black Rock.

Our First Pastor

God loved the struggling Black Rock Flock so . . .
That He sent the Zieglers to tell us so.
There were Earl and Vivian and Karen, so demure,
And Randy and Doreen and Michael, for sure.

Earl was our first full-time pastor then.
We were not certain what to do or when
To aid a pastor as a church is due,
But they got acclimated in the parsonage so new.

Into our hearts they crept so sincere
As we learned to know and love them so dear.
We listened to inspiring sermons each Sunday
And were challenged to Christian living on Monday.

Some of us were elected to serve on commissions
So that each could know his or her real mission,
That the load of the work of the growing church
Would rest on each shoulder without a lurch.

Our pastor's chores were many and varied.
He visited the sick, the troubled, the harried,
Those mourning loved ones, the aged and lended
Counsel for marriages and meetings he attended.

His concern for each soul made him evangelistic,
His untiring efforts were not those of a mystic.
When his smiling face appeared at your door,
You could be pretty sure there was some job in store.

Many a time he was away ministering to others
When he should have been home with the sisters and brothers.
Vivian kept the home fires brightly burning
Until the time of Earl's sure returning.

Not many of us could keep up with his pace
As he met each sticky problem face to face,
But with God to strengthen what could he lack,
So he worked each one out without even a slack.

There were youth, the elderly and lonely one,
The children came in for their share of fun.

*The community singing was an inspiration,
Many a choir he led with rich interpretation.*

*As a Director of tours, there are few to equal;
To Ecuador, the Holy Lands and now the sequel,
Around the world to the other side
Are just the beginning of many a ride.*

*Now God must have glanced at Mechanic Grove
And said, "Earl, it is your time to move,
There is much you can do and so much to share
To show to them just how much I do care."*

*Now, Earl, as you and your family cross the River so wide,
Do give us an occasional thought on this side.
We pray for you God's richest guidance and care,
As you meet the problems at Quarryville there.*

Our family when we said "Goodbye" to Black Rock in 1970. Left to right: Randy, Earl, Mike, Karen, Vivian, and Doreen.

WE NEED MORE BOARDS IN THE TABLE!
Chapter Nine

*"We couldn't help all the orphans in the world,
or even some of them,
but perhaps God was calling us to help *one* of them!"*

Vivian –

In July 1966, we tearfully bade goodbye to our Korean exchange student, Hyun Joo Yun (Audrey), and she entered Seoul University as a voice major. One of the highlights of the Around the World Tour we led in 1970 was a visit to South Korea where we were met at the airport by Audrey and a large delegation of her friends and relatives. Onlookers might have thought we were celebrities! Audrey had planned our Korean itinerary, which included seeing a country village, a Korean dance performance, the Jung Won school, the U.S. Army Base located at the 38th parallel between North and South Korea, several deluxe native-style meals (complete with sitting on the floor and eating with chopsticks), and an unforgettable and heart-rending visit to an orphanage.

When we approached the orphanage in the school bus which was our mode of travel, we saw the children lined up on both sides of the driveway to welcome us. As our tour members stepped from the bus, each was "claimed" by one or two orphans of varying ages (but most seemed to be between four and nine years old). The children would take the Americans by the hand and lead them on a tour of the orphanage grounds.

Words were not understood, but a lot of communication occurred through smiles, finger-pointing, charades, hand squeezes and hugs. They showed us their dining room, sleeping quarters, school rooms, and even the gardens where vegetables were growing in neat rows. Some children were so eager to show the garden that they would lift and even break off tiny green eggplants, and our tour members would say, "No, no, don't do that. You need to let them grow so they will get big and you can eat them." But the children just smiled broadly and didn't understand.

We were led indoors to a large meeting room and soon an orphan chorus came in and presented a concert with some songs in Korean and some in English to surprise us. (A few weeks later Bob Hope's visit to this same orphanage was broadcast on American television, and we saw this group singing the same songs for him.) At the end of the visit, some orphans wanted to go home with us, but of course, they couldn't. As our bus departed, they again lined the driveway and waved goodbye as long as we could see them. Many of our group were very emotionally touched. One single lady, Grace Baker, from Manheim, PA, openly cried and said they were tears of joy for having had this experience but also tears of sadness as she thought of the uncertain futures of these precious children. Memories of that visit remained vivid in our minds.

* * * * *

Marjorie Margolies was the guest on a television show I was watching one morning in April 1971. As a single television journalist, when she wanted to adopt a Korean orphan girl, she contacted the Holt Adoption Agency in Oregon. Through them, she was able to actually go to South Korea, visit an orphanage, and choose the child whom she would ultimately grow to love and raise as her own. In telling her story, she made the observation that most orphanages had only the means and facilities to keep orphans until age fourteen. At that point, boys sought employment and were on their own. Girls had just two choices: becoming a domestic helper in a home as a cook or housemaid, or beginning a life of prostitution. I thought, "How sad!"

When the program ended, Ms. Margolies gave the address of the Holt Agency and I quickly jotted it down. During the rest of that day I did much praying and soul-searching. Was God calling us to do this? Could we handle a fifth child in our family? Could we love an adopted child just as much as our natural-born children? Could we love an Oriental child just as much as a Caucasian one? We were thinking that I would soon apply for a full-time job as a school librarian, and how would that work with another child in our family?

On the other hand, when we thought of all the parent-less children in the world, needing love and attention, we felt we must do *something*! We couldn't help all of them or even some of them, but perhaps we could help *one*! Our family wasn't perfect, but we were strong in faith and strong in loving one another. Perhaps, with God's help, this was something we were being called to do!

That evening, Earl and I discussed it and talked about the pros and cons. Could we really afford it? Actually, we couldn't, but we believed our God has unlimited resources making Him capable of doing more than we could ask or even think! (Ephesians 3:20)

When we discussed it with our children, they were accepting and even enthusiastic about the idea of having another sibling. "It will be fun having a little sister." "We can teach her lots of stuff about America." "Can she sleep in my room?"

Mike, at age eleven, always hated when someone referred to him as the "Baby of the Family," and would always correct them by saying, "I am *not* the 'baby,' I am the *youngest*!" His comment in this discussion was, "I won't ever have to be called the "Baby" or even the "Youngest" member of this family any more, and that will be great!"

After sending in an application, filling out numerous forms and passing a home study, we received information and a photo of an eight-year-old Korean girl named Lee Kyung Ae whom they were assigning to us. Understanding that the Korean custom was to list the last name first, we realized that her western name actually was Kyung Ae Lee. We wanted her to always remember and be proud of her Korean heritage. We didn't want to give her a completely American name. As we repeated her name over and over, we noted that it sounded much like the name, "Connie." Deciding to keep some of the original spelling, we wrote and told her that Konnae Lee Ziegler would be her name, and sent along a photo of our family.

She arrived at New York City's LaGuardia Airport on Sunday evening,

Kyung-Ae Lee, 9, was renamed Konnae Lee Ziegler and entered third grade about a month after her arrival in the United States in August 1972.

August 20, 1972, at 7:39. We did not immediately recognize our new daughter, now nine, wearing sandals and a blue and white striped dress with a little red ribbon decoration on her chest. Just below the ribbon was a little plastic name tag with her name, Lee Kyung Ae, and our names, Earl and Vivian Ziegler, on it. She carried a little pink plastic shopping bag with handles and in it were the few "treasures" she had brought with her.

Wearing a big smile and showing no fear, she seemed completely poised, although she knew no English at all.

We meandered to the United Airlines ramp where we were to sign several papers showing that we had actually met Konnae and were taking her with us. Upon our arrival we witnessed one of the most memorable scenes of our lives. An 8 p.m. incoming flight was unloading, and eighteen Korean babies were arriving. There was a hubbub of excitement as the four- to eight-month-old babies were passed down the line and finally into the arms of their patiently waiting new American mothers. Everyone was laughing and crying. Some babies accepted it well and snuggled immediately into their new mother's arms; others sniffed and finally cried. It was a thrill to see.

On the way home, since none of us had eaten for a while, we were hungry, so we stopped at a restaurant. We ordered chicken rice soup for Konnae and a small coke. It was obvious that she loved the soup, and she finished that right away. Since she didn't know what to do with the straw that came in the coke, she peered down through it at the bottom of the glass. When we demonstrated how to suck the straw, she caught on, but after each sip, she took a swallow of water. After about four sips, she shook her head, "No," and didn't want any more.

After a few nights in an American bed, we got the idea that she may enjoy a sleeping bag on the floor more . . . and she did! That was more like the beds with which she was familiar.

* * * * *

In the next two weeks, our family taught Konnae a crash course in learning English. By the time school began, she knew more than one hundred words. One weekend we took her along to middle Pennsylvania where we attended a tour reunion, and we had Rev. Carl Zeigler with us. On the way home, Konnae started humming hymns. When we recognized the tune, we all joined her in singing them. Although she knew no words, as soon as we finished one, she started humming another one. We sang thirty or forty different ones, and Carl was very impressed at her musical ability and early Christian training that she had obviously had at the orphanage . . . and so were we. We discovered that her favorite hymn was "Come, Thou Fount of Every Blessing."

* * * * *

Because of her age and math ability, Konnae was placed in third grade. She picked up English amazingly fast and by midyear had progressed to the point that she was able to give her classmates a perfect put-down.

Since she was the first oriental student in the Solanco School District, some of her classmates, in a form of bullying, made fun of her physical differences and difficulties in speaking English. After listening so long, Konnae turned to them and said, "Okay, so my eyes are different from yours, and I have an ugly face, and I am stupid. But these are MY problems, so why are YOU worrying about them?"

* * * * *

Earl –

In 1971 the Lybrook Indian Mission in New Mexico made an appeal for sponsoring homes for American Indian teenagers with whom they had been working. It was felt that many of them had great potential but needed a chance to get out of their environment and see "how the rest of the world lived." The Mechanic Grove Church volunteered to sponsor three Navajo girls, Jessie, Favie, and Annie. Esther Landis agreed to host Jessie, Favie lived with Amos and Ruth Cunningham, and Annie became a part of our family.

When she arrived in late August 1971, Annie was fifteen years old and in eighth grade at Swift Middle School. She and Doreen, who was fourteen and a freshman at Solanco High School, shared a bedroom. We soon discovered that she was a champion tether-ball player, excellent in art and in all types of handicraft. What she appreciated most and felt was a luxurious convenience in our home was having indoor running water!

When the school year was over, the three girls went home to New Mexico for about six weeks to visit with their families. Then in early August 1972, Annie returned. On Sunday, August 20, she went along to the LaGuardia Airport in New York City with my brother, Victor, his wife, Grace, and Vivian to meet Konnae, the Korean orphan we were adopting. (Since it was a Sunday, I felt committed to preach at the morning service at Mechanic Grove.) That gave Annie a chance to see a little of New York City and such "modern" things as escalators. When Konnae's plane was delayed,

Our family at Christmas 1972. Back, left to right: Earl, Doreen, Randy, Karen, Annie Chavez, and Mike. Seated: Vivian and Konnae.

Victor and Grace went back home, and Annie and Vivian waited in the airport until I got there and Konnae's plane arrived.

It was interesting to see the protective, motherly role Annie assumed around Konnae. One time when Vivian was grocery shopping with both girls, someone asked her, "Do those two girls speak the same language?" It really was a ridiculous question, but in one sense, they did both speak the same language, the language of love!

Annie wanted to go home to New Mexico for Christmas, so we allowed her to go. On New Year's Day 1973, she called to say they had a blizzard there and she was snowed in. When that happened, she decided to stay there. She had been a part of our family for a year and one-half.

We visited her once, and now and then she connects with us by phone. She has had five children and is now, in fact, a grandmother. Although she had a drinking problem in the past, she became a Christian in the mid-1980's and now her conversations and letters are filled with reporting about her children, her church activities, and her health, as she was diagnosed with cancer in 2010.

* * * * *

Vivian –

Around 1976, knowing that we had adopted Konnae, a Korean orphan, a young mother in our community, Michelle, (not her real name) stopped by at the parsonage to see if I could give her information to contact an adoption agency so that she could adopt a child also. When I discovered that she already had five children, a daughter about eight years old and two sets of twins, three-year-old boys and one- and one-half-year-old girls, I tried to discourage her. However, she was determined because she wanted a "twin" for her eight year old. Her applications at several reputable adoption agencies were all refused.

Just about that time, the American troops were withdrawing from South Vietnam, and Vietnamese refugees began coming to the United States. When a southern doctor felt called to clear out several orphanages and bring those children to America, he chartered two planes and filled them with children and their nurses and caretakers. Tragically, one plane crashed on take-off and burst into flames, but the second plane was successful in reaching the U.S. When the doctor announced on television that he was looking for parents interested in adopting these children, Michelle quickly contacted him. She was able to get a 9-year-old Vietnamese girl and tried to assimilate her into their family. However, the harmony for which she had hoped never happened. Her daughter and the Vietnamese girl did not get along, and everyone was miserable.

After about two years, Michelle visited us again and asked if we would keep this Vietnamese child, SuLien, for a week to give their family a "break." We said, "Sure, we'll do that." At the end of that week, she asked if we could keep SuLien a couple weeks more. Coincidentally, the next week was when her age group was welcomed at our church camp, Camp Swatara, so we told Michelle that we would send SuLien to camp for that week to have that experience. During the week following that, Michelle asked if we could keep SuLien until school began, then later—until Christmas vacation—and finally until Easter. We kept her all that time.

On the Monday after Easter, Michelle and her husband met with us in Earl's study and said they had decided they didn't want her back. We could keep her or take her to the County Family Services. Earl and I both felt that we did not want her to experience another rejection. Besides, she got along well with our children and we had grown to love her, so it wasn't a difficult decision to decide to add this 12-year-old seventh grade Vietnamese girl to our family permanently. Several years later we offered to officially adopt her and actually began the procedure. When SuLien learned of the cost, she protested and said she didn't need or want that because she already felt totally accepted in our family, so we dropped that idea. However, in every respect, we consider SuLien an equal to each of the other five children in our family. Ever since, we have enjoyed explaining to people who ask about our family that we have six children: "four homemade and two adopted."

* * * * *

Now they are sisters! SuLien, from Vietnam, and Konnae, from South Korea, in 2000.

Earl –

In 1980, we heard that a number of Cuban refugees needed sponsors, so Vivian and I decided we would take two single men. We had a hide-a-bed in the basement of our home, the Mechanic Grove parsonage, and we felt that Roberto and Lionel could sleep there and eat their meals with us.

When they arrived, we discovered they knew virtually no English. Although Vivian minored in Spanish in college and was technically qualified to teach it, she was never able to speak it and had a very limited vocabulary. She got out her English/Spanish dictionary and we communicated with these men by pointing, hand gestures and writing.

Lionel discovered he had a relative living in New Jersey, so he only stayed with us about two months, preferring to go and live with them. Being a painter by trade, Roberto did odd jobs for people in the congregation for pay. He even painted the walls of our living room, the hall and the ceilings. He was a cheerful, happy-go-lucky guy whose main fault was that he smoked like a chimney. Vivian tried to give him English lessons, but quickly discovered he was not dedicated to learning. In all, he was with us about four months.

The funniest thing that happened with Roberto was that one day Vivian came home from school and found him carrying a lamp into the basement. Then she noticed that his car was stuffed with clothing, small appliances, etc. as though someone were moving. He then explained that his "girlfriend," Marta, from Lancaster, was moving in with him *in our basement* along with her five-year-old son, Michael. Of course, this was news to us! When I came home and learned of this turn of events, Vivian and I looked at one another and asked, "What do we do now?"

First, I had a long talk (as well as I could with the communication difficulties) with Roberto and explained we don't do things that way here. Roberto, who was divorced in Cuba, said he and Marta, also divorced, were willing to get married. So, we set a date about two weeks later, in early February 1981. During that brief interim, they lived together in our basement! Imagine! An unmarried live-in couple in a parsonage basement!

At the wedding in the Mechanic Grove Church, Marta wore a gown our daughter, Doreen, had once worn as a bridesmaid. Vivian baked a cake and bought them flowers at the grocery store. It was an economical, simple wedding, but a nice one. A couple days before the wedding, they moved to an apartment in Lancaster. After less than a year, we heard they had moved to Florida because of its warmer climate and more Spanish-speaking people, and since then we have lost touch with them. It certainly was an interesting experience while it lasted.

* * * * *

Vivian –

Phillippe, 27, lived with us for almost two years in the early 1990's. We had received a call from New Windsor that this man, a Haitian, had experienced the loss of his father during a political upheaval in his country and was looking for a home. His story was that after his father was killed, his wealthy mother sent him to Belgium for his own protection and to be educated. He had come to the United States with a camera he had invented, hoping to manufacture and market it, but upon his arrival at the Baltimore/Washington airport, the camera was stolen from him. Now he was here without a job, possessions, family or friends.

We agreed to take him into our home and helped him get a car. Soon he told us he had found a job in Harrisburg. Every day he would dress in a suit and leave for "work," and every evening he would have stories to share about what happened at work. Later, he said he had been transferred to Lancaster. After several months, Earl asked him to show him where he worked. He took Earl to a business office in Lancaster, walked in confidently, and showed Earl his desk, etc., but when Earl asked a secretary about him, she said she had never seen him before. We began discovering that most of his stories were not true.

Although he often went along with us to church and actually joined the Lampeter Church in November 1991, at home he spent most of his time in his bedroom, right across the hall from ours. He cooked his own food, as he preferred Haitian foods to ours, and actually ate very little. When he got an actual job at a local restaurant, he moved to an apartment in Strasburg, and after a period of time, we lost track of him. We are still puzzled about who he really was and what parts, if any, of his whole story were true.

* * * * *

Along our journey, there were a few families who were willing to expand *their* bloodlines and welcome us as some of their own.

When we were at Woodbury, we were almost three hours driving time from all of our relatives. With four small children and the time, distance, and cost involved in making that trip, we didn't visit them very often. However, the Ross Snyder family invited us to join them on most major holidays. What fun it was to feel we were a part of their big family—and our children enjoyed playing with their

Above: "Grandparents" to our children when we lived at Black Rock: Raymond and Mabel Walker and their son, Bob. Right: Doreen and Mike had a fun visit with Raymond and Mabel Walker when Mike got the honor of wearing the Daniel Boone hat! (Spring of 1962)

grandchildren. The Lester Sell family welcomed us frequently by inviting us to come to their home for Sunday dinner or after evening church services to enjoy ice cream and visiting together.

At Black Rock, it was the Werner family. They made us a part of them to the extent that we were included in the family name exchange for Christmas gifts! Every summer a huge potluck picnic-style family reunion dinner was held on the Chestnut Level Church premises near Spring Grove, and we were always invited. What wonderful memories we and our children have of those times when we were "Werners."

Raymond and Mabel Walker loved children. They had two of their own and taught children's Sunday School classes at Black Rock. They fell in love with our children and often came to us after morning worship and asked if they could take all four home with them for the afternoon, giving Earl and me several hours free of parenting responsibilities.

Their love was contagious, and our children loved them like another set of grandparents. Whether they walked along an old railroad track hunting discarded spikes, visited a nearby church camp which had a playground and ponies, wore "Daniel Boone hats" and played pretend games, or simply discussed and compared baseball cards with their son, Bob, our children loved spending time with the Walkers. Without fanfare, they had the knack of making the pastor's family feel loved and accepted by putting their love into actions.

* * * * *

Earl –

Three years ago, the Lititz Church of the Brethren sponsored two "Karen" families of five from Myanmar (formerly Burma). Diamond Johnny and his wife, Angel Kenneth, arrived first after living in a refugee camp in Thailand for eighteen years. Vivian taught them their first lessons in English, in handling American money, etc. and I worked with them for the next three years, helping them get a car, a job, filling out documents, caring for their medical needs, etc.

About seven months later, the Shee Sho family of five arrived in Lititz from a Thailand refugee camp, having lived there for eight years. The father, a younger brother of Diamond Johnny, is named Shee, his wife, Bway Hser Ku, and their children are Poe,11, MuMu, 8, Ester, 5 and Michel, 2, born since they are here. Similar attention and support was given to this family by the entire church and the refugee committee.

Both families are Christian. The Johnnys have two daughters: Fairy, 17, and Honey Dew, 14, and a son, Bush, 10. They like to call us Grandpa and Grandma, but in the Karen language, the word for Grandpa is "Pu-Pu," and the word for Grandma is "Pee-Pee." To see them succeeding in school, singing in the church choirs, and growing in their understanding of American culture and the English language, and to know that they feel so warmly toward us that they call us Pu-Pu and Pee-Pee is a real joy (in spite of what those words mean in English)!

* * * * *

Also important family members, whom we mentioned earlier, are Hyun Joo Yun (Audrey), our Korean exchange-student daughter, her husband, John Choi, their two children, and grandchild, Bethany; Avon McCree, our "Baltimore Sun," as well as the former New Zealand exchange student, John Willis and his wife, Glenda, their four children, and their grandchildren.

God has given us a truly international family, and we love each one of them. With a growing family like this, it is no wonder we had to keep extending our table with more and more boards!

"A HEAP O' LIVIN'"
Chapter Ten

"One hundred years from today
these won't mean a thing: the house we
lived in, the money we made, the clothes we wore,
the kind of car we drove, but the world will be
a better place because our children were loved."
(Bill Keane in "Family Circus")

Vivian –

We borrowed the title of this chapter from Edgar A. Guest's poem, *Home*, in which the first line is, "It takes a heap o' livin' in a house t' make it home . . ." Each of our homes certainly had in them "a heap o' livin'." Our children were born in Chicago, Illinois, and Roaring Spring (near Woodbury, Bedford County), Pennsylvania, raised at Black Rock where they attended schools in the South Western School District (in Hanover, York County), Pennsylvania, and the younger ones had their teen years at Mechanic Grove and were students in Solanco School District (near Quarryville, Lancaster County), Pennsylvania. The following anecdotes are just a sampling of the types of interaction that went on in our family throughout the years.

In 1961, Earl and I were conducting a weekend Family Life Institute in the Springfield Church of the Brethren. We took six-year-old Randy with us, and my mother stayed with the other three children, as Karen had the measles. On Saturday night Earl and I both used a blackboard as we spoke on recent changes in family life. I spoke first, with Randy sitting in the second pew. When I sat down and Earl rose to speak, Randy leaned over toward me and giggled as he whispered this observation in my ear: "Mommie, when you wrote on the blackboard, your behind wiggled a little bit!"

* * * * *

The youth of the Black Rock Church were decorating our parsonage basement very attractively in preparation for a "backward" party. Six-year-old Doreen watched them for a while and then asked excitedly, "When they have the party, can we go?"

I replied, "No, it's just for the young people."

"But," she persisted, "why can't *we* go? *We're* people and *we're* young!"

* * * * *

At age five, Mike liked to make kool-aid, especially the pre-sweetened kind. All he had to do was add water. One day he had our permission to make some and being unable to read, he chose a packet which needed sugar added. He had often seen me add a few drops of a non-calorie sweetener, and so he did the same. He tasted it and quickly called Earl, "Come out to the kitchen and taste my kool-aid; it tastes *horrible*!"

Earl came and agreed. Then he discovered Mike had added a few drops to his unsweetened kool-aid from a sucaryl bottle, but one in which I had been storing vinegar! For a long time, he enjoyed laughing about this "mistake" he had made.

However, this little incident was a lesson for us. We were lucky this time because vinegar isn't poisonous, but this incident was *a warning to us to not store certain more dangerous liquids in familiar bottles!*

* * * * *

Vivian –

It was 2 a.m. and 9-year-old Randy was feeling sick. He was sitting on the commode with a bowl on his lap, and using both to get relief! In his misery, he sighed and with great emphasis said, "I sure wish this was somebody else instead of *me* that is sick!"

(Can't we all identify with that feeling!)

* * * * *

Although our children were PK's (Preacher's Kids), we are only aware of two incidents when they were ridiculed because of that. One day when Karen was in high school, a male student teacher prepared to tell a mildly dirty joke. Prior to telling it, he remarked, "Now I'm going to tell you this, and most of you will think it is hilarious except for Karen Ziegler who, since she is a preacher's kid, will probably be offended by it." Of course, he probably meant it kiddingly, but that hurt her and us, when we heard about it.

In junior high, Randy had a teacher who distributed a test to the class, and then decided to leave the room for a few minutes. Before he left, he told the class, "I'm going out for a few minutes, but I'm going to ask Randy Ziegler to watch and when I get back I'll ask him if anyone cheated while I was gone. Since he is a minister's son, I know he'll tell me the truth."

* * * * *

Pastor's families are just as accident prone as other families.

When she was still in high school, Karen drove our red Renault car to an activity at South Western High School and came home on a curvy, less-traveled, back road. Moments later, Dale Fuhrman, a Black Rock Church member, was on his way to church down that same short-cut road and at a curve came upon our car, resting on its side beside the road and a shoe lying in the center of the road. His heart jumped into his throat, and he later told Karen that seeing that shoe really scared him. He discovered Karen had gone, but he did pick up her shoe and bring it to our house.

Shaken, trembling, and confused, Karen had emerged from the wreckage holding her left arm. Not knowing what to do, she started walking home. A male stranger driving by, saw the accident and realized she needed help, and brought her home. Between gasps, Karen explained that while driving around the curve, the wheels hit gravel at the side of the road and she lost control. The car had rolled over one and one-half times (and was declared demolished). Karen had been driving with her arm out the open window and the incident happened so fast that when the car rolled over, it went over her arm. Miraculously, no bones were broken, but the muscles in her forearm were crushed and were very painful and slow in healing. She went all summer for physical therapy to be able to open the fingers on her hand and even today still has somewhat limited movement in that hand.

* * * * *

About three years later, Randy demolished the white Renault we had at the time. After some flash flooding resulting from a heavy rainstorm, he was enroute to his work in Lancaster and was driving via Gypsy Hill Road. He noticed the stream under the bridge was so high that the bridge was about to be covered but decided to venture forward slowly. However, the water was rising faster than he realized. As he descended from the bridge on the other side, water began entering the car and kept rising. Fortunately, he was able to open the door, and exit the car before it sank more deeply into the water and floated several hundred feet downstream, a total loss.

* * * * *

When Randy was 22, he bought a house in Hessdale and moved into it, living alone with a minimum of furniture. On August 20, 1977, at 11:30 p.m. we were awakened by a phone call from the Lancaster General Hospital that Randy had been in an accident, admitted to the hospital and was in a coma. After a date, he had been on his way home, driving south on Millersville Road (Route 741), when a drunk driver in a speeding pickup truck driving north hit him from the front so forcefully that the truck came up over much of his car. Emergency workers had to cut the car apart to get Randy out, and he was rushed to the hospital.

Interestingly enough, the police told Earl that at that hour of the night, they expected to find evidences of alcohol use in Randy's car also, but all they found was an empty milk shake container and straw. They also said that if the emergency workers had arrived twenty seconds later, he would have died.

Randy's coma lasted four days, which were anxious ones for our family. Many prayers were offered on his behalf, and when he became conscious and was well enough to come home, the doctors said he should not live alone, so he moved back home with us in the Mechanic Grove parsonage and rented his Hessdale house. For years he had periodic severe headaches, and to this day still has some hesitations when telling a story. However, thankfully, he thinks clearly and is as witty and quick thinking as ever.

Meanwhile, the driver got a mere "slap on the hand" and warning from the courts and virtually got off free of penalty for what he had done. He was later convicted of a similar but less damaging DUI offense, and his record goes on.

* * * * *

Earl –

When we moved to Mechanic Grove in 1970, Karen was in college, but we still had three children at home. Konnae joined us in 1972 and SuLien in 1978. Five children and two adults needed to get ready for school and for work with only one bathroom and one powder room.

Vivian was the first to leave and needed to be out of the house and on her way to Swift Middle School by 7 a.m., so we decided that I would make breakfast for the rest while the children took turns in the bathroom. The last one left the house at 7:40 a.m., and that gave me twenty minutes to eat, take a shower, get dressed and arrive at my office in the church across the parking lot by 8 a.m.—and I was usually on time!

Consequently, I mastered making a variety of breakfasts, and we all learned to live with a tight schedule.

* * * * *

Vivian –

In April of Konnae's third grade year, she was playing with a classmate on a see-saw in her school's playground when she fell off and broke her leg. It was the day before her tenth birthday, and she had to wear a full-length cast on her leg for several weeks.

Amazingly, during the raising of our six children, that is the only broken bone that anyone in our family experienced.

* * * * *

After SuLien (age 12) had been with us for a couple weeks, a travel friend of ours, Art Knaub, from the New Fairview Church of the Brethren near York died. We had no one to stay with SuLien and didn't want to leave her alone, so Earl and I took her along to the viewing preceding the funeral. We stood in line and when we got to the casket, SuLien burst into tears. She began crying convulsively, uncontrollably. We wiped her eyes and hurried to a seat in the sanctuary. We were completely baffled by her behavior, as she had never known Art or even seen him before. During the service, she still wiped her eyes occasionally.

The burial was in the cemetery beside the church, and because of her reaction, we debated whether we should watch it, but SuLien wanted to go. Being small, she was able to wiggle through to the front row to a position where she could observe everything. After it was over, she asked for and received permission from Art's widow, Pauline, to take a flower from the large spray that had been on the casket.

In talking to her about it since, she has no idea why she reacted that way. However, we think she must have seen someone she knew or perhaps even her Vietnamese family be killed and still had that image deep in her psyche.

Another reason why we suspect that is that the Mechanic Grove parsonage was right beside the cemetery. During hunting season, when we were in our backyard, we could hear gun shots in the distance, but we thought nothing of it. One day SuLien was outdoors and heard it and reacted instantly shouting, "Those are guns! Those are gun shots!" She came running into the house terrified. For days, she wouldn't go out the back door or even walk by the cemetery.

Who knows what may have caused her to have that reaction? To this day, she doesn't have an answer, but we know that both she and Konnae experienced untold tragedies as child orphans, and both are survivors, fighters, resulting in their being strong, self-reliant women. We love and admire them both for those qualities.

* * * * *

SuLien's favorite response whenever someone was correcting her or anyone else in her hearing was: "*Nobody's perfect!*" (A good reminder for all of us!)

* * * * *

When Mike was in high school, he gave me a Mother's Day card that said, "You have something that no other mother in the world has." Inside it simply said, "ME!"

* * * * *

Upon arriving home from the photography studio with an order of reprints of his senior pictures in natural color, Mike was surrounded by the family, all eager to see them. Someone quickly noticed that each photo had a flaw—a small white speck on his cheek. Earl asked, "Did the original have this mark on it?"

As I shuffled through the proofs, Randy observed, "MIKE is the original, and he doesn't have a white spot on his cheek!"

That settled it. We returned the order.

* * * * *

Earl –

In 1985, when Doreen and Konnae earned a trip to Europe by working as couriers, Karen decided to fly there on her own. Since they each had to fly alone, Doreen, the bravest, left first, followed by Karen, and finally, Konnae joined them. Together the three of them toured Europe for two weeks, staying in homes, hostels and traveling by train.

One day, while they were riding on the train, some friendly fellows joined them. In introducing themselves, our daughters (with three different last names, one a blue-eyed blond, one a brown-eyed brunette, and one oriental) explained that they were sisters.

Immediately, the guys assumed a more serious attitude, and our daughters then realized these fellows thought they were nuns!

* * * * *

Vivian –

One day, shortly after our oldest daughter, Karen, became a grandmother, we were discussing the subject of raising children. She complimented us, and said that, considering everything, she feels we had done a pretty good job of raising her. We had shared our faith, exposed her to the world through travel, taught her to work and to save, but we made one big mistake.

Of course, we were curious to know what that was.

"You allowed me to quit piano lessons," she responded.

"But you begged us to allow you to quit," I protested.

"Yes, I know I did, but you shouldn't have given in to me," she insisted.

Our reasoning in allowing her to quit was influenced by my own childhood when I took piano lessons, which I did not enjoy. I especially hated it when we had company and I was asked to play for them. However, in my early teens I began playing the piano for Saturday night hymn sings when our family attended the Mt. Joy Gospel Tabernacle, and then played for Sunday morning worship services. Today I'm grateful that I can play most hymns if a pianist is needed. Had we known then that Karen would minor in music in college and be actively singing in groups and worship teams most of her life, we probably wouldn't have given in to her pleas to quit taking piano lessons.

For Randy, it was trumpet lessons, which he took long enough to be able to play in a trumpet trio at church. In junior high, he preferred drums, and quickly became discouraged when his teacher insisted that he begin with a drum pad instead of actual drums. Growing impatient with that, he quit. Today, he still occasionally gets out his trumpet when he is serving as worship leader at theHempfield Church of the Brethren and surprises the congregation by playing "All Hail the Power of Jesus' Name." (He says that is the only song he still knows how to play!)

I tried teaching Doreen piano lessons, but that soon fizzled out. Later, she took clarinet lessons, but her interest ended with her high school graduation. With Mike, it was trombone. He began enthusiastically, but grew tired of it quickly. Konnae enjoyed her piano lessons and actually practiced, resulting in becoming a good player. Being a music-lover, she took clarinet lessons (on Doreen's neglected clarinet) and also learned to play the bassoon and participated in the school orchestra. Music was not one of SuLien's interests, so she never took music lessons of any sort.

* * * * *

Earl –

On Father's Day, 2008, our oldest son, Randy, told this story about me in his church, the Hempfield Church of the Brethren.

"In 1962, I was seven years old and began a lifelong love affair with the sport of baseball and the New York Yankees. My goal in life was to succeed Mickey Mantle as their center fielder. However, first I had to learn to play the game. To do this, my dad began with pitch and catch with a rubber ball. Beginning by standing just a few feet apart, I progressed in my ability until we could stand a distance apart and used a softball.

"Then I had to learn to bat the ball. My dad got a board about six inches wide, about thirty inches long and about ½ inch thick and had me use it like a bat. Beginning with underhanded pitches, I seldom missed hitting the ball. I did wonder why I didn't have a bat like my friends had and questioned in my own mind if we were too poor to buy one, or what?

"Now, fast forward to 2006. My dad and I were discussing some of the things that happened when I was growing up and I asked the question, 'Why did you have me learn to bat by using a board instead of a bat? Were we too poor to afford one?'

"'No, Randy,' he assured me. 'I could have easily bought you a bat, but you were only seven years old. I wanted you to be able to *hit* the ball and feel good about yourself, to encourage you, to build up your self-esteem, to be sure you would not fail.'

"Immediately, when he said that, I saw the wisdom in his reasoning, and my estimation and admiration of him mushroomed. He was smarter than I thought he was! What a caring, loving, and thoughtful thing for a father to do."

* * * * *

Vivian –

Tony Campolo, sociologist and evangelist, has said that one of the best ways of teaching values within a family is through traditions. They give each family member a feeling of *belonging*, which is so essential to self-worth and self-confidence. A few that we practiced were:

- Each Sunday it was understood that all family members would attend Sunday School and church—no excuses!
- Every Sunday noon, we *sang* our grace for the noon meal . . . a practice Earl and I began shortly after our marriage and still do.
- When we lived in the Mechanic Grove parsonage beside the church, each weekend I would prepare a large casserole and bake a cake. That way, I was always ready if we got unexpected company for our Sunday noon meal.
- After any of the children participated in a school program, sports event, or received a report card with all "A's," the family would go for ice cream to celebrate. We still do this with the grandchildren whenever we can.
- I made chore lists which the children were asked to do each week. These included such things as sweeping the side-

walks, cleaning their rooms, making a meal, feeding pets, dusting, pulling weeds, folding the wash, etc. When their lists were checked off and completed, they received an allowance.

- From their allowance, they were expected to tithe at least 10% and to put at least 10% in a savings account in the bank. To encourage saving, we told them that any amount they put in the bank, we would double.
- When they reached high school age, their allowance increased, but then they had to begin buying their own clothes, except for occasional larger items like a coat or shoes, which we continued to buy for them.
- In preparation for Easter, the children loved to dye and decorate hard-boiled eggs. After we had attended church, had our noon meal, and washed and put away the dishes, we would always have an egg hunt. We remember fondly one Easter at Mechanic Grove when Earl's parents were with us, and his dad helped to hunt for the colored hard-boiled and plastic eggs for the *first time* in his life! What fun he had! And it was even more fun for us—just to watch him!
- Every Easter I prepared an Easter basket for each child, but we didn't just hand it to them. Instead, they had to work for it by going on a scavenger hunt. Younger children had fewer and easier clues, while older ones had up to ten clues at harder places to find. I would make a master chart showing *all* clues and then make individual notes for each one and hide them at all the various places. It was tricky getting the numbered clues in the right places and in the right sequence and was quite an exercise hiding them around our house and property, but when we observed

the fun the children had hunting them, it was well worth it. Today the grandchildren look forward to their scavenger hunts! As time went by, the contents of the baskets, (actually just colored paper bags), have changed from all forms of candy to healthier choices, such as individual kids' drinks, peanut butter and/or cheese crackers, individual puddings, fruits, small packages of raisins, peanuts and nutritional bars plus non-food items.

- On Memorial Day, my mother would usually take her four children to the Chiques Church of the Brethren Cemetery and walk my sister, two brothers and me through it as she placed a single white peony on the graves of my dad, baby brother, her parents, her siblings, grandparents, great-grandparents, and numerous aunts and uncles. Because of ancestors resting there, Earl and I have chosen to have our ashes buried there also.
- For several years on July 4th, we had a "Cauliflower Planting Party" and invited my mother, sister and two brothers and their families to come and help us plant 1,500 cauliflower stalks in a lot next to the Mechanic Grove parsonage and cemetery. After the planting, we would enjoy a picnic lunch together, making a fun experience out of what could have been quite a chore.
- At Thanksgiving every year, we invited my mother, and included my siblings, and their families. Before saying grace, each one stated things for which they were especially thankful.
- As long as the children were still at home, Earl would pack them up at Christmas and take them out to a tree farm where they would choose and then cut down our Christmas tree. That was always a highly anticipated event, but I never

went along with them, probably because the car wouldn't hold us all AND a tree!

- Because I never liked the expense, the wastefulness, and the mess of cleaning up fancy Christmas gift wrappings, I began saving the colorful comic sections of the Sunday papers. By December, we had enough comic "gift wrap" to cover all of our gifts. However, we still had to gather all the waste paper. Then I began buying Christmas-patterned fabrics inexpensively at after-Christmas sales and making bags of various sizes. We put our gifts in those bags and tied them shut with a ribbon. When they were saved from year to year, we accumulated a box full, so that now there is no cost for gift wrap from year to year, the gifts look colorful and beautiful under the tree, and there is no waste to pick up afterwards.

- At Christmas, before any gifts were opened, the breakfast dishes had to be washed and put away, or at least placed in the dishwasher. Then we gathered around the tree and someone read the Christmas story from Luke 2. After designating a "mailman" and the gifts were distributed, the youngest person opened his/her gifts, followed by the next youngest, and proceeding until the oldest was last, with everybody watching (and often making funny comments)! It took long, but everyone got to be the "star" briefly, and all could see what everyone received and his/her reactions.

- A joyous Christmas tradition was for our children (and later, grandchildren) to help make water crackers, an old family recipe similar to sand tarts. After rolling out the dough and cutting them in different shapes with cookie cutters, many different decorations were added according to the whims of the "baker's assistants." Some snowmen had a lineup of twenty "red heart" buttons down their front! What fun! (Look for the water cracker recipe at the end of this chapter.)

- On Christmas Day we have a standing invitation to share the evening meal of a turkey with all the trimmings with our daughter, Doreen, and all the Creightons. We look forward to this annual treat of a wonderful visit, one on one, with their family.
- Although Ann Landers and other syndicated columnists did not encourage it, we began sending a family Christmas letter in 1956 and have continued this annual tradition each year since. About ten years ago, I made notebooks for each of our children with a copy of each of our letters in its own plastic sheet protector as reminders of our family history. A recently discovered added benefit was that in gathering data for this book, the old Christmas letters helped to stimulate our memories.
- Birthdays were always celebrated with a cake as our dessert, complete with lighted candles, and a gift. As the children

Vivian and grandson, Ben Creighton, baking cookies in 1993.

got older, to treat everyone alike, we began giving a gift of the same amount of money to each one, and we continue to do that today for all our children, their spouses, and our grandchildren.
- About ten years ago, our son, Mike, and his wife, Mary, started the tradition of "singing telegrams" on birthdays and anniversaries, singing "Happy Birthday to You" when the honoree answers the phone.
- Our daughter, Karen, has started a lovely tradition of her own. Each year on December 19th, *her* birthday, she sends me a floral arrangement with a note thanking me for giving birth to her! The flowers grace our table during the Christmas holidays and are a beautiful reminder of her love.
- One of SuLien's traditions is that for every special day—our birthdays, anniversary, Mother's Day and Father's Day, she faithfully insists on taking us out for lunch—usually at an Asian restaurant. If we object or offer to pay, she always says, "No, I am just so *grateful* for all you did for me and for accepting me into your family that I want to do this." So we let her do it, and are thankful.

* * * * *

Earl –

Our oldest son, Randy, sent me this email on Father's Day, June 21, 2009:

"This morning one of the hymns we sang in church was 'How Great Thou Art,' and I had to think back to the year at Black Rock when, after a Sunday morning service during which we had sung that hymn, wanting a little feedback on the service from your family at the noon-time meal, you asked, 'Didn't I have a good sermon this morning?'

"You made that comment to spur some responses from your kids, whom you knew would not hold back or patronize you, and we broke into singing, 'How Great Thou AREN'T!!!' I was thinking of that while we were singing it this morning, and thought it would be a good Father's Day memory to share with you.

"I thank God for each day, week, month, and year that He allows you to remain accessible to me here on earth!"

* * * * *

How grateful I am for a family that loves to laugh!

* * * * *

Water Crackers
Cut-Out Christmas Cookies

2 cups sugar	1 tsp. soda
¾ cup shortening	1 tsp. cream of tartar
3 eggs	3½ cups flour
7 Tbsp. water (just under ½ cup)	

Blend the sugar and shortening. Beat 2 eggs and add the water to them. Combine the dry ingredients. Alternate adding the dry and liquid ingredients to the egg/sugar mixture. This makes a very stiff dough. Roll as thin as possible and cut out shapes. Place on cookie sheet covered with non-stick foil. Beat one egg. Dip a teaspoon in the beaten egg and rub the back of the egg-coated spoon on top of the cut-out shapes before decorating them with colored sugars, raisins, chocolate chips, red cinnamon candies, sprinkles, crushed nuts, etc. When decorating is finished, bake cookies in a 375 degree oven for 10 to 12 minutes. Makes about 150 cookies that are approximately 2¼" in diameter. (Note: These are economical to make and great for dunking!)

Freshman trio at The King's College, 1947-49. Left to right: Vivian Snyder (Ziegler), Genive Smith (Underwood), Marjorie Siddron (Ohman).

Heidelberg Male Quartet, 1946-50. Left to right: Earl Ziegler, Harvey Weik, Melvin Krall, John Kegereis.

Woodbury Male Quartet, 1954-60. Left to right: Earl Ziegler, Chester Erb, Dean Snyder, Jay Guyer.

*Great Master,
Touch us with Thy skillful hands;
Let not the music
That is in us die."
(Horatio Bonar,
1808-1889)*

Brethren Village Male Quartet, 2005-08. Left to right: Stuart Kauffman, Donald Charles, Earl Ziegler, Jim Eshelman.

182

Our wedding party/35th wedding anniversary.

Left to right: Roy Forney, Jr., Lloyd Gingerich, Lena Ziegler (Kreider), Nancy Swope (Fitzkee), Vivian and Earl Ziegler, Victor Ziegler, Fanny Ruth Snyder (Reider), John Drescher, and Dale Hylton. The day of our wedding, August 12, 1951.

*Thirty-Five years later.
(Absent from photo: Dale Hylton)*

Some of the houses we called "Home." 183

Front and Back of Woodbury Parsonage, 1954-1960.

Black Rock Parsonage, 1960-1970.

Solar room we built on Pioneer Road home, 1983-2002.

184

Woodbury Church of the Brethren—Before and after renovations made in 1958.

Black Rock Church of the Brethren, 1876-1964.

Black Rock Church of the Brethren, 1965-present.

Lampeter Church of the Brethren.

Black Rock Church of the Brethren Youth Choir—1969. Back Row: Karl Lehman, Michael Brenneman, Tony Measley, Rodney Wentz, John Werner, Dale Fuhrman, Ronald Fuhrman. Third Row: Shirley Baughman, Sue Mummert, Karen Ziegler (Director), Pearl Nace, Sandi Riebling, Connie Meckley, Linda Beckner, Sandi Brant, Esther Kipple (Pianist). Second Row: Brenda Garvick, Barbara Rappoldt, Sharon Werner, Diane Lehman, Connie Brant, Sharon Sunday, Barry Stremmel, Randy Stremmel. Front Row: Joan Beckner, Debbie Mancha, Terri Sunday, Paula Sackett, Norma Lockamy, Sally Sterner, Glenn Kipple, Kevin Lehman, Randy Brant, Randy Ziegler. (Absent: Karen Amspacher, Suzanne Fuhrman, Jennie McElrath, Robin McElrath.)

Reunion of the Black Rock Youth Choir, 2010.

All of our family attended the wedding of Ken and Doreen (Ziegler) Creighton, June 15, 1980 in the Mechanic Grove Church. 1st Row, Left to right: Randy Ziegler, SuLien Nicodemus, Marianne Zimmerman, Jimmy Choi, Audrey (Hyun Joo) Choi, Konnae Ziegler, Avon McCree 2nd Row: Jim and Karen Zimmerman, Ken and Doreen Creighton, Vivian and Earl Ziegler, Mike Ziegler.

2001—50th Anniversary photo of Earl and Vivian and their six children. Left to right: Konnae Berces, Mike Ziegler, Karen Ungemach, Vivian and Earl Ziegler, Doreen Creighton, Randy Ziegler, and SuLien Nicodemus.

Past Moderators attending the Wichita, Kansas, Annual Conference in 1994, the year Earl served as Moderator. Back Row, left to right: Earl Ziegler, Bill Eberly, Phil Stone, Earle Finke, Elaine Sollenberger, Donald Rowe, Dwayne Ramsey, Curtis Dubble, Harold Bomberger. Front Row: Charles Bieber, Ira Peters, Wayne Geisert, Charles Boyer, Blair Helman, Dale Brown.

Dominican Republic Bible School and Work Camp group in 2008. Standing, Left to Right: Karen Ungemach, Dean Lengle, Irvin Heishman, Sue Ream, Megan Wenger, our Dominican driver, Susan Dundore, Arial Rosario, the assistant driver. Front: Molly Wenger, Matthew Ream, Rebekah Miller, Earl Ziegler.

Haiti Work Camp group in September 2011. Standing, Left to right: Ken Hess, Nancy Wenger, Carl Martin, John Knepp, Harold Hershey, Jim Eby. Front: Earl Ziegler, Cheryl Garner, Earl Mull.

Dominican Republic Work Camp group in February 2012. Back Row, Left to right: Scott Garner, Chris Peifer, Jeff Grubb, John Knepp, Bill Kettering, Art Kreider. Front: Cheryl Garner, Mark Peifer, Lena Ziegler, Grace Ziegler, Todd Christophel, Earl Ziegler

190

The wall hanging assembled and quilted at the 1994 Church of the Brethren Annual Conference in Wichita, Kansas, and presented to Earl K. Ziegler, the Moderator that year. Each square represents a segment of Earl's life journey.

5th (Top) Row: Solanco Area Men's Chorus which Earl directed for about 12 years; the Mechanic Grove Church of the Brethren; the Lampeter Church of the Brethren.

4th Row: Springfield Church of the Brethren; our immediate family with our six children; the Woodbury Congregation consisting of three churches: Woodbury, Curryville and Holsinger.

3rd Row: Puerto Rico interests; Annual Conference logo for 1994—"Come, Drink the Living Water;" Hispanic Ministries.

2nd Row: Elizabethtown College; the A. H. Ziegler milk wagon and Earl's birth family; Heidelberg Church of the Brethren.

1st (Bottom) Row: Prairie City, Iowa, Church of the Brethren (chosen to show that the Moderator serves ALL churches across the nation); Atlantic Northeast District Executive; Black Rock Church of the Brethren.

BITTEN BY THE TRAVEL BUG
Chapter Eleven

"The more of God's world that you see,
the more you realize you haven't seen!"

Vivian –

When I was eight years old, my aunt, Ida Snyder, who lived in California, traveled to Europe. When she returned to the United States, she visited us before she returned to her home and I thought that being able to travel overseas was absolutely awesome. That same year, 1938, her sister, my aunt Emma Snyder, sailed to Nigeria to begin working as a missionary nurse with the Sudan Interior Mission. When she returned to the United States on one of her furloughs, her flight connections took her through several European countries. I asked her how that was possible for a missionary who was always short on funds and her reply was that this was part of the "exceeding abundantly above all that we ask or think" that the Apostle Paul refers to in Ephesians 3:20. Likewise, this describes the way we've been able to travel and to see what we've seen. We certainly *never* planned it that way from the beginning!

*****

We thought the trip to Ecuador in 1965 had been the trip of our lifetime! We had no dreams or intentions of going on more trips. We had wonderful memories of the beautiful snow-capped mountain peaks, the plants and animals of tropical areas, and observing various cultures and Indian tribes in their native habitat. Ecuador had it all!

One of the most lasting impressions was that we saw firsthand that the role of a missionary was not just to preach the gospel verbally but to show God's love to the people by helping them improve their lives in practical ways. Consequently, Merle Crouse and others initiated the raising of poultry as a means for poor families to make a living and also provide protein for their diet. In other words, the missionaries went there with a Bible under one arm and a chicken under the other. To present the gospel, it was necessary to use a combination of both approaches. Earl has often used this imagery in presenting talks on missions.

* * * * *

Earl –

On our trip to Ecuador, we rode a train from Quito to Guayaquil via a route locals called "the Devil's highway" because of its steep inclines and sharp turns with deep ravine drop-offs at the sides. Since our group of twenty-one were the only Caucasians, we were of great interest to the native passengers, most of whom were of Indian descent. It was a very hot day, and at various stops along the way, "vendors" holding a large jar of orange juice tried to sell the train passengers a drink of it poured into a glass tumbler. The unusualness of their sales technique, from our perspective, was that after one buyer drank his cupful, he would hand the glass tumbler back to the juice-seller, who would promptly refill it and offer it for sale to another buyer! Everyone drank from the same glass!

After our train arrived in Guayaquil, we boarded a public bus to go to our hotel. Since it was a hot day, the bus windows were all wide open. One of our male tour members sat down by a window and propped his elbow on the ledge. Moments later, as people were still boarding, a young man ran by the bus and quick-as-a-wink snatched our tour member's watch from off his wrist and ran away with it. A few passersby who witnessed the theft chased after the culprit, but he darted down an alley and got away. We quickly learned that traveling in the city was quite different from traveling in the countryside, and we had to keep alert.

* * * * *

Shortly after we returned from the trip to Ecuador, I received an invitation from Wholesale Tours International in New York City to lead a fifteen-day tour to two European countries plus Egypt, Israel, Lebanon and Syria at the cost of $875 per person. We decided to accept, so in July 1966, we both flew with twenty-eight people, including Vivian's sixty-five-year-old mother and our thirteen-year-old, ninth-grade daughter, Karen, on KLM Royal Dutch airlines. We were beginning to become aware that travel is addictive—*the more of the world that we saw, the more we wanted to see.*

* * * * *

Vivian –

Because Earl preferred working with a local travel agency with whom he could communicate face to face, he decided to take his third trip in July 1968, with Menno Travel Service of Ephrata, Pennsylvania. This time he had a group of twenty-five who traveled to six European countries plus Israel and Egypt for twenty-two days at the cost of $1050 per person.

Although I didn't go along on that trip, Earl wrote a trip summary which he called, "The Parson's Epistle," and inserted the account in the September 1968, issue of "The Black Rock Flock," their monthly newsletter. He mentioned some interesting facts about that tour group. "The oldest member was seventy-three with two claiming the distinction of being the youngest at twenty-one. Five were under thirty years of age; only three were of retirement age. Seven were schoolteachers, two ministers, successful businessmen, factory workers and a secretary. The greatest single bond common to all was our faith as Christians. We had in our group those who 'fell for' things or people, those who had the gift of getting lost, jokesters, and those who were always hungry. In a very short time, the group was knit as a family."

After a glowing account of all the things they had seen and done, he ended his report with this paragraph: "Arriving at 5:00 a.m. at Black Rock after having already lost our Canadian, our Lancaster County bachelor, and our seven friends from the New Fairview Church of the Brethren, the rest of the weary pilgrims faced another day with lots of enthusiasm but *no sleep!* Indeed it was such a day that when I stood in the pulpit, I couldn't find my sermon which had been hatched just hours before above the Atlantic Ocean. How embarrassing! (It was located after I stumbled through the introduction!) After a wedding and several hospital calls, the family and I arrived at Cowan's Gap State Park (in middle Pennsylvania) late that evening for two and one-half days of family reunion."

In 1970, between pastorates, we escorted an Around-the-World Tour for thirty-three days for thirty-six people at the cost of $2,395 per person. Bob Young, a fundraiser for Elizabethtown College for many years, and his wife, Dorothy, were among this group. Being "typically Pennsylvania Dutch frugal" in their personal finances, the Youngs thought long and hard before sending in their reservation. About twenty years later, Bob told Earl, "That was one of the best investments we ever made!"

* * * * *

Earl –

Since Vivian's widowed mother, Kathryn Zug Snyder, had been a Sunday School teacher for years, Vivian and her siblings knew that to be in the Holy Land and actually walk where Jesus had walked would be a thrilling and inspiring experience for her, so they joined together and paid for her trip in 1966.

In Germany, we took the Rhine River cruise and were met by our bus, but when we got to our hotel after dusk, the hotel didn't have room for all of us. However, after phoning other hotels, everyone finally had accommodations. Consequently, some had rooms that were not too great, and one room had in it a double bed and two singles. I didn't want to ask two couples to share a room, nor did I want to crowd four singles together, so we decided that Grandma, Karen, Vivian and I would share that room. It was equipped with a small washbowl but no private bathroom, so we had to share one down the hall.

We joked about our arrangement, and in the morning Grandma pretended to make a big deal about how she would get dressed with a man in the same room. I said she could get dressed while I was shaving at the small bowl and I would have my back to her. Grandma thought that would be acceptable, so she began to disrobe from her nightie. Just then, I added, "Remember, Grandma, although I have my back to you, I can still look in the mirror!"

* * * * *

Vivian –

The German hotel operator was very embarrassed that our reservations had been messed up and they'd had to scramble to find sleeping arrangements for everyone. To apologize for that inconvenience, the next morning they gave Earl a large bottle of white wine, a product of that area of which they were very proud. As a teetotaler, Earl didn't really want it, but he knew the courteous thing to do was to accept it, so he did. He then set the bottle down while he checked everyone out of the various hotels, counted to make sure that all the luggage had been put aboard the bus, and talked with our bus driver about plans for that day.

Everyone boarded the bus, and Earl would have forgotten his "gift" if my mother hadn't prodded someone to ask him, "Where is your bottle of wine?"

Since the bus hadn't started yet, he jumped off and ran into the hotel to look in the area where he had placed it . . . but it wasn't there. He looked all around, and then came on the bus and asked, "Did any of you notice what happened to that bottle that the hotel here gave me?"

He was about to assume that some German had seized the opportunity and stolen it when he noticed a naughty twinkle in his mother-in-law's eyes. Incredulously, he asked, "Mother, do *you* have it?"

Without replying verbally, she smiled and pulled it out from under her sweater. "I wanted to keep you from getting in trouble with it," she explained. "I was just protecting you!"

Of course, he mockingly scolded her and acted shocked "to think a Sunday School teacher of many years would stoop to doing a thing like that," and everyone enjoyed a good laugh at her little prank.

* * * * *

Before we left for our first trip to Europe and the Holy Land in 1966, we warned our tour members to take lots of dollar bills along and very few bills of larger amounts. We had been told that in many places in Europe, if we didn't have their local currency, many establishments welcomed American dollars and one could make small purchases, like a soda or a postcard, using them. However, they always returned any change due tourists with their local coins. If we gave a larger bill, we had a greater chance of being swindled since we usually didn't know the value of what they gave us as change.

One of our tour business men thought this was silly advice. On our first day in Rome, he got up early and went out of the hotel and down the street to a small restaurant to get a cup of coffee. Since he had not exchanged his money yet, he only had American money, so he gave the waiter a $10 bill. Later, when he told our guide about his experience and showed him the change he had received, he was told that it was practically worthless. By not heeding the advice to use smaller bills, he had paid almost $10 for a cup of coffee!

When we left our hotel in Rome and were traveling toward the airport on a bus, one of the women in our group called Earl frantically and said, "I can't find my airplane ticket!" Each person had been told to be responsible for his/her own tickets, and Earl had just announced they should get them out and have them in hand when we arrived at the airport.

After being quizzed about what she had done that morning, where she had been, when she saw the ticket last, etc., this woman said, "Well, I *did* clean out my purse this morning and threw away some old papers and receipts and things like that."

On hearing that, Earl stopped the bus, and he and the woman caught a taxi to take them back to the hotel. They rushed in, requested her room key, and got there just as the cleaning lady was about to empty the waste cans. Sure enough, amidst the papers she had thrown away was the lost airplane ticket! What a close call!

* * * * *

Earl –

On our first trip to Cairo, Egypt, we stayed in a beautiful hotel along the Nile River. Most of our rooms had a balcony overlooking the river. Seeing the falukas sail slowly up the river was an impressive sight, especially at sunset. However, the view lost much of its charm because the Nile was so dirty with filthy things floating in it such as old boards and even a dead goat!

In 1977, on another trip to Cairo, we enjoyed an evening cruise on the Nile, complete with refreshments and entertainment provided by an exotic and scantily-clad Egyptian bellydancer. Without a stage, the dancer performed her abdominal gyrations in the narrow aisle between our tables. For a long time, she positioned herself in front of 80+ year old Clayton Kreider and his wife, Sadie, as we sat at an adjacent table watching and giggling. I was planning to tease Clayton afterwards about how he enjoyed the show, but Clayton beat me to it. As we disembarked and headed toward the bus to our hotel, Clayton leaned toward me and remarked, "Didn't that girl have *beautiful* hair!" (She did have beautiful waist-length hair, but that wasn't what octogenarian Clayton was watching during the show!)

* * * * *

On a long overnight train ride from Cairo to Luxor in 1966, our train accommodations were narrow bunk beds in tiny compartments, closed by a curtain from the walking passageway that led to the single unisex toilet that served the entire car. The rails seemed uneven and our car was obviously not new. Between the bumpiness of the ride, the noise of the wheels on the tracks, and the frequent jolts when we would stop at little stations along the way, it was almost impossible to sleep.

At one point, we rounded a curve and at that moment, there was a loud banging noise followed by the usual clanging of the wheels as the train chugged along. Right after that, there was a knock beside our curtain and one of our older male tour members, Paul, called loudly, "Earl, Earl."

I sat up in bed and sleepily answered, "Wha-a-a-t? Who is it?"

Paul pushed aside our curtain and excitedly said, "Earl, you have to go up to the engineer and tell him that we just lost a wheel back there. Didn't you hear that sound? Didn't you feel that jolt? I *know* that's what happened. You *have* to go up and tell him."

"Paul, don't worry about it," I replied in as calm a voice as I could muster. "We're not in America; we're in Egypt, and this is a noisy train. Everything's okay. You just go back to bed."

And after a little more persuasion, he did.

Not every big noise on a foreign train means that the train has lost a wheel!

* * * * *

On a trip to the Soviet Union, our group was waiting in the Leningrad Airport on August 13, 1988, for a flight to Helsinki, Finland. Several of us decided that while we were waiting, we may as well get some money changed. I happened to be standing in line behind Faye Kreiner from Manheim. When we approached the window, the teller asked if we were a couple.

"Oh, my, no!" exclaimed Faye, a single and pleasingly plump redhead.

I turned to her and said, "My 37th wedding anniversary was yesterday, and I always carry Vivian across the threshold of wherever we are on our anniversary. If we were a couple, I would have had to carry you."

"Well, it's good we aren't, because you never could do it without getting a hernia," she retorted.

That was like throwing out a challenge to me.

I rounded up Harlan Keener and we decided to give Faye the surprise of her life. I told Vivian what we were going to do and told her to get her camera ready.

"But we aren't allowed to take pictures here in the airport," she protested. "Don't you see the signs over there?"

Two sober-faced women were behind a counter watching this group of Americans suspiciously. I went over to them and asked if it would be okay with them if we played a trick on one of our tour members, and I pointed out Faye to them. They nodded their heads, but did not smile. Then I described what we planned to do—lift Faye and carry her from one row of chairs to another row. Now their lips turned up a little at the corners, and their eyes got a sparkle to them as they began to be part of the plot and saw that this might be quite funny.

"That is my wife," I explained to them, pointing at Vivian. "Could she take a photo of us when we carry this lady?" I asked. I demonstrated taking a picture and added, "She will only turn the camera that way, nowhere else."

They both smiled and said, "Okay."

So, Harlan and I approached Faye from the back, and in that noisy airport, she didn't see or hear us coming. We got behind her and joined hands beneath her, picked her up and carried her across the aisle (about ten feet). Of course, she yelled, and we all laughed so hard that Harlan and I almost dropped her! Vivian and others got photos of her with her mouth wide open.

When we put her down, and she caught her breath, she shook her finger at us and warned, "You guys are going to get hernias from doing that!"

We all just laughed even harder.

The most amazing thing was to watch the two formerly straight-faced ladies at the counter. They were laughing as much as any of us, and we all had a great time—at Faye's expense. Although we knew she's good at giving people a hard time, this incident demonstrated that she's also a good sport at taking it when they get back at her.

As we continued our wait, someone got the idea of singing, and our group began singing hymns. Strangers walking by looked at us and smiled. The two ladies at the counter kept smiling approvingly and seemed to know enough English to understand that we were singing religious songs. We felt our group did one small bit that day to improve the "Cold War" conditions between our two countries by changing the atmosphere and bringing smiles into one Russian airport.

* * * * *

Vivian –

From August 6 to 21, 1984, we took a group of thirty-two people on a fifteen-day tour of Western and Eastern Europe, including the Oberammergau Passion Play, for a cost of $1,975 per person. For some reason, on that tour I must have felt especially poetic, as I wrote a number of poems describing various sights and experiences. They may bring back memories for those who have visited these places.

Two Views on Flying
(Guess which is Earl's and which is mine!)

One View:
Feeling apprehension,
Filled with lots of tension,
How can this big airplane ever fly?
Sitting there white-knuckled,
With my seat-belt buckled,
Will this be the way that I will die?
Winds may turbulent be,
Water soon engulf me,
Ocean waves are known to be quite high.
What if we would crash now?
We would all be mashed now;
Seas so vast would have no help nearby.
How can others laugh so?

Sleep—or through the aisles go?
Would it help at all if I would cry?

* * * * *

ANOTHER VIEW:
Great anticipation,
Filled with much elation,
Finally, the time has come to fly.
See the mighty motors
With their roaring rotors,
Eagle-like, we soar into the sky.
Flying o'er church steeple
See the ant-sized people,
Looking down from windows up so high.
Good food we are eating,
New friends we are meeting,
Sounds aboard are like a lullabye.
Faith in God is strengthened,
As the trip is lengthened,
For we know His love is always nigh.

(Both views were written 8/8/84
while flying from New York to Frankfurt.)

* * * * *

STORY-BOOK TOWNS

What fun to walk through an old story-book town
With window-boxed houses lined up street and down.

The steps are foot-worn and the streets cobblestone,
All bordered by vineyards where grape-vines are grown.
The smells from the bake-shops invite us to eat,
And smiling French dolls await shoppers to greet.
The story-book towns cast on all quite a spell,
What wonderful stories their old walls could tell!

(Written 8/9/84 after walking through Riquewihr, France.)

* * * * *

Tourist Attractions

A tour group flew over the sea
The sights of old Europe to see,
But the sight of renown
That was sought in each town
Was always the W-C!

(In Europe, toilets are called W-C's or "water closets.")

* * * * *

Street Girls

Girls with young faces that are black and blue,
What brought you here? What has happened to you?
Eyes just half open, your gaze just a stare,
Cigarettes dangling from mouths once so fair.
Men hang around you, unkempt and unshorn;
Your lives are young but your bodies shopworn.

You look unhappy. Oh, where is your smile?
Sin marks its victims in such a short while.
Girls with young faces that are black and blue,
What brought you here? What has happened to you?

(Written 8/9/84, after eating lunch in Basil, Switzerland, at a sidewalk café where street girls were sitting and looking miserable.)

* * * * *

Visiting the Casino

While at the casino, what is it we do?
We sit dipping bread cubes in creamy fondue,
And savor each mouthful, a gourmet's delight,
And eagerly wait for the show for tonight.
Accordion music with Tyrolean beat
Soon starts our hands clapping and tapping our feet.
A pretty girl yodels; a lad plays the spoons,
And soon we are humming the same catchy tunes.
Some volunteers try blowing the alpine horn
Or hit a small target, thus having reborn
A new "William Tell," as the legend of old.
We're so fascinated our coffee gets cold.
For many, the pleasures of both sight and sound
Are part of the folklore in that show we found.

(Written 8/12/84 after seeing a folklore show in Lucerne, Switzerland.)

* * * * *

Rainy-Day Blues

Rainy-day weather depresses us so,
Hides gorgeous views . . . but it makes the grass grow!
Tree-covered mountains stand hidden in clouds,
Draped in their fog-laden, wispy-gray shrouds.
Ancient stone castles on hilltops so high
Seem to be built from the earth to the sky.
Legs with umbrellas are passed on the street.
Faces are hidden; there's no one to greet.
Stamps stick together, and writing gets smeared;
Colors on houses look faded and weird.
How we miss sunshine with its warmth and its light
Perking our spirits by making things bright.
Rainy-day weather depresses us so,
Hides gorgeous views . . . but it makes the grass grow!

(Written 8/11/84 after four consecutive days of rain. Ingrid, our guide in Innsbruck, Austria, told us not to complain about the cloudy weather. During World War II, Germany planned to bomb Innsbruck. Because it was cloud-covered, they postponed it for three days. On the third day, the war was over and so Innsbruck was spared because of the clouds.)

* * * * *

The Oberammergau Passion Play in Germany has an interesting history. During a deadly plague epidemic of Europe in 1632, the people of the little village of Oberammergau prayed and vowed to reenact the story of the Passion of Christ every ten years if God would spare their town. Miraculously, the plague stopped just short of their village, and the first Passion Play took place in 1634. Through the generations since, the people have kept their vow, producing the play on each decade year. The one exception occurred in 1984 when they performed an extra one to honor the 250th year after their productions began.

Earl and I have had the privilege of seeing it six times (in 1970, 1980, 1984, 1990, 2000, and 2010). Each time I see the crowds of people attending it, of all races and nationalities, and hear the commixture of languages, I think of Revelation 5:9 which states that "You (Christ) were slain, and with Your blood You purchased men for God from every tribe and language and people and nation." (NIV) It is thrilling to be a part of that mixed crowd, most of whom, I assume, are part of that same family to which I belong, the family of God.

Although the words and music are spoken and sung in the German language, there is no problem in understanding because, as Christians, we know the story. In addition, the actors put such emotion into their lines that without being able to translate the exact words, all who are familiar with the events of the last week of Jesus' life, *know* what is being said. Booklets containing side by side translations in many languages are also available for purchase.

Since all of the actors are natives of that immediate area, many of them are woodcarvers during the winter and have gift shops to sell their carved works during the tourist season. One year we were privileged to purchase something from the man who had the role of John the Disciple in the Passion Play, and in 2010, we bought something from "Caiaphas." When we asked him what role he had, he explained, "I'm a bad guy in the play."

I don't remember the year but I do remember which production was most impressive. During the crucifixion scene, just when Jesus died on the cross and said, "It is finished," there was actual thunder and lightning, followed by a short rainstorm. It truly seemed that God was listening and participating in telling the story of His only begotten Son so that whosoever might believe.

* * * * *

THE OBERAMMERGAU EFFECT

Oberammergau photos reveal
Its main attraction is the "Passionspiel."
A vow was made here a long time ago:
If God would save lives, the people would show
The world an enactment of Christ's life and death
Each ten years as long as God granted them breath.
So, tourists have come over three hundred years
To hear the old story and shed a few tears.
They see how the many out-shouted the few,
Condemning our Savior to die in full view
Among mocking soldiers and women who wept
And fearful disciples who had overslept.
The anguish of Judas and Peter is shared
By all who today have their faith not declared.
Again they're reminded of God's boundless love
Who wants all earth's sinners to join Him above.
This story of Jesus each Christian revives
And many vow henceforth to live better lives.

(Written 8/14/84, after seeing the Passion Play.)

* * * * *

Morning in a German Village

Under the feather-tick, sleeping so well,
Wakened so suddenly by the church bell.
After a wash-bowl bath, walk down the stairs,
Eat cheese and hard-crust rolls and say our prayers.
Women on bicycles ride down the street,
Purchase in baker's shops more rolls to eat.
Music from cow-bells chime, ringing through town,
Walking on cobble-stones, up hills and down.
Men wearing knicker-pants pass on the street.
Smoke from each chimney-top, a sign of heat.
Flowers greet passers-by. Oh, hear them call
Down from each window-box: "Gut Morgan" to all.

(Written 8/14/84 after two nights in Oberammergau.)

* * * * *

Prague's Old Town Clock

On the Old Town Hall in Prague
Is a sight you'll want to see:
A clock whose message spans the ages,
"Come now with me. Come now with me."

Life for all of us is short;
Death is beck'ning you and me.
Since fourteen-ten the clock reminds us,
"Come now with me. Come now with me."

Riches cannot add more years;
Beauty soon will also flee.
We'll stop our singing when death calls us,
"Come now with me. Come now with me."

Great apostles pass by too;
We'll soon join them, they agree.
The skeleton of death invites us,
"Come now with me. Come now with me."

When the cock crows, we're released,
From the pow'r of death set free.
An angel beckons us to Heaven:
"Come now with me. Come now with me."

Like an hour-glass, lives are spent,
Minutes, hours, go swiftly by.
Though none of us knows when we'll hear it,
"Come now with me," the old clock's cry.

(Written 8/19/84 after seeing the Old Town Clock in Prague.)

* * * * *

Gertrud

We met our guide in Rothenburg and Gertrud was her name.
She mixed some fun with history, so touring seemed a game.
Beneath the flower-laden walls of houses on the street,
Her high, "Yoo-Hoo," brought faces out of windows we could greet.
She told the slow to "shake-a-leg," to come see the "dumb clock."

With her umbrella up ahead, we followed like a flock.
Within the St. James Church, we saw the figures carved in wood.
She then explained the story well so that we understood.
She said she was a Christian, too, led to it by her son
Who was unwanted, but through him, her new faith was begun.
She feels her work's a mission field, for as she says her speeches,
She witnesses of Jesus' love and thus all races reaches.

(Written 8/21/84 after having Gertrud
as our guide in Rothenburg, Germany.)

* * * * *

One European guide told the story that she observed a tourist in her group frequently writing "ABC" in her memo book. Out of curiosity, the guide asked, "Why are you writing down 'ABC' so often?"

"Oh," the woman laughed. "That's just my shorthand for 'Another Beautiful Cathedral.'"

* * * * *

On my first trip to Australia, we exited the plane at Sydney and waited for our baggage. Before we could touch it, it was placed in a large room, and we observed men leading police dogs that were sniffing the bags. Then they called us by name and those people were allowed to get their suitcases and proceed through customs.

When they called my name, I was directed to a special lane. The attendant asked what I had in my bag.

Puzzled, I said, "Just clothing, toiletries, and things like that."

"Would you open it, please?" he asked politely.

When I did that, he reached immediately into one certain corner and came up with a bottle of saccharine tablets. "What are these?" he inquired.

I probably blushed and laughed nervously as I confessed, "Oh, those are just saccharine tablets."

"Why did you bring them?" he asked in a stern voice as though he had never heard of them.

Again, I smiled guiltily. "Those tablets make beverages taste sweet and don't have as many calories as sugar does. Because I'm fat, I take them along so that I won't get even fatter."

He obviously didn't think it was humorous, nor did he think it was wise for me to have them, so he confiscated them. I moved on having felt soundly rebuked and humiliated because I was the co-tour leader, some group members were watching, and mine was the only suitcase singled out for inspection. That experience taught me to highly respect the drug-sniffing abilities of trained dogs. That dog not only smelled those tablets in the bottle through my closed suitcase but also indicated to the authorities exactly where they would find them. Amazing!

* * * * *

Earl –

In all our years of traveling, we've seldom had a problem with lost luggage. However, one time when we arrived in Moscow, two suitcases were missing: Kathryn Plowfield's and Vivian's. I called the Russian airline several times the first afternoon and evening and kept getting evasive, non-satisfactory answers as to where they could be.

The following morning, Kathryn and I went via taxi to the airport to do some detective work on our own. Since I could recognize Vivian's luggage as well as she could, she didn't come along. After we inquired at the lost luggage department and described the two pieces, the Russian man went to look for them. He returned and stated emphatically that the luggage was not there. In our desperation, I insisted that he permit us to search. He then waved his hand, allowing us in the baggage area while he watched us. We were amazed at the large collection of luggage that was there, and sure enough, in the midst of them all, Kathryn spied her suitcase and I found Vivian's. If I hadn't been aggressive, we could have gone home from Russia before the suitcases were "found."

* * * * *

Carl and Ann Diller from Lampeter were in our European Tour Group in 1984. A reluctant traveler, Carl feared going through the border patrol most of all. We tried to assure him that as long as he didn't have contraband liquor, arms or drugs with him, he had nothing to fear. Besides, at that time, when an officer faced a tour group, rather than question and search everyone, he would often choose one or two which he'd consider as representative of the group and go through only those. The rest he would wave through. The chances of Carl having to open his suitcase were slim.

When we approached Checkpoint Charlie in Berlin, the men came out with their dogs and their long-handled mirrors so they could check that we didn't have some illegal person hanging somewhere beneath the bus. We were all ordered off the bus as they searched inside and then checked us individually. At their command, the driver opened the baggage compartment and then they pointed at one suitcase and asked for its owner to step forward. Wouldn't you know, they chose Carl's!

Nervously, he unlocked it and opened it. As the officer felt around among Carl's clothes, he came up with a Bible.

"What's this?" he barked.

"That is a Bible, the Word of God," Carl answered boldly.

The officer looked at it, shuffled through the pages, made a face and threw it on the ground in utter contempt. After searching a bit more, he walked away, leaving Carl's clothing scattered and disheveled. Carl quickly swept up his belongings, including his precious Bible, and packed them back into his suitcase.

Then we all boarded the bus again and after another long wait were permitted to move slowly through the gate. That was an experience none of us, and especially, Carl, ever forgot.

* * * * *

Vivian –

Crossing the Border

What is it we need to pass border control?
Just passports and patience and time.
They search through our luggage and pockets and soul
Without any reason or rhyme.

And what do we feel when we're told to move on?
Just thankfulness, relief and joy
That birth in America guarantees hope
And freedom for each girl and boy.

(Written 8/19/84 after waiting almost two hours to get through the Czech/German border.)

* * * * *

Another tough border patrol was at the Allenby Bridge crossing between Jordan and Israel. Leaving Jordan was no problem as the Jordanian guards were usually friendly and their questions and searches were perfunctory. The bridge, itself, was short.

However, on the Israeli side, it was another matter. We were guided into an open pavilion filled with tables in rows. At the end of each row was an inspector, so we placed our luggage on a table and stood in line, moving slowly toward the inspection site. When we got near the officer, we were to take *everything* out of our suitcases for him to inspect. (We had been warned that they might puncture toothpaste tubes and remove flashlight batteries.) No matter if it was dirty laundry, sanitary napkins, underclothes, Bibles, or magazines, it was all spread out on the table for the world to see. Though embarrassing and humiliating, that was what it was meant to be.

When I was in front of the officer, he asked to see my camera. I hoped he wouldn't open it and ruin my 35mm film and was surprised when he simply said, "I want you to take my picture."

"What?" I asked in amazement.

"Yes, I want you to take my picture. Don't take a picture of anything else. Just take a picture of me."

"Okay," I said, and did it. Obviously, if it had been rigged somehow, it wouldn't have clicked or it might have blown up, and that is why he made that request. It did make an interesting addition to my slides taken of that trip. Note: He didn't smile!

Some persons, especially Palestinian Arabs, had to go to a walled-in area to be strip-searched, but as Americans, we were spared that.

* * * * *

Earl –

On another trip, when my brother, Victor, was along, he had bought a case of oranges. When a border patrol guard saw it, he said the oranges couldn't be taken across the border. So, Victor simply handed out oranges to all the tour members, and we ate them right there. *Then*, ten minutes later, we were allowed to move forward and go across, taking the oranges with us . . . in our stomachs!

* * * * *

European hotels have the same rules that we have at most buffet meals in America: we can eat whatever and as much as we want, but we are *not* to carry food out. However, in one of our tour groups, we had a man who brought a 2-quart thermos to a breakfast buffet and had the audacity to fill it with orange juice to take on the bus with him. When a hotel employee saw this, he reported it to our driver who alerted me. I confronted the man, but he was very arrogant and saw nothing wrong with what he had done. Before we left, the hotel billed me $26, and I had to pay it out of my own pocket. I was never repaid by the man who stole the orange juice.

On another trip, we were warned that we could not take any fresh fruit out of the country. One lady had just bought a couple lovely apples and had eaten one, but still had one left. She boldly declared, "I am *not* going to throw away this perfectly good apple."

During the inspection, it was found, and she was fined $200.

Some of us learn the rules the hard way!

* * * * *

Doc Harnish and Helen Sealover were both widowed singles on one of our trips to Alaska, and they had never met before. As we prepared for a short jaunt in four vehicles from our hotel to an Alaskan Salmon Bake dinner, Helen had no place to sit. All the seats were filled. One of the tour members yelled, "Helen, sit on Doc's lap."

She obeyed, and he seemed pleased as they took that short ride to the Salmon Bake, where they sat next to one another for dinner. Shortly, the group noticed a mutual blossoming relationship developing between these two. The following February, on Valentine's weekend, I performed their wedding before family and friends. Both Helen and Doc have since passed away, but they were rewarded with several years of marital bliss.

Sometimes one can discover more than beautiful scenery on a tour!

CIRCLING THE GLOBE
Chapter Twelve

"You know when I sit or stand.
When far away you know my every thought.
You chart the path ahead of me,
and tell me where to stop and rest.
Every moment you know where I am . . . If I ride
the morning winds to the farthest oceans,
even there your hand will guide me,
your strength will support me."
(Psalms 139:2,3,9, 10) TLB

Vivian –

Before we left on our trip to China, Hong Kong and Thailand in October 1996, we had a strange request. Alicia Kofroth, a fourth grade student in the Quarryville Elementary School gave us a little plush stuffed chipmunk named "Chipper" and asked if we would let him accompany us, take his picture now and then on his travels, and send her postcards. Upon receiving them, her class would follow our itinerary on a large map. We thought it was a neat geography project for a public school class, so we agreed to take Chipper along.

Consequently, Chipper was photographed on the Great Wall of China, among the terra cotta soldiers, watching the passing scenery as we cruised on the Li River, looking down on Hong Kong's high-rise buildings, visiting the Grand Palace in Bangkok, and other sites. After we got home, we received this note from Alicia:

Dear Earl and Vivian,
    Thanks for taking Chipper with you to China. I really appreciated it. My teacher and I loved the postcards. I'm glad Chipper had a great time. You guys are very nice people.
                              Thanks with love,
                                Alicia Kofroth

* * * * *

In Guangzhou, China, we went through a street market and saw all kinds of caged mammals, reptiles and birds that were for sale. Our guide told us, "In China, we eat everything that has legs except tables, and we eat everything that has wings except airplanes."

* * * * *

Earl –
    One evening when we were in Hong Kong, our tour group had dinner on a floating restaurant, accessible only from sampans in the harbor. After a delicious Asian meal of several courses, the group exited and I hung back to pay the bill. Suddenly, I heard someone from the floor above me call out, "Earl!" (I thought it might be the good Lord, Himself, calling me!)
    When I looked up, who should I see but Bud and Sarah Ritchey who had been youth advisors in my first pastorate in Curryville, Pennsylvania! What a shock for them and for me, for

neither of us knew the other was traveling in China at that time. How nice to see a familiar face!

Just another illustration that *you never know whom you might meet when you travel.*

* * * * *

Vivian –

At the conclusion of our trip to China, Hong Kong and Thailand with Chipper, our tour group was scheduled to fly home from Bangkok around midnight on Thursday, Oct. 31, 1996, on United Airlines. As we approached the airport, our Thai guide, Jimmy, announced that she would be coming through the bus to collect our passports so she could go in and check us through as a group. Marianne Smith, in her mid-sixties, was sitting in the back of the bus, and her passport was the last one Jimmy collected.

Inside the airport, the airline representative said they must speak to each of us individually for security purposes. This meant that Jimmy had to return our passports to us, along with our air tickets and airport tax receipts. When all the passports had been distributed, Marianne's was missing. We backtracked where we had walked and searched everywhere, but couldn't find it.

Meanwhile, Earl and I tried to decide what to do. We agreed that we didn't want to pull the entire group from the plane but we couldn't leave Marianne stranded there alone. It would have been inappropriate for Earl, a male tour leader, to stay in Bangkok with Marianne, so the only alternative was for me to stay with her. Earl and I had both shown our passports and checked in our suitcases, so I had only my hand luggage with me. Without a passport, Marianne still had both her suitcase and her carry-on. Earl and I said our goodbyes with sinking feelings in our hearts, uncertain what the future would hold, but knowing that our God was loving, omniscient, omnipotent and in total control.

Within the airport, Jimmy took Marianne and me to the airline office to cancel our tickets. Then she took us by taxi back to the Rembrandt Hotel to the same individual rooms in which we had slept the night before. By that time it was 1:30 a.m., and neither of us slept well.

Before going to our buffet breakfast on Friday, I met Marianne in her room and we prayed together. Until she had made a reservation to travel with us, I had never met her. I discovered she was of Italian descent, a Roman Catholic, a diabetic, a widow, a mother and very emotional. However, we agreed that we needed to work together to the best of our combined abilities, and that we needed God's help most of all.

Jimmy drove us in her own car to the American Citizen Services downtown, a branch of the American Embassy. We told our story and applied for a new passport for Marianne. They seemed skeptical and didn't seem to trust Jimmy, and at that point, we didn't either, but she was our translator, chauffeur, and virtually our lifeline. After Marianne's new passport photos were taken, Jimmy took us to the Northwest Airlines office to get new air tickets that had us leaving near midnight, going through Seoul.

With her new photos, the American Citizen Services gave Marianne a new passport. Thinking everything was now in order, we were taxied by Jimmy to the beautiful Rama Garden Hotel near the airport, and she rented us a room so we could rest until about 10:30 p.m.

After dinner, Jimmy took us to the airport where we checked in Marianne's baggage, but then hit another snag. Although we already had our boarding passes, we were told we couldn't leave without an "entering stamp" on Marianne's passport. Jimmy pleaded with the officer to allow us to go through, but he firmly said, "No," and literally turned his back on us. Case closed.

On seeing this exchange, the airline girl requested our boarding passes and smiled as she tore them up in front of us. Marianne's luggage had been pulled off the plane, so we had to reclaim it at "Lost and Found." At 2 a.m. Jimmy took us back to the Rama Garden Hotel for the night.

On Saturday, we left the hotel by 7 a.m. At the Thai Immigration Office we were told that the entry stamp *must* be confirmed by computer, and that department was closed until Monday. Marianne tearfully pleaded with him, explaining that she was diabetic and running out of her medications, but he seemed unimpressed and just laughed. Obviously, he was enjoying his *power* over two Americans, even if they were just two older ladies.

In late afternoon, Jimmy phoned us at the hotel, promising to take us sightseeing the next day. After dinner, Earl called and I explained our predicament while Marianne phoned her mother and discovered her Uncle Fred was dying.

On Sunday morning, Jimmy arrived and drove us north of Bangkok to the town of Ayutthaya where the three of us had an enjoyable day visiting Buddhist sites built in the Thirteenth Century and destroyed by the Burmese in the Seventeenth Century. We saw damaged Buddha images, the phenomenon of a tree whose roots had grown around a Buddha statue head, a golden Buddha, and many large Buddhist temples with people worshipping in them. Since Queen Elizabeth from England had just visited Ayutthaya two days earlier, we saw many streets still lined with flags and colorful banners strung overhead. Jimmy explained things well and even took us for lunch at a floating restaurant.

That evening Earl phoned again and informed us the Lampeter congregation was praying for us and that Menno Travel Service (MTS) was going to increase their pressure for our release.

Early Monday morning we were at the Immigration Office waiting until it opened. The man at the counter greeted us with a smile, spoke softly with Jimmy, and began putting many stamps in Marianne's passport. I winked at Marianne as we both felt that he was finally giving us what we needed. It took about a half hour, and he waved us out with a smile. Our first miracle!

At our next stop, the Northwest Airlines Office downtown, we received all negative news. They said *all* flights from Bangkok by every route imaginable (through Seoul, Hong Kong, and Manilla) were filled, and forty were on standby to leave that night through Tokyo. Nevertheless, we requested to be added to the standbys.

Just then, Jimmy got a phone call. She went outside to talk, and when she came in, she talked in Thai with the Northwestern Airlines representative. The girl quickly removed our standby tickets from her typewriter and put in new ones. With a different demeanor, she turned to us, smiled, and said, "Your husband just called and now there *is* room, and you can leave tomorrow going through Tokyo!" A second miracle!

(After we got home, we learned that the head of the MTS agency had phoned Jimmy's agency and threatened to discontinue his business with them if they didn't get us on our way home promptly.)

The girl from Northwest continued, "You can go . . . no problem. Would you prefer a window seat or an aisle seat?"

Marianne and I were dumbfounded . . . but joyful! We had not heard those words, "No problem," for five long days! The cost of changing our flight was seventy-five dollars.

Over lunch in an Italian restaurant, Jimmy pleaded with us to not send a letter of complaint to her travel agency employers because if we did, she would be fired. Marianne assured her that we wouldn't complain as *all three of us* were victims. In tears, Jimmy explained that she, personally, had been paying for all our bills for lodging, meals and transportation because "I can always earn money, but if I lose my good name, reputation and/or career, I lose them forever."

Tuesday, November 5, was Election Day in America with the presidential contest between Bob Dole and Bill Clinton, and Marianne and I were hoping we wouldn't miss voting. When Jimmy arrived at 4:45 a.m., we were waiting. She checked at the desk to see if our bill was paid and made no comment when she discovered I had already paid it. After she took us to the airport for our 6:25 a.m. flight, no one questioned Marianne's passport, and our check-in went smoothly. We hugged Jimmy, gave her a tip and thanked her. After one last wave to her, we boarded the plane and enjoyed one of the smoothest take-offs and landings I can remember. Interestingly enough, there were empty seats beside both Marianne and me! The flight from Tokyo to Detroit, where I then called Earl, took just over eleven hours.

When we arrived in Philadelphia, we were so glad to see Earl waiting to greet us and take us to Lampeter. Marianne's car was there, and it started with no problem and she headed home. Meanwhile, I went straight to the Lampeter Fire Hall to get in line to vote. It was 7:15 p.m., and the man in back of me said he had driven from Virginia to get there to vote. He was shocked when I told him that I had come from Bangkok! It had been a long day, but it was *so good* to be home! To God be the glory!

Marianne's Uncle Fred died three days later, on November 8th, but she did get to talk to him before he died. His brother, another of her uncles, died suddenly on November 18th, so that month was one she would *never* forget.

At the time this happened, we were told that a stolen American passport could be sold in that part of the world for five thousand dollars. In retrospect, Marianne and I still suspect that Jimmy, in spite of her denials, may have been the culprit who stole it. Who else could have done it?

* * * * *

Earl –

In January 1996, the Ministers of Music (Lamar Dourte, Dale Engle, Robert Kettering, Ron Ludwick and Alice Lauver) hosted a Caribbean cruise for eighty people on the *Regal Princess* and invited me to be their Chaplain. Two happenings made that experience unforgettable.

Barbados was one of our stops, and Vivian and I took a bus tour of the island including a stop at the Andromeda Gardens containing exotic tropical plants and gorgeous blooms. As the bus was loading to move on, an announcement was made that someone had collapsed in the garden. Being the Chaplain, I thought it would be wise to check if it was one of "our" people, and soon discovered that Dr. Robert Stone, 77, from our group but whom I had not known, had suffered a fatal cardiac arrest. He and his wife, Catherine, were residents at Brethren Village, and Catherine, who suffered from Alzheimer's disease, was traveling with him. On the cruise, Dr. Stone led the way and made the decisions, and Catherine calmly followed. Consequently, her problem could not be readily detected, and I remembered having seen her playing the piano on the ship.

An ambulance was called, and Catherine went with her husband to the hospital while I sped there in a taxi, arriving a half hour later. When it became obvious that Catherine didn't grasp what had happened, I realized she was suffering from serious dementia. In Dr. Stone's wallet, I discovered the contact information for his son, whom I then phoned and informed of his father's death. Fortunately, he was an airline pilot and suggested that I secure a nurse-companion to accompany his mother to Miami and he would meet her there. Amazingly, I was able to complete all those arrangements and get back on board the cruise ship five minutes before it sailed away.

The second event was that while we were sunbathing on Caribbean beaches and enjoying balmy breezes, Lancaster County received a thirty-three inch snowfall dubbed "The Blizzard of '96." When we arrived back home, what a time we had digging out our cars from all that snow!

*****

Vivian –

On our trip to Europe in 2000, we took along our grandson, Tim Creighton, who was 13. On the final evening, we had a talent night, featuring several duets and the sharing of favorite happenings on the tour. Tim had forgotten to prepare anything, so he quickly jotted down a poem on the paper tablecloth in about fifteen minutes and titled it, "An Ode to Europe."

An Ode to Europe

"Ah, Europe, O grand continent in the Eastern Hemisphere,
But let us look at its grandeur by looking at it here.
Iceland, the smallest, yet westernmost of Europe. It's an island.

Earl and Vivian with grandson, Tim Creighton, 14, with the village of Gebenbach, Germany, in the background in 2000.

*It's warmer than its name implies, and all Vikings say, "It's **my** land!"*
Ireland, a fine island, containing lots of greens,
Once Catholic, then Protestant, under English kings and queens.
With clover and Saint Patrick's Day and a land that is snake-free
And a stone that gives great eloquence—Oh, what's its name—
BLARNEY!

~ ~ ~ ~ ~

Circling the Globe 229

*Great France, home of great crepes Suzette, the Eiffel Tower, too.
In France, the Tower's* La Tour Eiffel *and each street is called a rue.
Their language is very ornate. Their literature is great.
Unfortunately, it's all in French, so for translations I must wait.
Italy is Europe's foot, with Roma, Firenzi,
Venetia, Genova, Brindisi, Milano, Palermo, Napoli.
With pasta, pizza, Pisa, Sicily, Sardinia and the Colosseum,
If you want to see all the stuff down there, it takes a while to see 'em.
Germany has a history in this Teutonic land,
As shown in Berlin, Hamburg, Bonn, in which many had a hand.
Switzerland and Austria with folklore and the Alps,
Can make all present sit and think, sit back and scratch their scalps.
Slovakia and Hungary, Liechtenstein, Czechia, Romania,
I don't have much to comment on like Estonia, Latvia,
Lithuania.
Greece has a long, proud history right near the Aegean Sea,
But then Rome came and all was lost, sad in archaeology.
Ukraine, with capital at Kiev, Hail, O poor Ukraine.
I say poor, for centuries, the Russians drove them insane!
Russia has a part here, too, with Perm and then Moscow.
St. Petersburg, Yekaterinburg, it's cold up there! YEEOW!
So, that's Europe, slightly compressed. I have much more to say,
But Earl didn't want me to, for this night I might delay."*

Several lines about Great Britain, Scotland, Wales, Spain and Portugal were omitted here. When Earl noticed Tim writing hurriedly, he warned him, "Don't make it too long!" That is what he referred to in his last two lines.

* * * * *

Earl –

Herman and Beverly Ritchey from Woodbury were along with us on one of our trips to Alaska. During the last few days of the trip, we cruised on a Holland America ship down the Inland Passage from Juneau to Vancouver. In the middle of one night, a storm came up, and the ship rocked. The motion awoke Beverly, and she was terrified. "What will we do?" she asked Herman frantically.

"Go back to sleep, Beverly. Everything's under control," Herman advised.

But Beverly was too frightened to do that. Instead, she took off her nightie and put on her Woodbury Church of the Brethren sweat shirt and pants.

Noticing her activity, Herman asked, "Why are you putting that on?"

She replied, "Because when the ship goes down and my body is found, then they will know where I was from!"

Herman just laughed, rolled over in bed, and said again, "Go back to sleep!"

* * * * *

When we spent a couple days in Fiji in 1993, I thoroughly enjoyed the beach. With its clean sand, sloping gradually into the clear aqua-blue waters of the Pacific, sunny skies and warm breezes, it was a tropical paradise. On our last afternoon there, Bob Guyer, my friend from Woodbury, Pat Cooper, a pleasingly plump, fun-loving, retired elementary teacher, and I had some fun in waist-deep water with an inflatable raft. While we tried to assist Pat to get on and ride the raft (and repeatedly failed), Delma Over took a video of our antics. The result could almost qualify to be shown on "America's Funniest Home Videos." What a time we had! But that is not the end of the story!

Because men usually have their ankles covered with socks, they are often tender to the sun's rays. Neither Bob nor I were aware of that, and after a few hours we had blisters on our ankles the size of an egg! I sported the largest one and didn't feel it would be wise to puncture it. On the flight home, the stewardess suggested that I lounge on the empty back row of seats with my leg elevated, and one of my first visits upon getting home was to our family doctor. Years later, those areas of my ankle are still extremely sensitive.

* * * * *

Vivian –

The most extravagant and entertaining show we have ever seen was in Beirut, Lebanon, in 1970. Our guide told us that we had the option of seeing a very outstanding show at a night club at the outskirts of the city at a cost of $30 per person, which at that time, seemed very expensive. After a busy day touring Baalbeck, most group members chose to retire early, but Earl and I and Annabelle Werner reasoned, "We are only here one night—let's see what we can see."

Forty-two years later, the acts I can still remember seeing from our front-row seats were two motorcycles circling within a large clear (glass?) sphere, large horses pulling a chariot through a simulated "snow storm," an elephant act, and the edge of the stage opening to reveal a "canal" of water and out of the water rose gilt-coated dancers. Although we have seen many shows all over the world since then, none of them came close to the fabulous show we saw that night.

* * * * *

On one of our trips to Oslo, Norway, we toured the museum where Thor Heyerdale's original Kon-Tiki boat and other old ships, some of which were salvaged from the bottom of the sea, are on display. After walking among the artifacts, I went to an area where numerous postcards were for sale. At that time I was an avid postcard collector, so I was engrossed in choosing which postcards I would purchase. Other tourists were doing the same thing, and when a woman bumped me on the left hand side, I thought nothing of it. I apologized briefly, took several steps away from her and continued to peruse the card display.

A little later, she bumped me again, and again I quickly apologized and stepped away. A short time later I finished making my choices and went to the cashier to pay for them. I was surprised to see that my shoulder-strap purse was open, as I didn't remember opening it. I was even more surprised when I couldn't find my wallet in my purse. After finding Earl, we retraced my steps in the museum, looking to see if it had dropped out somehow somewhere. We reported to the cashier that we believed my wallet had been stolen, and she claimed that although Oslo is noted for the slick work of pickpockets, they almost never had a problem in the museum before. I then remembered being "bumped" twice, and now I understood why. Having something stolen is always a disappointment. It's tricky replacing everything, and it's even more complicated if it happens when you are on a trip in Europe.

The moral of this story is—if you travel in Oslo, beware!

* * * * *

Earl –

On a trip to New Zealand in 1993, our itinerary said we were to see Mt. Cook, and stay in a nearby hotel with a gorgeous view of that high, snow-capped mountain. However, the day we arrived, the skies were overcast, drizzling, and it was so foggy that the mountain was completely hidden.

As night fell, the spirits of our tour group sank with disappointment. As the tour leaders, Vivian and I decided to have an "Un-Birthday" celebration and chose tour member, Preston Walker (in his seventies) to be the "honored guest." We purchased a card and all the other tour members surreptitiously signed it, including Preston's wife, Delena, and we ordered a cake through the hotel.

After the main course of dinner, the waitress brought in the cake and set it in front of Preston, and we all sang "Happy Birthday" to him. Of course, he was *very* surprised, because it wasn't really his birthday. However, nobody likes a joke more than Preston does, and after his initial confusion, he played right along as if it really were his birthday. After he was given the card, group members had their own talent show featuring a comic skit, recited poems, and a vocal solo. The funniest part was when other guests, including a couple from Germany, exited the dining room and wished Preston a Happy Birthday, he politely thanked them. What could have been a dud of a travel experience turned out to be an evening filled with fun that is still joyfully recalled by those who were there.

Actually, we had several "un-birthdays" in our travels. One time in Europe the honoree was Hannah Clouse, a retired schoolteacher from Waterside, Pennsylvania, and on a trip to Branson, it was Anna Jane Glisson from Quarryville, Pennsylvania. We always picked on people whom we knew could take a joke, and everyone left with a nice memory.

* * * * *

On a Three-Continent Tour in the summer of 1974, we had a retired schoolteacher with us who didn't want to comply with the group activities. When we went on a safari tour in the Masai-Mara Game Reserve in Kenya, we were divided into groups of six in jeep-like vehicles. The Kenyan men who were our drivers were also our spotters, skilled at seeing the animals in the trees and tall grass. This woman, whom I'll call Marian (not her real name) immediately sat in the front beside her driver, and from the beginning began engaging the driver in conversation. Consequently, the others in her vehicle began noticing that other jeeps had stopped to view animals here and there, but they seldom stopped as their driver was distracted.

At one of our stops, some of those passengers approached me and said, "You need to talk to Marian. We are not getting to see all that the others are seeing because she is monopolizing our driver's attention."

I wanted to have a witness, so I asked Richard Thierut (who later was elected and served as Mayor of Spring Grove, Pennsylvania, for many years) to go with me for this confrontation. Although I broached the subject as tactfully and yet as directly as I could, she immediately became defensive. She said she was teaching the driver to speak German, and he was an eager learner. As we parted, in a very derisive and almost mocking tone, this woman, who was old enough to be my mother, reluctantly agreed to not interfere with the driver/spotter doing his job by saying, "All right, *Father* Ziegler!"

The next day she handed me a handwritten letter in which she said, among other things, "I do <u>not</u> travel to <u>meet</u> or <u>learn to know</u> thirty other Americans! . . . In a good family, the father does not dictate behavior. . . . Our driver said he could understand me and talk to me better than most people and that he was happy to learn from me. Apparently, you do not consider it good to become friends of the 'hired help,' especially if they are black. . . . You need never be concerned about turning me down for another trip because I will not ask to go along. . . . I will try hard not to criticize you or the trip but please try a little at least to let me be me."

Not all aspects of being a tour director are fun! But when there is a problem, somebody has to intervene. Marian did cooperate during the rest of the trip, but she never did choose to travel with me again . . . nor did I invite her!

* * * * *

Vivian –

While Earl was serving churches as their pastor and I was working in the public schools, we only took one trip a year or less. In the 1970's and 1980's, we took a total of nine trips per decade. In the 1990's, we took nineteen trips, and in the 11 years beginning with the year 2000, we have taken around 82 tours . . . so far! In addition, Earl's mission trip to the Dominican Republic in February 2012, was his sixteenth time there, plus he's been on a work camp in Haiti once, and had several trips to Puerto Rico. Since we're both retired, we've accelerated our tours, adding more one-day tours to accommodate seniors in the North Atlantic District of the Church of the Brethren. We do hope to begin slowing down soon . . . but not yet!

What began with a trip to visit missions in Ecuador that we thought would be a "once in a lifetime" opportunity, has resulted in our visiting more than sixty countries!—and many of them more than once! We have also been blessed to have visited six of the seven continents (skipping Antarctica), gotten wet in four of the five oceans (missing the Antarctic Ocean) plus dipping in the Blue Lagoon in Iceland, the Mediterranean Sea in Spain, and both the Dead Sea and the Sea of Galilee in Israel.

In addition, we've been to such exotic places as Bethlehem and the Garden Tomb of Jesus in Israel; Anne Frank's home in Amsterdam, Holland; the concentration camps of Auschwitz in Poland, Dachau in Germany, and Breendunk in Belgium; Mt. Kiliamanjaro in Tanzania, Mt. McKinley in Alaska, and Mt. Cook in New Zealand; the peaks in the Alps of Jungfrau, Matterhorn, and Pilatus in Switzerland, the Dolomites in Italy, the Rockies and the Tetons in the U.S.A.; St. Peter's Cathedral in the Vatican; TienAn Men Square in Bejing, China; a salt mine in Poland; and attended the World's Fair in Osaka, Japan and a church service in Westminster Abbey in London. We've seen such wonders of the world as the Great Wall of China, the Grand Canyon, the Pyramids in Egypt, the Acropolis in Greece, the Colosseum in Rome, the Taj Mahal in India, the Eiffel Tower in France, Stonehenge in England, Petra in Jordan, the Christ the Redeemer Statue in Brazil, the Statue of Liberty in New York City, St. Basil's Church in Moscow, the Neuschwanstein Castle in Germany, and the Sydney Opera House in Australia. We've been north to Point Barrow, Alaska, and south to Stewart Island, New Zealand, where one can behold some of the most gorgeous sunrises and sunsets in the world. We've walked on icy glaciers, ridden a camel, and taken an African safari, observing numerous wild animals in their natural habitats. God has created such an interesting, beautiful and amazing world, and we praise Him that we have been blessed and privileged to have seen so much of it.

What wonderful friends we have made among those who traveled with us and those we met around the world. For example,

Earl and Heinz Karner, our Austrian coach driver in Europe, posing and color-coordinated with the "ZIEGLER" coach in 2000.

since 1992, whenever we go to Europe, we request Heinz Karner, an Austrian, to be our bus driver. He has taken our tour groups to visit his parents, tour his new home under construction, and meet Regula, his fiancé. He pointed out and explained interesting sites along the way that we would otherwise have missed, and has visited us in America. In 2000, he was especially pleased because he was able to surprise us by getting a bus for our tour from a "Ziegler" company and we toured through various countries in a bus with a huge Ziegler name painted on its sides!

Our lives have been so enriched by all these experiences and it is amazing that two people who started out with so little resources and virtually no travel goals were still able to travel and see so much! **If we could do it, so can anyone else!** This illustrates two of Earl's favorite quotes: *"If it is to be, it is up to me!"* and *"You shall have what your faith expects."* (Matthew 9:29, Phillips translation)

LIVING IN "RUFUS P. BUCHER COUNTRY," 1970 - 1983
Chapter Thirteen

"People with vision know where they're going and how to get there."
(Bob Kettering, pastor of Lititz Church of the Brethren)

Earl –

Flying from Honolulu, Hawaii, on the last leg of our 33-day "Around the World" tour in 1970, we landed in Baltimore and headed straight toward our new home south of Quarryville, Pennsylvania. I had been called to pastor the Mechanic Grove Church of the Brethren, which had an average attendance of 230, in rural agricultural Southern Lancaster County, beginning on September 1st.

I soon discovered that this was "Rufus P. Bucher Country." Rufus (1883-1956) had been the first pastor of this church with a total ministry of fifty-five years, either in free ministry or paid ministry. During that time, he was perhaps best known as an evangelist, having held revival meetings in thirteen states, in forty congregations in eastern Pennsylvania, resulting in nearly three thousand conversions including that of Vivian's mother, Kathryn E. Zug, when she was nine. When someone objected to baptizing a child so young, Rufus retorted, *"If she's old enough to serve Sa-*

tan, she's old enough to serve God." This same Rufus Bucher, when serving as chair of the Elizabethtown College Board of Trustees, handed us our college degrees in 1951 at Commencement. Drawing illustrations for his sermons from common everyday life and relationships, and including much humor, he was a popular speaker. Stories about him and his wife, Naomi, are legendary.

Immediately after the Easter season in 1970, Vivian and I had motored to the Mechanic Grove Church where we met in a congregational interview on Saturday night with several hundred members. During a question and answer period, Pauley, an older and somewhat eccentric farmer, addressed the group saying, "When we were both boys, I worked together on a farm with Earl's father, and I can tell you, he comes from *good stock*!"

The next morning I preached the sermon, and at the conclusion of the worship service, Vivian and I headed back to Black Rock to our home and family. Several days later, Harold Bomberger, the District Executive, phoned and relayed the message that I had received an almost unanimous vote to come to pastor the Mechanic Grove Church. One negative vote had been cast. Did that ever raise my curiosity? However, I accepted the call even though the financial package was exactly what I was getting at Black Rock.

Two considerations shaped us to respond positively and leave the Black Rock congregation after ten and one-half years. One was very personal. When I was a senior in high school, my family had moved, and I had to finish my education in a totally new environment with new classmates and faculty. I promised myself that I wasn't going to allow that to happen to my children. In the spring of 1970, our oldest daughter, Karen, graduated from South Western High School and matriculated to Elizabethtown College that summer. Randy was entering tenth grade, Doreen eighth grade, and Mike sixth grade. A decision had to be made to go . . . or to stay another seven years to adhere to my promise.

The second factor was that the call from Mechanic Grove was two-fold: They needed a creative worship leader and one who related well with youth. Since those were two of my greatest strengths, I had felt moved to answer God's call to leave my comfort zone and enter the land of Solanco (Southern Lancaster County).

* * * * *

The first year went great, but the second year was more challenging. A search committee member graced my office one morning and told me how disappointed he was in my leadership

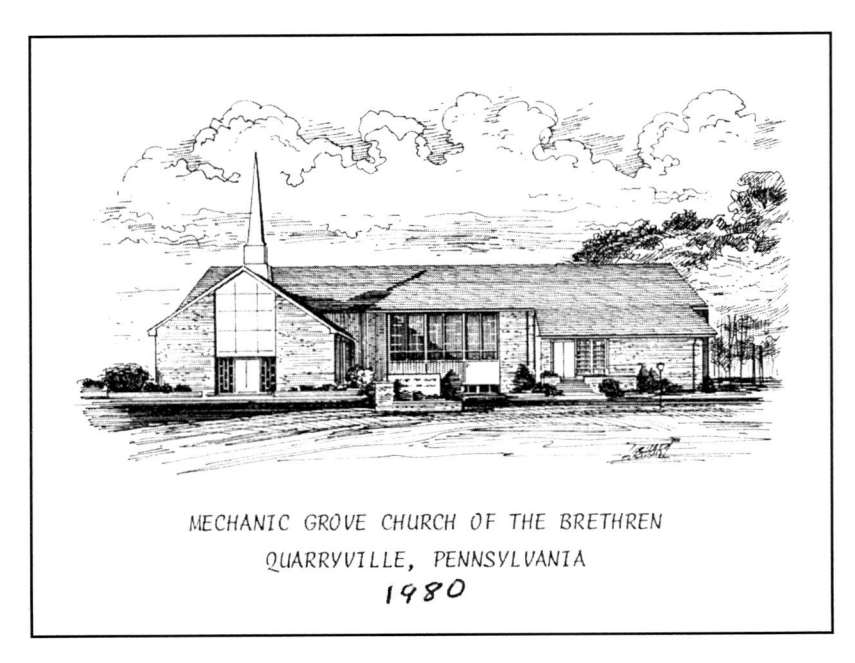

Sketch of the Mechanic Grove Church of the Brethren. Drawn by Joyce Bushong.

and that some of his family problems stemmed directly from my lack of attention. To complicate things further, when one of the organists played out of sequence one Sunday during the worship service, she was so embarrassed that she wrote a resignation note, placed it on the organ bench, and left the church with her family, never to return. It was also called to my attention that a small group was meeting regularly in secret. How does a pastor respond to allegations and behaviors like that? I was questioning more and more my initial call for innovation and creative leadership. What seemed to be wanted here was little change, simply maintaining the status quo.

One spring Saturday night, the Deacon Board met in the home of a deacon couple. I realized from the agenda that we were simply coasting, "doing good enough," and there was no desire to grow! Upon leaving the meeting that night, I was discouraged and questioned my own calling. Why did I leave Black Rock where things were going so well and come to this church with such strong resistance to change? After discussing the dilemma, Vivian and I retired for the night.

At 3:00 a.m. I awoke hearing someone calling my name, "Earl." I looked over at Vivian, and she was sound asleep. I pondered this and laid down again when the second call of my name occurred and I sat up straight in bed. What followed was shocking and humiliating. A voice said clearly, "Earl, begin with yourself."

The next morning at the breakfast table, I was convicted that I needed to begin with myself by surrendering my life to God more fully and inviting the congregation to do the same. Before the morning service, I alerted the organist that I may wish to speak before the last verse of the closing hymn. And I did just that! After sharing the night vision, I issued an altar call. In answering my own call, I knelt down on the step leading to the altar and was soon surrounded by forty-five people as we knelt together in repentance and commitment. That day the church blossomed and began to grow! In the ten years that followed, our average attendance doubled to 423 on a Sunday morning. As the saying goes, *"God moves in mysterious ways His wonders to perform."*

* * * * *

God has a sense of humor! While we were struggling to figure things out, God was already planting the seeds for something much greater. We saw division and turmoil; God saw beauty out of the ashes of human conflict. We experienced a house divided, the body of Christ at a crossroads; God was at work within to do a good thing!

The place was the Congregational Business (Council) Meeting of the Mechanic Grove Church of the Brethren on November 13, 1974. The time was in my fifth year as pastor there. In a personal letter, Moderator Amos Cunningham had already alerted the members to the fact that two issues were on the agenda: One was theological, the other, a future growth strategy. People came to the meeting with prejudiced and strong opinions.

As a result of the Jesus movement in the early 70's, a strong charismatic influence was very alive in Lancaster County, Pennsylvania. The issue was pinpointed to the inappropriate speaking in tongues and the claims of powerful healings. Members were meeting in unofficial small groups and practicing unusual behaviors. The result was that brothers and sisters in the same family found themselves on opposite sides of the issue, thus straining family relationships. We needed to decide if our congregation would remain a Church of the Brethren, continuing our Anabaptist heritage.

Paradoxically, at the same time, the church was gaining members, and the second issue to be addressed that evening was how to accommodate a growing congregation. How could one congregation at the same time be involved in such turmoil over a Biblical issue and yet continue growing so solidly?

The conflict had future theological ramifications for the Mechanic Grove Church. The first question was: "Shall the church become Pentecostal in its theology and practice, or shall it remain a Church of the Brethren with a strong New Testament emphasis?" The decision to remain faithful to the Anabaptist traditions and teachings was overwhelming. That issue had watershed reverberations. A few members absented themselves and began another church in the Willow Street area. Out of this conflict emerged several strong charismatic leaders who later established the Worship Center in Leola and the Lord's House of Prayer in Lancaster. God's hand of blessing and direction was laid upon all who found a special ministry in their communities.

In that same Council meeting, when the proposal came to build on to the current structure, a lively discussion ensued. At the appropriate moment and in God's timing, Sadie Kreider stood up and challenged the congregation with these words, *"If we feel we have something good to share and if we like what we have, why not share it with another community?"* Her vision became the decision that night for the Mechanic Grove Church to be the "Mother Church" of a new congregation.

* * * * *

With the use of professional research services and in cooperation with the Lancaster County Council of Churches Comity agreements, the Lampeter community was chosen as the site of the new church plant. Sponsored by the Mechanic Grove Church financially and spiritually in accordance with District policies, the next logical question was, "Where shall we meet?" After contacting a school, a funeral home and a store, the Lampeter Fire Hall was the most logical place. When we contacted the fire company official, Mr. Henry, he said an emphatic, "No!" He explained: "Two other religious groups have also asked in the prior six months and were refused."

That door was slammed shut! But with the power of God at work and the resurrection spirit in the people, even slammed doors can come ajar.

Several weeks later, in the middle of one of the Bible study/prayer services being held in the Carl and Ann Diller home, the phone rang. It was Mr. Henry of the Fire Company inviting us to come to the fire hall because they were in the midst of their regular meeting. Could it be? Is it possible? Do they have more questions?

The three, Carl Diller, Ervin DeLong and I, left the Bible study immediately while the rest spent time in prayer waiting for an answer. The sixty men in the fire hall welcomed us warmly. Chief Henry was the spokesman, "Yes, the fire hall may be rented!" The committee could hardly contain themselves. The "Yes" answer was so great but the words of Mr. Henry that followed were even more exciting, both complimentary and challenging. He said, "If you want to know why we changed our minds, let me tell you. We know the Brethren. We love the churches in our town. We want to keep them strong. There is room for another church in our community. There are two reasons we are willing to rent the facilities to you. One is that the Brethren have the reputation that they do not steal sheep and the other reason is that they are community-minded people."

With that statement of challenge, the fire company agreed to rent the building for $30 per week for the Sunday morning service only. The committee went back to the Bible study group and reported the good news. What an explosion of emotions filled with praise and gratitude to God for the answer to prayer—a miracle indeed and a challenge!

* * * * *

The morning of April 2, 1978, was filled with emotional electricity as we anticipated the first worship service in the fire hall of this new "yet to be born" organism now called the Lampeter Fellowship. Thirty-six people had gathered by five minutes to 9 a.m., the designated time for the worship service to begin. Naomi Wenger and I were standing on the steps into the building, wishing for more people. When we were about ready to turn and go and begin the worship service, suddenly there appeared a pickup truck with three people in the front and three teen-aged boys in the back. It was the Tim Brown family, responding to an invitation given to them by the Harlan Keener family. That made 42 persons attending our first service. Wow! The assembled group was ecstatic!

* * * * *

Pondering a location for the building of a sanctuary, Harlan Keener relates:

"One morning, sitting at the breakfast table, prior to going to the barn to milk the cows, an inspiration came to me. Why not go across the road and research ways to turn the swampy land into an appropriate building lot? The land was swampy because the creek was redirected, and a spring located west of the land fed into the swamp—not a particularly desirable spot on which to build a church. Nevertheless, while I was milking the cows, the thought of the land across the road became an obsession. I finished the milking, drove directly to the home of Glenn and Mary Jane Herr who owned the swampy land, and knocked on the Herr door at 8 a.m. Mary Jane answered the door knock and said to me, 'I know why you are here. I had a dream last night that the land next to our flower business will be bought for a church.'

"I felt a tingling in my spirit because this was a 'God moment' for me. How could she possibly know what I was thinking? Here I was at 8 a.m. to bring a request that she already had known was coming! I left the Herr residence feeling Divine guidance."

Ten acres of the Herr's land (part of it swampy) was bought by the committee for $8,000 per acre or a total of $80,000. The church building stands today as a legacy to that God-inspired vision.

* * * * *

I was "on loan" to the newborn Lampeter Church from the first day of its life in April 1978, un-

Marriage of Tim Jones and Jill Zook on May 27, 1978, in the Mechanic Grove Church of the Brethren.

til the middle of June when Tim Jones, a Princeton Seminary student minister, came as a three-month summer intern. At the same time, his fiancé, Jill Zook, also a student at Princeton, served as an assistant summer pastor at Mechanic Grove. They were married by me in late May and moved into a house owned by John and Evie Burkholder near Mylin's Corner, Willow Street, Pennsylvania.

When they left in the middle of September, I again assumed the pastoral role until December 1 of 1978 when Earl H. Kurtz came to serve in a half-time pastoral position. I served as the Moderator of the fledgling congregation for the first five years.

* * * * *

Besides Tim and Jill, other student ministers whom I mentored as summer pastors or interns during my thirteen-year tenure at Mechanic Grove were Don Hollinger, Jim Hutchinson, Del Keeney, Judy Kocher, Leroy Martin and Tim Morphew. In addition, other student ministers called from our congregation during my years or shortly thereafter were Jim Chinworth, Mark Cunningham, Audrey (Wagner) Finkbinder, Tracy (Wenger) Sadd, Blaine Wenger and Todd Wenger.

* * * * *

In 1975, the year of the downfall of Saigon to the Communists, many Vietnamese who had cooperated with the U.S. government in its prolonged war had to flee for their lives. Some thirty persons were sponsored by the Mechanic Grove Church that year. The first family was that of Dan and Lai Lai, a family of five. The second was a married man, Lam, whose wife was left behind in Vietnam. The third family were the Trinh family, a set of parents with four daughters, followed by the Duc Tran family of ten. The fifth family was the Phat Trang family of four. Other single Vietnamese persons were invited into the family circles of several members. All have worked hard, progressed to home ownership, began successful businesses, and have been a great asset to our communities. The first Vietnamese wedding in Lancaster County was performed by me in the Mechanic Grove Church on September 16, 1975, joining Tuyet Thi Lai, the bride, and Chau Viet Do, her groom, in marriage with the church sponsoring the reception. The local Lancaster newspaper carried the wedding as a feature article.

* * * * *

Vivian –

After the Mechanic Grove Church had sponsored their first two Vietnamese families and a single man (12 persons), the church members and the refugees were beginning to bond well. Then, on a Friday morning, Earl received a phone call directly from Fort Chaffee, Arkansas, where many refugee families were held until they were sponsored. A young man working there as a Brethren Volunteer Service worker ("BVS-er") knew Earl and called with an urgent request.

"We have a large family here who desperately needs a sponsor. The only problem is that it's a family of ten; this couple has eight children. We've contacted churches that have shown interest in sponsoring, but none are willing to take a family this large. We know your church has recently sponsored two families, so they've gone through this process several times, and we're wondering if they'd be willing to stretch themselves even more to help this family also?"

Upon hearing that, Earl felt a familiar tug at his heart wanting to help them, so he said, "I understand your problem, but I don't feel authorized to commit the church to this without consulting them. How much will it cost to get them here?"

"For a family this size, it will be $1,500," was the reply.

"Let me speak to the congregation on Sunday," Earl requested. "I'll phone you back one way or the other by Monday noon."

He took the challenge to Amos Cunningham, the church moderator. Earl suggested, "How about I 'throw out a fleece' to the congregation?" (Referring to the story of Gideon seeking direction from God via a fleece in Judges 6:37-39.) He continued, "On Sunday morning I'll explain the situation to the congregation and then invite people to call me with a pledged amount. If I have $1,500 by noon on Monday, I'll call Fort Chaffee and say we'll sponsor the family. If I receive less than that, I'll call and say our congregation isn't able to sponsor more at this time." Amos agreed.

By 11:30 on Monday morning, Earl had received $1,100 in pledges.

At 11:45 a.m., Earl was working in the church office when Clayton Kreider walked in. He was a successful farmer in his seventies who usually had a twinkle in his eye and enjoyed heckling and teasing. After a brief period of "small talk," Clayton asked, "How much did you get in commitments toward the refugee family?"

"$1,100," Earl replied.

"That's too bad. What are you gonna do?" Clayton inquired.

"Well, I put out the 'fleece,' and if more doesn't come in, I'll take that as God's direction that we're not to sponsor them."

Clayton paused, looked out the window thoughtfully and slowly made his way toward the door. Soon he disappeared around the corner.

However, in a few minutes he returned, and his eyes had that familiar happy sparkle in them. "Earl, I'll give you $400. You go ahead and make that call and tell them that our church will be their sponsors."

And a few minutes later, Earl did just that, changing the lives forever of the ten members of the Tran family.

After they arrived in the Philadelphia airport, we discovered that Mr. Tran, the father, had been a high school French teacher in Vietnam, and his wife, a businesswoman. They were Christians, and had seven sons and one daughter, who was the youngest in the family. One church family allowed them to rent a house they owned, another gave them a car, and many shared furnishings, linens, clothing and food.

While they lived in our area, the children attended the Solanco schools, and the family attended our church regularly. For some time, the father worked as a janitor at Lancaster General Hospital, and although her grasp of English was minimal, the mother found a job as a seamstress at a clothing factory in eastern Lancaster County. Several months after she was working there, her boss called Earl and said, "Pastor, any time your church sponsors families who have workers as good as Mrs. Tran, you can feel free to send them to me for a job." The older sons also got good jobs, and the family saved their money for their future.

By working, living frugally and saving together, in time, they were able to purchase a small house on a corner in Lancaster. They lived upstairs and made a small oriental grocery store on the first floor. Later, they moved to Philadelphia and started a growing business there, and for a while, they had two grocery stores. When they closed their Lancaster store, we lost contact with them.

* * * * *

Fast forward *thirty-one* years. *We never know how acts of kindness will be multiplied.*

One day in 2006, the present secretary of the Mechanic Grove Church of the Brethren was working in her office, and she got a Vietnamese visitor. It was John Tran (formerly known as Dung, the second from youngest in the Tran family) from Philadelphia.

"Is Pastor Earl Ziegler here?" he inquired.

Secretary, Pat DeLong, explained that Earl had left Mechanic Grove in 1983 and gave John our current address and phone number.

John then related to the secretary that the Mechanic Grove congregation had sponsored his family in 1975 and that sponsorship was the doorway to the American Dream for them. In Philadelphia, the family had a grocery store which gradually became a supplier of meats and supplies to oriental restaurants along the eastern United States' seacoast from New England to Virginia. Several brothers together now own a fitness center that serves 3,000 clients. One served as a pastor in Canada for many years. Several are working as computer technicians, and their only sister is now a schoolteacher married to a doctor and living in New Jersey.

He concluded his story by saying, "In appreciation to the Mechanic Grove congregation for sponsoring us, our family wants to give this church a gift." As he said that, he handed Pastor Rhen a check for $1,500, *exactly the amount* the congregation had paid to bring them here. That's amazing because when the family arrived, John was only a ten year old and had no idea of the dollar amount the church had paid. In fact, Earl doesn't think anyone in the family, including the father, knew that amount. But God did, and in our view, that was a "God-moment," one of life's unexplainable little miracles.

Two years later, in 2008, the Mechanic Grove Church hosted a reunion of all the Vietmanese families they had sponsored. In addition to those the church aided, the Jesse Wood family had sponsored two young brothers who also had become a part of our community. The single married man, Lam, had finally been able to bring his wife to the United States, and they now had several grown-up children. Dan and Lai Lai added a daughter to their family and two of their sons had graduated from West Point. Once again, the Tran family gave the church another check, and many of the other families did also. Those gifts were used by the church to help refugee families they were currently sponsoring.

* * * * *

Earl –

Another poignant moment of truth with refugees was when the Adam Zytkowiak family of four from Poland arrived in the Quarryville community sponsored by the Mechanic Grove

Left to right: American citizens who were former refugees sponsored by the Mechanic Grove Church: Christine, Gia, Phat, and Cynthia Trang, 2005.

Church. For the first two weeks, they lived with us in the parsonage until a house was found for them. Adam, the Polish husband and father, a former journalist, was very apprehensive about believing what I told him about the forms he had to complete, medical shots that were necessary, and all the rules and regulations about the resettlement of refugees.

On his second day with us, Adam was standing in the parsonage doorway when Phat Trang happened to stop by. I introduced Phat to Adam, and explained that Phat, who had arrived from Vietnam with his family several years earlier, also had had to fill out numerous forms, but that had led him to a job where he saved his money and eventually he'd been able to buy his own house. Recognizing fear in Adam after our brief conversation, Phat turned to Adam and said, "Don't be afraid. These people will treat you well. They have helped me so much, and you'll find them to be very caring and understanding."

One could see Adam's anxiety level diminish with those reassuring words, and I thought, "What a powerful testimony from someone from another culture but who has had a similar experience!"

* * * * *

The need for more office space and a small chapel prompted an addition to the entrance of the church in 1976 when a secretary's office, two pastoral offices, a chapel and an enlarged narthex were added. Dedication of this addition was during the fall of 1976 and as of December 31, 1976, its cost was $114, 840.

In the middle of my pastoral stint at Mechanic Grove, I felt the need to push myself academically and so enrolled in the Doctor of Ministry program through Lancaster Theological Seminary. I chose Lancaster because of its proximity, the staff gave me six years to complete it, and because it was a theological discipline outside of my denomination and experience.

Beginning in the fall of 1976 with my study focus on "Family Systems," my doctoral dissertation, printed in book form, was entitled, "Divorce among the Church of the Brethren Clergy." It was a pleasure to be able to exercise an emphasis on family life in my ministry by having space for family and personal counseling for couples within the local church parish but also from the wider community as I served on the staff of the Pastoral Counseling Services of Lancaster. One night a week was dedicated for counseling for a fee as approved by the executive committee.

I received the doctorate degree on May 15, 1982. Although I had completed my work a year earlier, I was absent for graduation due to spending part of my sabbatical in the South Pacific area.

* * * * *

Vivian –

Speaking of education, the year of 1973 was especially noteworthy for our family. That was the year Mike "graduated" from eighth grade in Swift Middle School to enter Solanco High School, Randy graduated from Solanco High School, Karen got her Bachelor of Arts degree (B.A.) from Elizabethtown College, and I received my Masters of Science in Library Science degree (M.S.L.S.) from Shippensburg University. Interestingly enough, that all happened exactly fifty years after my mother, the former Kathryn E. Zug, had graduated from Elizabethtown College in 1923.

* * * * *

Earl talking on "eye level" with some Lampeter youngsters, 1990.

Earl –

    Name retention was a great game for me. One of my practices was to know the name of every child in church from the moment of birth. I would consciously repeat the names every time I saw a child just as one of my favorite Bethany seminary professors, Dr. William H. Beahm, had done.

    When Teddy Hershey was in second grade, I received a profound, friendly and very complimentary note from him which said, "You are the only preacher who noes (sic) my name!" I still have that card from Teddy!

* * * * *

    Marlene Eckman, Annetta McCardell and Miriam Krantz were three personalities that stood the test of time in the church Nursery School. Founded in 1973, hundreds of children, ages two through pre-kindergarten, passed through those

Education Becomes A ... For The Zieglers Of ...

By CINDY SCHUSTER
Intell Staff Writer

Education is currently a unique term in the Earl Ziegler family, Quarryville R2.

Within the past week, three members of the family have received degrees and the Rev. Earl Ziegler delivered the graduation message at his son's high school and was included in the processional of his daughter's ceremony.

Mrs. Vivian S. Ziegler, wife of Earl, mother to five, and

Members of the Ziegler family are shown above at Karen's graduation from Elizabethtown College on Sunday. They are left to right, foreground, Mrs. Kathryn E. Zug Snyder, grandmother and graduate of Elizabethtown College; Mrs. Vivian Ziegler, Mrs. Karen Zimmerman, and in the rear, the Rev. Earl Ziegler, and his son Randy.

Intelligencer Journal Photo By Richard Reinhold

Family Affair Quarryville

librarian at Swift Junior High School, received her masters degree in library science from Shippensburg State College on May 19. "I had been working on my master's since 1969 at nights. It took me four years and was a difficult thing but I made it," Mrs. Ziegler said proudly. She added that the whole family seemed to be in gear for it and there was much cooperation at home.

On June 3, daughter Karen, 21, graduated from Elizabethtown College earning her bachelor's degree in elementary education. Mrs. Ziegler pointed out that Karen is a third generation member of the family graduating exactly 50 years after her grandmother, Mrs. Kathryn E. Zug Snyder (Mount Joy R2). Both the Rev. and Mrs. Ziegler are 1951 graduates of Elizabethtown College.

Future Teacher

Karen is the wife of James Zimmerman, a welder, Campbelltown. She is presently working at Hershey Estates as a mail carrier and hopes to teach in the near future.

On June 3, the Rev. Mr. Ziegler, who is pastor of the Mechanic Grove Church of the Brethren, Quarryville, preached the Baccalaureate sermon for Solanco High School where his son, Randy, 18, graduated. For the past few years Randy has been working on Bill Guhl's farm. "For the early part of this summer I will be working at the farm and then vacation and after that I may enter some type of business, but I don't plan on going to school right now," Randy explained. His father's speech was eintitled, "It's Your Life ... Live It."

The Rev. Mr. Ziegler expressed his happiness at the family graduations falling together. "We never thought that they'd all end together,

but I feel proud of all of them It took lots of time and energ for everyone," he said, and " think it's really worth though because education ca never be lost."

Other Children

The Zieglers have thre other children. Michael, wh has just completed the eight grade at Swift Middle Schoo will move into Solanco Higl School in the Fall. Michae works part-time on the farn of Jason Weaver, a neighbo: of the Zieglers.

Doreen, 16, is president o her sophomore class at So lanco High School. She is member of both the hockey and track teams, is a membei of the color guard at schoo and is on the Church Govern ing Board for a three-year pe riod at her father's church The Rev. Mr. Ziegler feels i important for young and old t have a say in church oper ations.

The Zieglers' last daughter Konnae, is a Korean orpha: who will be legally adopted or June 14.

When asked where they came upon Konnae, Mrs. Zieg ler replied, "In 1965, we had Korean exchange student herc and we just loved her. Since that time we have done a lo of travelling. In 1970, we went around the world and saw a lot of poverty and visited ou exchange student who took us to an orphanage. After seeing the poverty and realizing that in Korea orphans can only be kept until they are 14 years o age, we went away different people. I guess it was our part in helping," Mrs. Ziegler noted.

She explained that it took a year and a half until Konnae arrived last August . . . "but very shortly she will be our daughter," Mrs. Ziegler added happily.

walls. Many families joined the church as a result of the nursery school connection.

The Nursery School gave me a memorable experience. A four-year-old boy was misbehaving in class for three days in a row. His behavior was unusual. In desperation, Marlene, the teacher, brought him down to my office, told me briefly about the situation, and left, closing the door behind her. I seized the moment, knelt down and met the young boy eye to eye and inquired, "Tell me about your morning. Your teacher tells me you are unhappy."

The scared young lad looked at me and blurted out, "My mother is having a baby, and *I don't like it!*"

Surprised, I tried to console him and assure him that some good things may happen when he gets his brother or sister. After our brief conversation, I took his hand and led him back upstairs to his classroom.

His teacher told me later that, as soon as he walked in, a little girl classmate ran up to him and asked what happened downstairs. His answer: "I met a man downstairs who loves me."

* * * * *

Vivian –

Driving home with one of our deacons, Lester Kreider and his wife, from an evening service in another church, we were engaged in conversation and scarcely noticed the small, creaky, plank bridge until the car stopped.

"Excuse me a moment," stated our driver. "I drove over this bridge earlier today and noticed a large nail sticking up from one of the boards." Reaching under his seat, Lester added, "I brought a hammer along tonight so I could stop and pound it in on our way home. I wouldn't want someone to have a flat tire or an accident because of that nail."

What a lesson that was to us of someone who took citizenship seriously!

* * * * *

Earl –

A third-of-an-acre of the cemetery plot located behind the church and the parsonage lay idle for many years. Approaching the cemetery trustees, I requested permission to till the ground and plant cauliflower. A member of the church, an expert in cauliflower growing, had agreed to help me.

Mike, 14, asks, "Is this enough cauliflower for your family?"

With permission granted, we planted between 1,500 to 1,750 plants each July Fourth. Vivian's mother, brothers and sister and their families came annually for the "Cauliflower Planting Party." In late September and all of October, hundreds of heads of cauliflower were sold from the back of the parsonage to members and community folk alike. I was always accused by my family of giving the cauliflower away . . . and I admit, I often did! My prices were always ridiculously low, but oh, it was fun! I can name a few converts who began coming to church through my "cauliflower ministry."

* * * * *

Dean and Jeanne Small moved to the Quarryville area from New Jersey where they had been Presbyterians. They had two older sons who were out of the home and a daughter, Marjorie, who had just graduated from high school and was still living with her parents. The first Sunday they worshipped at the Mechanic Grove Church of the Brethren was on a very hot summer morning. In fact, because of the extreme heat, the service was moved outdoors to the pavilion in the adjacent woods behind the parsonage. The Smalls sat near the back but were impressed by the sermon and the friendliness of the people, and in time, decided to make it their church home. (The fact that Jeanne, a nurse, and Vivian discovered that they were second cousins may have also been a *slight* influence.) The church family soon discovered that Dean had a great sense of humor, a hearty laugh, and the gift of teaching.

Their daughter, Marjorie, appeared to be the daughter that every couple would be proud to claim as their own. In high school she had been very popular as a cheerleader, a student government leader, and the football homecoming queen. She became a nursing student at Lancaster General Hospital, an accomplished water skier, and was beautiful, inside and out. But she had one big problem; she had contracted leukemia during her senior year in high school. Despite that handicap, she lived life to the fullest. From time to time, this insidious disease would flare up and take her down. She would experience mountaintops of extremely good health and vitality and also frequent sudden drops into the valley of sickness. The family's hopes would rise and fall along with these cycles.

In one of her last low times, Marjorie called for me to visit her. I was appalled to discover that this vibrant and beautiful girl wanted to discuss her funeral plans. She chose these verses from 1st Corinthians 4:8-10 to describe her life: *"We are pressed on every side by troubles, but not crushed and broken. We are perplexed because we don't know why things happen as they do, but we don't give up and quit. We are hunted down, but God never abandons us. We get knocked down, but we get up again and keep going. These bodies of ours are constantly facing death just as Jesus did; so it is clear to all that it is only the living Christ within who keeps us safe." (TLB)* Planning her funeral to be an expression and witness of her strong and unwavering faith, she chose the hymns she wanted sung and which friends were to sing a special number as a quartet.

However, she and those who loved her noted that each time the disease manifested itself and became active, her valleys would be a little deeper. On several occasions, it was thought she was near death, but she would seem to recover . . . for a while.

One time she recovered so much that she went water skiing with a group of friends and had a great time. Within two or three days, the disease had once again pulled her into its grip, and she told me that she was sure this time she would not recover. And she was right. In September 1977, less than a week after she had water skied, she went to meet the Savior who had died for her and whom she loved so dearly.

Sadly, Dean and Jeanne struggled for years to accept this loss of their only and beautiful daughter. It permeated their conversation and their very lives. Although they had a strong faith and later traveled to Europe and the Holy Land with us, their lives were shortened by the weight of their daughter's death.

* * * * *

Earl and his brother, Victor, connived together to purchase this quilt at the Church of the Brethren Annual Conference in Seattle, Washington, July 7, 1979.

Vivian –

In 1979, Annual Conference was held in Seattle, Washington, and I wrote a letter to my mother reporting our activities. I wrote: "The ladies here collected the quilt patches that had been made by many churches in the brotherhood and sewed them together, making four beautiful quilts. Yesterday a quilt auction was held to benefit the Arts emphasis of the church. Earl's brother, Victor, bought the first one (the one we thought was most beautiful) for $1,100. After the other three were sold, Victor offered his to be sold again. He asked Earl to bid against him. This time, it sold for $1,375, and Victor was again the buyer! What crazy brothers!"

* * * * *

During our years at Mechanic Grove, I taught adult Sunday School classes regularly, and was elected by the District to serve a two-year term as one of two delegates to the national Standing Committee. On my second year, I was elected to the Nominating Committee and the following year was chosen as chairperson. At that time, many in the church were concerned about the inequity of males vs. females serving in leadership roles. For several years, every time that a female had been nominated for Moderator-Elect, she lost. In an attempt to change that, our committee brought to Annual Conference a ballot of four female names and no males. The Standing Committee, voted first, and narrowed it to two names. However, during the Conference, a male was nominated from the floor, and he was the one elected. During that whole process, I heard many pro and con discussions about these issues, and it was an eye-opening experience.

During these years, Earl and I also attended as well as led numerous marriage enrichment workshops. Often we would arrive at a motel on a Friday and have get-acquainted games with the five to twelve couples who had registered. After breakfast on Saturday, we would have a morning class with Earl and me co-teaching and later we had an evening session. We discussed subjects like the importance of self-esteem, communication, openness, spiritual unity, and common goals in marriage. Saturday afternoons were usually free to tour the area, swim in the motel pool or relax in their room. Sunday morning we'd have a final meeting followed by a closing worship around noon. Our emphasis was always that persons attending a marriage enrichment were not coming because they had problems, but "to make good marriages better."

One funny experience occurred when we were working with couples from a rural southern Pennsylvania church. A man in the group told this joke:

A lecturer was speaking to a class of adults about the frequency of sex in marriage. He asked them to raise their hands if they usually had sex every night, and several hands went up. He noticed one man on the front row had twinkling eyes and a wide smile. Then the lecturer asked if they had sex twice a week, and a few more hands went up. The man continued to smile. "How many have sex about once a month?" he asked. Again a few hands went up, and the man on the front row was still smiling. So far, he hadn't raised his hand at all.

The lecturer turned to him and said, "I don't mean to embarrass you, but I've noticed you haven't raised your hand at all. How often do you have sex?"

"Just once a year," replied the man, still smiling.

"Only once a year!" exclaimed the lecturer. "How can you keep smiling when you only experience sex once a year?"

"Well, tonight's the night!"

With that story, the group burst into laughter, and we used that story at most of our marriage enrichments after that.

* * * * *

Earl –

Scouting over the countryside on routine visitation in the Mechanic Grove parish one afternoon, I thought of Bill and Liz Baughman, a couple approaching retirement age.

A Lukens Steel employee and a nurses' aid at the Quarryville Presbyterian Home respectively, they indeed were a delightful, interesting couple. They had appeared in a worship service about two years before and had become regulars. To nurture their spiritual longings, I visited them occasionally in their home as their pastor. We had become comfortable with each other. Liz was ready to make a commitment, but Bill was hesitant.

One day, while visiting Bill, I risked wading in on the question of accepting Christ as Lord and Savior feeling I had earned the right to do so, and Liz was working. When I posed the question, he looked straight at me and forcefully responded with the words, "Bug Off, Earl." Thereafter, I did just that because I had a real respect for him and he for me. I lost that round and never asked him again.

They kept coming to church faithfully, and one morning about two years later, as the last hymn was being sung, I saw Bill take Liz's hand and pull her out of the pew, and they walked forward together. I greeted them with hugs and he said to me, "Now I'm ready. I want to be baptized." Liz was ecstatic.

During the preparation time and before they entered the baptistery waters together a few weeks later, Bill explained, "When you asked me to commit my life to Christ, I was still drinking a bit and I felt I had to conquer that habit completely before I could be baptized." What a powerful testimony and lesson in integrity!

* * * * *

Charles Groff, a special needs fifteen year old, attended the Mechanic Grove Church with his mother and sister. One morning after the worship service, I was greeting people back at the door. Charlie came by, stopped, looked straight into my eyes and asked, "When can I be baptized?"

Not sure that he understood what he was asking, I told him, "Please go to the bottom of the steps and wait for me. I'll talk with you as soon as I can." He went and stood there patiently, watching me, until I joined him and inquired, "Why do you want to be baptized?"

His dramatic and sincere response was, "Because I love Jesus."

What a testimony! It can't get better than that, and he was baptized in an outdoor stream several weeks later.

* * * * *

One day I was driving (in a hurry, as usual) on May Post Office Road from Quarryville to Strasburg for an appointment. Halfway there, I encountered a road sign which declared, "Detour—Road Closed Ahead." Shrugging off the sign and reasoning that there must be a way around it, I continued to drive toward Strasburg.

Sure enough, as I came over a small hill, there it was—the bridge was out! I drove slowly up to the site to ponder my predicament. A road grader was parked perpendicular across the road. As I turned around, I noticed that someone with a sense of humor had planted a small handwritten sign which said, "It *was* closed, wasn't it?"

* * * * *

In 1982, Vivian and I both took 8-month sabbatical leaves from our respective duties as pastor of the Mechanic Grove Church and Swift Middle School librarian. On Dec. 31, 1981, we packed our car to the roof and headed west to an apartment at Bethany Theological Seminary, then in Oak Brook, Illinois. (Rev. Wilbur and Evelyn Martin from Florida moved into the parsonage at Mechanic Grove and served there while we were gone.) For the first three months of 1982, I'd been invited to serve as Bethany's first campus chaplain and taught several classes. Vivian shared with me in teaching a course for pastors' spouses and also took a full load of seminary classes for that quarter.

In March we flew from Chicago to Tahiti, Australia and New Zealand for three weeks to lead a tour group of eighteen persons.

After they returned to the United States, we remained in New Zealand, staying six more weeks touring the country, serving a 2½ week "Presbyterian pastorate" on Stewart Island living in the manse, and having our base at the home of former exchange student and current sheep farmer, John Willis, his wife, Glenda, and their four children.

After returning to the United States and traveling through numerous states visiting friends, "taking the long way home," we returned to Pennsylvania and spent the last month of our sabbatical living with our daughter and son-in-law, Doreen and Ken Creighton. From there we took numerous day trips as well as helped them finish woodwork in their brand new passive solar home in Gap, Pennsylvania. We moved back home refreshed and inspired to resume our respective jobs again on September 1, expecting to work in both for many more years.

However, that was not the plan God had for our lives!

The title of the monthly newsletter while we served at Black Rock was "The Black Rock Flock." When we were in New Zealand in 1982 on John Willis' sheep farm, Earl posed in the midst of a REAL flock! Can you find him in this photo?

GOD-MOMENTS
Chapter Fourteen

"Mommie, when men fly up high in the air in airplanes, can they see God a little plainer?"
(A question our son, Mike, asked when when he was four years old.)

Vivian –

In February 1964, the six of us and a doctor and his family (members of the Black Rock congregation) got tickets for the Ice Follies at the Hershey Arena. Although it had begun to snow, we left home in an adventurous mood with four adults and seven children in the doctor's van. The Follies had beautiful color effects and outstanding performances of skating skills, and we had a great time.

Upon leaving the arena after the show, we discovered a real blizzard was in progress. A normal trip to Hershey from our house in York County usually took an hour, but that night returning home required two and one-half hours of slow and hazardous driving.

At Loganville, we left Route 81 with its friendly snowplows and red tail-lights ahead to make original tracks on a road almost impossible to find in the driving snow. A stalled car caused us to lose speed so that we couldn't turn and continue to go up a hill in the road ahead. Backing and beginning again didn't help, so three of the adults got out to push. By now it was 1:00 a.m., and we were alone. After we pushed and grunted, the car climbed the hill and the "pushers" walked up behind it with the snow blowing into our faces.

Near a street light several feet ahead, I spied a dark object lying in the other lane and asked, "What's that?"

The doctor's wife laughed and said, "I bet you thought it was a man."

Walking ahead of us, Earl approached the object and called to us, "It IS a man!"

The doctor got out of his van, checked the man's pulse, and finding none, declared the man was dead. Being near a motel, Earl trudged there through the falling snow to call the police.

He discovered that the deceased man was the owner of the stalled car we had seen. Having just walked to the motel to call a neighbor for help, this man had been returning to his car when he had a heart attack and died instantly. We had to wait for the police and coroner to arrive before we could continue toward home.

We got new insights that night concerning God's guidance in our lives. If we wouldn't have been *on foot*, we would never have seen the man. WITHIN MINUTES, in that driving snow, he would have been snow-covered, and the first snow plow or automobile traveling down the hill *couldn't* have seen him and would definitely have run directly over him!

God's timing is perfect!

We got home at 3:30 a.m. and felt we had experienced a night we would never forget!

* * * * *

After we had been at the Black Rock Church several years, in the mid-1960's, I was invited to be the Sunday morning speaker at a church in nearby Lineboro, Maryland. Besides their pastor, I knew very few people there.

The next Sunday a new young couple appeared in the Black Rock Church service, and as usual, Earl obtained their names and address and made arrangements to visit them that week. During his late Saturday afternoon visit with them, Richard and Carla Bradford said they had heard me speak the week before and decided they would like to visit the church where my husband was pastor. During their conversation, Earl discovered that Richard enjoyed music and Earl asked if he sang.

"Yes, I do," Richard replied.

Moving on cautiously, Earl inquired, "Do you sing solos?"

"Yes, I do," Richard answered, with a smile.

Continuing to press on, Earl proposed, "Would you sing a solo for us tomorrow morning?"

"I'd be glad to," was the response.

Arrangements were made to practice with the organist at 6 o'clock that evening.

Earl met with them at the church, and when he came back to the parsonage that night, he came in the door and just rolled his eyes at first. "Just wait until you hear him! He's a professional! He's great! What a blessing he will be to our congregation—if we can keep them!"

And they did stay—and continued to be a blessing.

After we moved from Black Rock, we often spoke of them and learned they had moved, but we never heard where they had gone, so we lost touch with them.

Fast forward about forty years and in 2010 Earl had a speaking engagement in the Westminster, Maryland, Church of the Brethren. After the service, a man had a conversation with Earl, reminiscing about the years when Earl had served at the nearby Black Rock Church. One thing led to another, and they got on the subject of music. Earl asked if he ever heard what happened to Richard and Carla. The man replied that he didn't know where they were but he knew someone who did. That led to Earl getting their phone number, and he phoned them.

To our surprise, Richard had gotten training and became a pastor on the Delmarva Peninsula along the Virginia border of the Chesapeake Bay. Carla is actively leading a Bible Study group, and they are now grandparents. Sometime after that phone conversation, they visited us and how wonderful it was to meet them again and catch up with one another's lives! We all marveled at how God brought us together and the mutual blessings we had received . . . Another series of God-Moments.

* * * * *

As an adult Sunday School teacher, I discovered long ago that I could learn much from my students. One example: I was teaching from 1st Peter, verse by verse, and came upon chapter 5, verse 8. "Be self-controlled and alert. Your enemy the devil prowls around like a roaring lion looking for someone to devour." (NIV)

Since whenever one is engaged in warfare, it is important to *know* the enemy, I asked the class to describe the devil and started writing a list of their answers on the chalkboard. We agreed that the devil *doesn't* look like cartoons and comics usually picture him, with a hideous face, horns on his head, dressed in black and carrying a pitchfork. I was taken aback, however, when one man said emphatically, "The devil is *beautiful!*" Until that moment, I would never have used that word to describe him. However, how true that is! The Bible even supports that description. (Ezekiel 28:12-19, 2 Corinthians 11:14) That's why many people succumb to his wiles. He uses things that are pretty, attractive, and cute to detract us from following Christ, from focusing our attention on Him, from giving Him praise . . . at any time, but especially at Christmas and Easter. That was a profound insight that I never forgot.

* * * * *

Moving is always hectic. Moving with all the trappings, possessions, and paraphernalia of three teenagers and an eleven year old is even more so! Then, imagine at the same time preparing suitcases for all six members of the family to be away for the next 33 days! As I worked at this in mid-July, 1970, I realized that there were some *really important* things like the children's birth certificates, the family's checkbooks, investment information, credit cards, driver's licenses, and such that we wouldn't be using the next month as Earl and I took a tour group around the world, but I wanted to keep them especially safe. As I thought of these *very important* documents, I collected them in a large plastic bucket, intending to take them with me on my last trip from the Black Rock parsonage and hide them somewhere in a closet in our future home, the Mechanic Grove parsonage.

As fate would have it, I completely forgot about the bucket until the first week of September 1970, when I received a phone call from Mary Beth Bieber, who with her husband, Charles, had begun pastoring the Black Rock congregation and had recently moved into the parsonage which we had vacated. Mary Beth said she had found a bucket on the kitchen table and was about to throw away its contents, when she saw the Ziegler name on certain papers and felt that *perhaps* these were papers we still may want. How right she was!

We had just returned home a few days earlier from our trip around the world and until her call, we hadn't missed them! What a miracle that they were still safe, undisturbed, and had been standing on the kitchen table for a month—while people were going in and out of the house, renovating it for the new pastor's family. Another one of God's miracles!

* * * * *

We had decided that when we returned from our 33-day trip around the world in 1970, I would not seek work immediately but would slowly unpack the stacks of boxes and turn the empty parsonage into a home. I needed time to learn to know the community, schools, doctors, grocery stores, etc.

Several weeks later, Esther Landis, a church member who taught at the Swift Middle School located just four miles away, gave me an invaluable tip. The school librarian, a young, recent college graduate, had become engaged. Esther didn't know the librarian's fiancé's name or his profession, but she said, "You may be doing a smart thing if you would volunteer in the library one day a week. You would learn to know the school, the principal and the faculty, and IF the present librarian would happen to get married this summer and move away, you could apply for the job and have an "in" because they would already know you."

So, that's exactly what I did. That summer the librarian did get married, resigned and moved to another area with her new husband. I applied for the job and was interviewed by Dr. Curtis Rohm, the supervising principal of the Solanco School District,

Robert Sepulveda, the principal at Swift, and Mrs. Edith Ankrum, the library department head. In that interview, I mentioned that I was in the process of taking courses toward a Master's Degree in Library Science. Dr. Rohm inquired about my husband's profession and the size of our family. Then he asked me, "Do you think you can handle being a pastor's wife, the mother of four children, taking classes AND taking on a full-time job in the public school?" I smiled, and said, "I think so. I did it before in our previous pastorate." He shook his head and seemed doubtful. Shortly after that, I was informed that I had the job. (Little did they know that we had already begun negotiating to adopt a Korean orphan, adding a fifth child to our household!)

The timing of this whole process always seemed like a miracle. Moving during that year, the tip about volunteering, the current librarian's resignation, and my securing the job seemed like the work of the Lord from beginning to end. As a result, I held that job from 1971 until I retired in June 1993.

* * * * *

In the early 1980's, after she graduated from Eastern Mennonite High School in Virginia, our daughter, Konnae, had a couple years when she was trying to "find herself," decide on a vocation and establish her goals and values. After moving to different states, dropping out of college and working at different jobs, she finally settled in the Washington, D.C. area as a secretary for patent lawyers and has kept in that profession for over twenty years.

During her period of searching, we very seldom heard from her and didn't always know where she was living or what she was doing. All we could do was pray that God was protecting and guiding her. Although we were unaware of it, she lived several months close to us in Lancaster, and during that time, she had an encounter with an angel. I'll let her tell about it in her own words:

It was such an amazing night to me. I was working as a cocktail waitress at the Holiday Inn and was headed to my home in my old Datsun around 4 a.m. All of a sudden, the car just died, but I had enough engine power to pull over to the side of the road. Sitting in the car, I didn't know what to do because it was SO early and SO dark. Being a girl, I decided to just wait it out in my car until it was lighter outside before I would start walking to get help.

No cars were around, but out of nowhere, suddenly a car was right beside me. (I can't remember what kind of a car it was or what color.) At the same time, I felt a strange, warm, and peaceful feeling come over me. I rolled down the window to talk to the driver, a man who was "old-looking," a Caucasian, with very white hair.

"Do you need a ride?" he asked.

I didn't feel any fear and answered, "Yes."

So, I got in his car and rode with him. I don't remember our conversation during the ride, but when he dropped me off, I asked him if I could offer him some money, and he said, "Where I go, I don't need any money."

I didn't realize it that same morning that I had encountered an angel, but only did so much later in my life. For some reason, God brought it to my memory, and I shared that story with my current church as a praise report. I will never forget that experience, because that taught me that God is always watching over us and protecting us.

* * * * *

Earl –

Dean and Carol Snyder were a couple our age and very active in the Woodbury Church. Carol served as my first secretary there, and Dean, whose vocation was truck driving, was a gifted singer and soloist. We shared many fun times in the late 1950's, and I always appreciated Dean's commitment to Christ and his messages in song. He and I and two other guys also enjoyed singing together as a quartet.

Years later, the Mechanic Grove Church of the Brethren planned a surprise celebration of the thirtieth year of my ordination on February 18, 1950. I like to think I know all that is happening in the churches I serve, so it is hard to surprise me, but somehow, they managed to do it. About 420 persons showed up for morning worship, a pot-luck dinner, and an afternoon "This Is Your Life" program for me on September 7, 1980. People from my past were brought in to participate, and Dean was one of them. After some brief remarks, he sang a song I love, "I Walked Today Where Jesus Walked." The entire program was taped.

In his mid-50's, Dean contracted cancer and spent some time in the Hershey Medical Center. I was serving then as Atlantic Northeast District Executive, and I visited him several times. His death happened to occur when his pastor was in Europe, so Carol, his widow, and their three children asked if I would participate in his memorial service. Because of these special circumstances, I agreed to do it.

In planning the service, we wanted to include much music because that was so important to him. Near the conclusion of the service, with the knowledge and permission of the family, the recorded tape of Dean singing, "I Walked Today Where Jesus Walked," was played. He sang for his own memorial service! What a God-Moment! How powerful that was! Especially, when we thought that perhaps he actually *had* enjoyed walking with Jesus that day, or even was doing it at that very moment!

* * * * *

Vivian –

It was about April 1989 and the Ziegler brothers and sisters and their spouses met together for lunch in the banquet room at the Country Table Restaurant in Mount Joy, Pennsylvania. Together, we enjoyed a delicious meal and great fellowship. Whenever Victor, Earl and Lena were together, there was always plenty of banter back and forth and lots of laughs, and this day was no exception. The in-laws in the group always enjoyed joking about how the Ziegler siblings were never at a loss for words, and it was often just fun to sit back and listen to them talk.

After the meal, the conversation got serious as Wayne Patches shared about some of his physical problems, which we may not have realized then were being caused by cancer in his body. His wife, Mae Ziegler Patches, had been recently diagnosed with Parkinson's Disease. None of us, including Mae, knew much about that disease then or what the best methods were of combating it.

About that time, Verna's husband, Norman Kline, one of the in-laws who seldom had much to say, spoke up and asked, "Do any of the rest of you have any prayer concerns in your families?"

At that time Earl and I were very concerned about our daughter, Doreen Creighton. She was between five and six months pregnant and was having difficulties. She had been spotting and the doctor said she had a placenta previa problem. To avoid a miscarriage, she was ordered to have complete bed rest. Since she

The Ziegler siblings and their spouses in 1993. Standing, left to right: Victor Ziegler, Irvin Kreider, Monroe Good, Wayne Patches, Earl and Vivian (Snyder) Ziegler, Norman Kline, Reba and Glen Ziegler. Seated: T. Grace (Cox) Ziegler, Lena (Ziegler) Kreider, Ada (Ziegler) Good, Mae (Ziegler) Patches, and Verna (Ziegler) Kline.

was normally a very active person, this was very hard for her. She had been in bed for about four weeks and still had at least three more months to go. In answer to Norman's invitation, we shared our concern about Doreen.

"I think we should go somewhere where we can pray together as a family," Norman suggested. All of us agreed it wouldn't be appropriate to do it there, in a public restaurant, so where would we go?

"How about going to the Florin Church of the Brethren?" Earl suggested. "It's close, and we can go in one of the Sunday School classrooms." So, that's what we did.

We arrived at the church, went into a classroom, and never even sat down. We joined hands, formed a large circle, and prayed together as a concerned family for our sister, Mae, our brother-in-law, Wayne, and for Earl's and my daughter and their niece, Doreen. Some specifically prayed that Doreen's bleeding would stop, that she and her baby would be healthy, and that she could finish her pregnancy without being confined to bed. It was just after noon when we met, and by 12:30, we had finished, talked a bit more, and then departed to our various homes.

The next afternoon I phoned Doreen to ask her how she was. "I'm feeling great, Mom," she replied, adding, "and I have good news. My bleeding has stopped."

"What?" I asked in amazement.

"My bleeding has stopped . . . completely . . . for almost twenty-four hours now. I called and told the doctor, but he said I should remain in bed at least to the end of this week . . . a couple more days . . . just to be safe. Isn't that wonderful?"

"It sure is. I can hardly believe it. Do you remember when it stopped?" I asked, feeling I already knew the answer but wanting to be reassured.

"Oh, yes. It was funny. Yesterday, around 12:15 p.m. I had a strong feeling of peace, a feeling that the baby and I were going to be okay, and at that same time, my bleeding abruptly stopped."

"Doreen, do you know what we were doing yesterday at that time?"

Puzzled, she answered, "No, Mom, what was happening then?"

"Your Dad and I ate lunch with his sisters and brothers. Several of them had prayer concerns and we shared about your pregnancy. Uncle Norman suggested we go somewhere and pray together, and we went to the Florin Church of the Brethren, met in a classroom there, stood in a circle holding hands and prayed for those in our family who were sick. We prayed that your bleeding would stop, and *at the very time* that we were all there praying, God answered our prayer and performed a *miracle* in your body and stopped your bleeding."

Both of us just praised and thanked God for His love, mercy and healing. When Earl's family heard about it, they, too, rejoiced. Beginning the next week, Doreen finished out her pregnancy participating in normal activities, and on August 5 her healthy son, Benjamin John ("Gift of God") Creighton, was born!

We feel that impromptu noon-time family prayer circle with the simultaneous answer from God in Doreen's miraculous healing was definitely a God-Moment in our lives.

* * * * *

Earl –

Around 1991, the Florin Church of the Brethren sponsored two Ukrainian brothers and their families and resettled them in Lancaster County. When we began planning a trip to Eastern Europe, including Ukraine in 1992, we met with these families. They asked if we would mind taking some gifts from them to their parents and siblings in Ukraine, and we said we'd be glad to do that. We didn't know what was in their packages, except they did tell us that there were several pairs of jeans! They said Bibles were very hard to obtain there, so we got Bibles in their language to share with them.

Our tour group was thrilled to be able to share the unique opportunity of crowding into their home in Ukraine, and experiencing their joy and gratitude which we understood in spite of our language differences. Living in evident poverty, they must have spent a month's salary to set their tables for us with their best china and crystal and to serve us their best foods. Although we didn't want to accept it all, we realized that, *"Sometimes we must receive so that others can know the joy of giving!"* Words were not necessary when they hugged the Bibles to their chest, and few dry eyes were in the house. What a privilege to be used to share God's Word in this way!

* * * * *

Vivian —

While visiting Fiji in 1993, we went for a morning tour of the island and stopped at a native village. We walked between the houses and saw women doing their laundry and making preparations for their dinner. Our guide took us to a small chapel at the end of the "street" and a small entourage of natives followed us inside. We noticed some men were humming, so someone in our group asked if they would be willing to sing for us. About eight of them stood together, turned toward us and to our surprise began singing, in harmony and in English, the chorus, "He is Lord, He is Lord, He is risen from the dead, and He is Lord. Every knee shall bow and every tongue confess that Jesus Christ is Lord!"

A thrill went through me as they sang because it seemed like a prophetic preview of that time in eternity when some "from every kindred, tribe and nation will be there" praising God. What a holy moment!

* * * * *

Earl –

One Sunday morning in 1993, I had the privilege of preaching in the Kennington Presbyterian Church near Invercargill, New Zealand. Among our tour group was Roy Gish, from Elizabethtown, Pennsylvania, whose business at that time was making Moravian stars. On this trip, he brought a large star to present to this congregation as a gesture of good will, our oneness in Christ, and in gratitude for their hospitality in hosting us for a pot-luck meal following the service.

We were in that church and community because of our relationship with John and Glenda Willis who were active members. Because John had been an exchange student in the Black Rock congregation when I pastored there and then traveled with our family for seven weeks across the United States, he and Glenda agreed to arrange weekend lodging for our tour group among their friends and fellow church members.

Don and Doris Dibert, Everett, Pennsylvania, members of our group, received a phone call during the Christmas season for the next fifteen years or more from their host family in New Zealand to tell them that "The star is still shining in New Zealand!" What a nice, reassuring testimonial!

* * * * *

Vivian –

In 1993, after I had retired, various tests revealed that I had stage one uterine cancer, and my gynecologist recommended that I have a complete hysterectomy. Although I'd undergone major surgery twice before, when the time of the operation got closer, I became very apprehensive.

I was a member of a small Bible Study group, and the day before my admission, I asked Earl if he would anoint me when the group met that morning. I'd never been anointed before any of my previous operations, but this time I felt the need for all the help and assurance I could get. For me, that anointing service was very meaningful, especially because it was done in the presence of that small group of only four or five people whom I knew would be faithful in praying for me.

On the day of my surgery, I was admitted to the Lancaster General Hospital, prepped, and told to lie on a stretcher. Then I was wheeled into a "holding room" where there were other people on stretchers, presumably also waiting for their summons to an operating room. The temperature there was quite cool, but I felt at peace and closed my eyes.

With my eyes still closed, I suddenly "saw" what looked like a very bright and colorful neon sign and on it were these moving words (like the news headlines keep moving on one of the buildings in Times Square in New York City, or like the moving captions under a TV screen) from Isaiah 26:3: "Thou wilt keep her in perfect peace whose mind is stayed on Thee because she trusteth in Thee." (KJV) I opened my eyes in amazement. I had not read, quoted or even thought about that verse for weeks, perhaps even months! And I was also amazed that the pronouns were feminine – when in the King James Version they are masculine. I had never thought of it in that way before. I felt that this was a direct message from God, so I concentrated in focusing my thoughts, my mind, on Him, just as the verse advised. And it worked. I experienced complete peace, absolutely no fear.

The operation was so successful in removing all signs of cancer that I didn't need to have any chemo or radiation follow-up treatments at all. Ever since, I have felt that this truly was an unexplainable "God-Moment" in my life and I praise God for speaking to me in that way at that time.

* * * * *

In 1994, our daughter, Doreen, and her husband, Ken Creighton, took their sons, Tim, 8, and Ben, 5, on a five-day vacation trip to Florida, and we kept their two-year-old, Emily. During that time, we had several precious "God-Moments:"

- Emily would come to me and say, "Hold me," meaning that she wanted to be cuddled. One day I was especially touched when she added, "Hold me. I need love." (I obliged with pleasure.)
- One night Emily slept almost fourteen hours. In the morning I anxiously checked on her frequently, and incredibly, each time she would still be sleeping. At 9:15, I stood by her bed, and Emily's eyes were closed. I whispered, "Emily," and her blue eyes popped open instantly, and she jumped up into my arms. I hugged her, and Emily announced, "I'm Mommie's 'Cutie Pie.'" I laughed and said, "Yes, and you are Grandma's 'Pumpkin Pie.'" Then we both laughed.
- I continued hugging her and said, "Mommie loves you, Daddy loves you, Tim loves you, Ben loves you, Grandpa loves you, and Grandma loves you." I thought I had included everyone, but then 2-year-old Emily added, "Yes, and Jesus loves me." I agreed and said, "That's right, Emily, He sure does!"
- As I was putting her to bed one night, Emily again went over everyone who loves her: "Mommie, Daddy, Tim, Ben, Grandpa, Grandma, and Jesus loves me. After a slight pause, she declared, "And I love me, too!"
If only everybody could say that!

* * * * *

For almost ten years, Sparky, a Pomeranian, was a part of our family. When he was still a puppy, he often reminded me of some aspects of God! How so? He had free reign in our kitchen and family room, but we put up expanding fences to prevent him from exploring our living room and bedroom areas. When I would step over the fence to go to those areas, Sparky would come as far as the fence and lie down and wait . . . and wait . . . and wait. Two hours later, he would still be quietly waiting there.

I thought that if our little dog can wait so patiently for me to come back to him, how patient God must be, waiting for us to talk to Him, thank Him, praise Him, come back to Him! The Prodigal Son's father probably looked up his lane every day, many times a day, hoping to see his son returning.

Sparky would lie there waiting, looking up at every little sound, hoping I would return, and when I did, what a tumultuous greeting I received. He was SO glad to see me! . . . and I believe God is like that!

* * * * *

Some "Spiritual Highs" that we experienced during our travels included:

- Singing "How Great Thou Art" together in Alaska while beholding a very rare and cloudless view of the magnificent snow-covered peak of Mount McKinley, locally known as Denali, "The Great One."
- Being in the ornate Weiss Church in Germany, known as the "Church in the Meadow," surrounded by great works of art depicting Biblical scenes and listening to their gifted organist and a vocal soloist practicing.

- Staying in the King David Hotel in Jerusalem on a Sunday night and wanting to have a worship service with our group. No one had a room big enough, but the hall around the elevators was spacious. We checked with the hotel if we could meet there for a half hour or so and got their permission. After singing a few choruses, we were soon joined by a small Christian youth group from South Africa. We sang several songs together and asked them to suggest one for us *all* to sing. They sang what to us was a new one: *"All Over the World, the Spirit is Moving."* What appropriate lyrics, and what a God-Moment! (During our short worship experience, we were watched from the sidelines by a man dressed in full military regalia with an expression of obvious disapproval and disgust. Years later, he would become Israel's Prime Minister, Izak Rabin.)
- Holding a Sunday morning worship service in Fiji in a thatched roof pavilion surrounded by "calendar views" of clear blue water and palm trees and asking the group members to share moments when they had been inspired. One who responded was Walter McGibbon who described in a very moving way how he had felt the presence of God with him when he was in Europe as a soldier in World War II, expressing feelings he had never shared before with anyone, even his family, during all the years since.
- Standing for the first time with several group members in what may have been the tomb of Jesus just outside Jerusalem and seeing the hewn-in-stone place for a corpse, but noting that *it was empty!* A woman who had recently become a widow was moved to tears and so were we as our

group sang together "He Lives" and "Because He Lives" in that setting prior to observing Holy Communion there.

* * * * *

Earl –

On March 17, 2000, I received a phone call informing me that no monies had been given for a scholarship fund for university students in the Dominican Republic. This had been a project of the Brethren World Mission organization to help worthy students who were in training for medical and/or pastoral careers. The amount needed was $3,000, and I had no idea where I was going to get it.

When I went to the Lititz Church of the Brethren the next evening, March 18, for a dinner meeting, I was totally *surprised* to discover that it was really a celebration to honor my fifty years in ministry. About one hundred and seventy-five persons attended and I heard persons from my past, much like a "This Is Your Life" program, share about my connections with them. As the program concluded, I was presented a check for $4,000 designated for the Dominican Republic. Representing the contributions from those present and others in recognition of my ministry, it not only covered, but exceeded the amount needed, and I was overwhelmed with gratitude at the way the Lord had met that need!

* * * * *

Vivian –

In July 2005, just a few days before I needed to submit my manuscript about the life of Earl's deceased brother, Victor, to the printer, I still didn't have a title for the book. By brainstorming,

I had compiled a list of about twenty possibilities, but none of them seemed like the "right fit."

One morning I woke up about 4:30 a.m. with a sudden thought. Whenever Victor went to town, whether it was Lebanon, Myerstown, or somewhere else, if someone greeted him saying, "Hey, Victor, what brings you to Lebanon (or wherever he was) this morning?" His answer would always be, "I'm on my way to heaven, but I just stopped here in Lebanon to get a part I needed for my tractor." Or he might have said, "I'm on my way to heaven, but I'm just here in Myerstown to mail a few letters." Whatever his mission was, he would always preface his answer with the phrase, "I'm on my way to heaven."

My early morning thought was very clear. All of us are "on our way to heaven." That could describe everyone's lifetime journey. Today I am closer to arriving in heaven than I was ten years ago. Each day we are all closer to our final and eternal destination. Why not use that phrase, so typical of Victor, for the title of a biography about him?

Moreover, his travel companion for over fifty years of his journey was his wife, the former T. Grace Cox. Why not complete the title by saying, "On My Way to Heaven . . . Traveling with Grace." In that context, "Grace" could represent his wife, Grace, or it could also be a description of the *way* he went on his journey through life, assisted by the unmerited favor of God or with a certain charm or appeal. In other words, traveling *with grace.* I liked both interpretations. This title felt so right that I wrote it down on a slip of paper.

The next day Victor's widow and I had arranged to have lunch together. During the meal, Grace asked, "Have you chosen a title yet for the book?"

I said, "No, but I have an idea for one."

"I have an idea also," she responded.

"You tell me your idea first, and then I'll tell you mine," I suggested.

"Well, it was funny, but yesterday morning I woke up about 4:30 a.m. and was thinking about a title. I thought about the way that Victor always used to say he was 'on my way to heaven,' and I thought perhaps you could use that idea in some way in the title," she explained.

A chill went down my arms as she spoke, and I picked up my purse and got out the paper on which I had written my suggestion for a title the morning before. Through tear-filled eyes, I looked at her, held up the paper and said, "Grace, here is my suggestion!"

She looked at it and broke into a wide smile. Then I explained how I, too, had wakened the same morning she had, at about the same time, and we both had the same thought, which I believe was not a coincidence but a direct message from God, an assurance of His blessing on the book. We *knew* immediately that that would be the title for the book. It felt so right. There are not many times in life that God gives His directions so clearly, but that time He did, and what a confirming thrill that was!

* * * * *

For our annual family Christmas gathering on December 22, 2007, the Saturday morning before Christmas, we invited all thirty-one members of our immediate family (at that time) to meet at the famed Shady Maple Smorgasbord Restaurant at 9:30 a.m. for a brunch, after which they would all come to our cottage for the traditional gift exchange and a time of fellowship. Earl and

I arrived early only to discover that there were four long lines of people waiting at the cash registers. It seemed everyone in Lancaster County had the same idea! Since our family is *not* known for its promptness, Earl took his place in line to purchase the thirty-one meals while I waited near the door to direct our family as they arrived.

By 9:30, Earl had the meal tickets but only half our family were there. "Let's go around the corner to get out of the way," Earl suggested, while I remained at my post by the door. About 9:50, the last ones came and we all went around the corner to meet up with the first group.

Meanwhile, a waitress told Earl, "Because we are so busy this morning, it will be impossible for your family to sit near one another. You'll probably have to sit here and there and over there." She pointed in different directions as she spoke. The group slowly shuffled along.

Then the male dining room manager approached Earl and said, "A very unusual thing is happening. There are three tables situated next to each other that each seat ten persons. All the people eating there are leaving at once, so I will have the waitress seat you over there."

What a surprising "coincidence!"

* * * * *

It was March 15, 2008, and we were headed to a Palmyra Junior High School performance of "Guys and Dolls," in which our 7th grade granddaughter, Rebekah, had a leading role, and decided to stop at a restaurant for a quick supper. Since there was a waiting line and we were running late, the five of us (Earl and I and our son, Mike, his wife Mary, and our grandson, Jeremy, 25) decided to sit at the bar for quick service.

Another man sat down at the bar at about the same time. Earl engaged him in conversation and told him that he is a retired pastor, and the man responded that he also had recently retired. "What was your profession?" Earl asked.

"I was a shop teacher," he responded.

Earl leaned forward and told Mike who was then in his 24th year as a shop teacher, "This man just retired and he was a shop teacher."

"Oh," said Mike, leaning forward with interest, "where did you teach?"

Smiling, the man said, "Did you ever hear of Hershey Industrial School?"

Mike's eyes widened and in shock he said, "Are you Mr. Englert?" and he slid from his stool in an instant and went over and hugged the man as he was nodding, "Yes."

Mike turned to his surprised family and said, "This man was my mentor in teaching industrial arts when I was in my senior year in college." It turned out that they had not seen or heard from one another for 26 years. What a warm reunion they had as they both talked fast, sharing all each had experienced through those years.

Mike and his family live near Hazelton, Pennsylvania, about 125 miles north of the restaurant, and we just "happened" to stop at that specific restaurant briefly, and chose to sit at the bar, etc. Was this just "luck?"

By the way, we reached the school and sat in our seats just as the lights dimmed for the production to begin!

* * * * *

Earl —

In the late 1960's, when we were serving the Black Rock congregation, I frequently attended conferences held in the New Windsor, Maryland, Service Center. On one of my visits there, I met a young woman, Tina (not her real name), a Christian Arab and native of Bethlehem. She was a frequently-requested speaker at women's meetings and church functions on the subject of Israeli/Arab relations.

One day she shared with me a concern about her younger sister, Nadia (not her real name), coming to America to attend college. As a trustee at Elizabethtown College, I was able to help her get admitted there. In appreciation, the two sisters came to the Black Rock Church kitchen and prepared a Middle Eastern dinner consisting of lemon-flavored chicken, stuffed grape leaves and other tasty dishes and served it to the church board and their spouses.

Both girls were very attractive, and in time, Tina told us that she planned to marry a young man from another state. Since I was the pastor she had come to know best, the young couple asked me to perform the wedding. So it was that Vivian and I traveled to the site and attended their beautiful wedding in the groom's farmhouse. She became an American citizen on July 4th, and in time became the mother of three children. Nadia attended Elizabethtown College just one year and then returned to the Holy Land to live with her aging parents in Bethlehem until their death.

In 1970, when we took a tour group around the world, we spent several days in the Holy Land. During that time, we had the privilege of visiting Tina and Nadia's parents in their Bethlehem home. Through the cooperation of their friends and neighbors, our entire tour group was invited to the Bethlehem Fire

Hall one evening where they served us a home-cooked Middle Eastern meal. We felt so privileged to have that experience and came away with an entirely different perspective on Israeli/Arab relations than what the media reported.

Although we visited each other a few times through the years and kept in touch via Christmas cards, we gradually grew apart. Vivian and I often spoke of Tina and Nadia, but made no further contact with them.

In July 2008, at the Church of the Brethren Annual Conference in Richmond, Virginia, an announcement was made that anyone willing to host some of the Nigerians who were attending the Conference were to meet with Earl Ziegler at a certain place and time. As we were exiting the coliseum, I heard a woman's voice saying excitedly, "There he is now."

When we turned in that direction, a woman stepped forward whom we instantly recognized as Tina, our long lost friend. What a joyous reunion that was! She had heard my name announced, and as she and some friends were walking, she had just said aloud, "I wonder how we could meet Earl Ziegler . . ." At that very moment, we walked by . . . Was that a coincidence?

We visited with her that afternoon for three hours, catching up with one another's lives.

* * * * *

In June 2008, we were members of the Lititz Church of the Brethren when that congregation welcomed to the United States the Diamond Johnny and the Shee Sho families who were refugees from Myanmar, formerly Burma. Over the next three years, I chaired a committee that helped these families find an apartment, a job, obtain a driver's license, get their required medical and dental checkups, learn American customs and language, and get a car as they struggled to adjust to a completely different lifestyle and culture. After their Burmese homes had been burned down twice by enemy forces, they had fled on foot through the jungles into Thailand to save their lives, and the Johnnys had lived in a refugee camp for eighteen years. Diamond Johnny had been a community health educator while his wife, Angel Kenneth, had been a middle-school science teacher. Together they have two daughters and one son. We discovered they were active Christians, attended church regularly, loved music, and their children were soon making the honor rolls in our local schools.

After three years here, the second-floor, two-bedroom apartment became too small for the Johnny family, and we started looking for a three-bedroom home for them. However, Lititz is a very desirable and beautiful community and rentals for three-bedroom apartments and/or homes were unavailable under $1,000 a month. Because of their limited knowledge of English, they had only part-time jobs and couldn't afford those prices. In addition, I felt that if they rented, they would be paying heavily and have nothing to show for it, so I began looking for a house.

In the meantime, a nephew of mine and his family had purchased a home in Lititz through a well-known local realtor, Dennis Beck. I noticed that Mr. Beck had many ads in the newspaper for homes in the Lititz community and specifically, Warwick School District, where the Johnny children attended, so I made an appointment to meet with him that next Wednesday morning at his office.

I had never met him before, and I explained to him that I was seeking a 3-bedroom home for under $150,000 for this refugee family.

"You won't find any place in Lititz for under $150,000," he responded. "Even duplex homes here are priced higher than that, and most of them don't have three bedrooms."

Perhaps he noted my crestfallen expression, because he paused and then said, "Let me check on my computer exactly what is available," and he turned on his computer screen.

"Well, this is interesting," he observed. "Just this morning a listing is coming in for a three-bedroom home on Main Street for $135,000! It hasn't been advertised yet, as it is just now being put on the market."

I got the address and looked at the place and was favorably impressed. Then I asked several church members and businessmen who understood home values, construction, plumbing, electricity, etc., to inspect the home, and all felt it would be a good buy. I stopped at the realtor's office later that afternoon and offered $125,000 for the house. The owners countered with an offer of $127,000 with the understanding that there would be a *cash* settlement.

Early Thursday morning Mr. Beck called me and said two other prospects had appointments to check out the house that evening, so if we *really* wanted it, we needed to make a deposit of $3,000 by Friday evening. Although I had to be out of town most of that day, I promised Mr. Beck that I would see that he got the payment by 4 p.m. Friday.

My next step on Thursday morning was to enlist a Christian lawyer and I told him the story. No way could I, personally, afford buying the place. He suggested that a partnership be formed; the buyers would be called "Friendship Partners." Together, we concocted a strategy to invite friends in my Sunday School class to provide cash at a 3% interest rate, each investor giving 1/10th of the purchase price plus closing costs which amounted to a total of $132,000.

Thursday evening, one day after my initial visit with the realtor, the Johnny family was given a tour through the house. They were excited, confused, felt their prayers were being answered but kept asking, "*How* can we buy this house? We have no money." Noticing the nice-sized backyard, the father, Diamond, exclaimed, "I could even make a garden here." At the end of the lot was also a nice garage.

With a risky faith, by late Friday afternoon I gave Mr. Beck the $3,000 from my own funds to hold the property for us. On Sunday morning I introduced the idea to my Sunday School class and by Wednesday morning, all ten shares were subscribed!

A few days later, as the refugee family and I were touring the house again, dreaming about their future there, the owner with his wife walked into the house. After casual conversation, the owner stated, "I hear that this is a ministry of your church to help these people. We've thought about this and want this to be our ministry too. So, we will leave all the furniture, including the appliances, dishes, linens, telephone, etc. in the house, except for several items like the microwave, grandfather's clock, and sports memorabilia from our youth. And, oh yes, since we forgot to tell the oil man not to fill the tank, he filled it a week ago with 500 gallons of oil (about a $1,500 value), and we will give that also."

What a miracle! This event was orchestrated by the Holy Spirit from its inception! Why did I go to this unknown realtor? Why was this house placed on the market that same morning? Why could $132,000 be raised in three days? Why would a "never met before" house seller give all the furnishings . . . AND the oil? "God moves in mysterious ways . . ."

* * * * *

It was Friday, December 30, 2011, the last day for the Lititz Church of the Brethren's end-of-the-year giving! The giving on Christmas Sunday to the building debt had amounted to $3,007. The time was 11:00 a.m. in the church office, and the random funds that had come in during the last week of the year toward the building debt had amounted to $1,240, thus reducing the debt to $102,508. I was serving as chair of the Capital Gifts Committee whose dream goal for the year had been to reduce the debt to $100,000 by December 31. We were short by $2,508. Close to our goal . . . but still short.

Financial Secretary, Walt Keeney, the church Office Administrator, Diane Lamborn, and Pastor Bob Kettering were closing the books on the 2011 giving, when at 11:30 a.m. the mailman came to the office with a pile of letters. In that pile was one more offering. When that envelope was opened, it contained a financial gift marked for the building debt, and there it was! A check for $2,508 reducing the debt to $100,000. WOW! Explain this one—not $2,500, but exactly $2,508.

When Pastor Bob Kettering was accused of orchestrating this, he vehemently denied it, declaring NO way could *anyone* have known the amount needed. I, personally, tackled Walt Keeney, the Financial Secretary, about this reality, and he insisted he knew nothing. The gift would have had to be put in the mail on Wednesday or Thursday, at least one or two days before.

So, I ask you, did this happen by chance, by luck or by God's direction? You figure it out! For me, it was a "God-Moment," Holy Spirit led, and all I could say was, "Praise God" and "Thanks" to all who shared their blessings throughout the year.

To top it off, Pastor Bob contributed one dollar more so we could claim that our debt was now _under_ $100,000 at $99,999!

SERVING AS THE ATLANTIC NORTHEAST DISTRICT EXECUTIVE, 1983-1989
Chapter Fifteen

"We are to be fishers of men,
not keepers of the aquarium."
(Unknown)

Earl –

Our life at Mechanic Grove as pastor and family came to an unexpected ending.

Harold Bomberger, the Church of the Brethren's Atlantic Northeast District Executive, retired from his position after serving twelve years, and the District was searching for his successor. When I was contacted, I wasn't the least bit interested. My goal was to stay at Mechanic Grove for at least twenty years. Life was good. Vivian was in her fifteenth year of teaching (the last twelve as Swift Middle School librarian in the Solanco School District), and our children were all graduated from high school. Our four "homemade" children were married, and our two adopted children were on their own. The church, which had given up sixty members to plant the Lampeter Church several years before, had gained back another sixty, plus many more.

Would you believe that someone as unsuspecting as I was would be tapped to become the next executive of the Atlantic Northeast District, the largest District of our denomination in the nation? I was afraid to pray for the Holy Spirit's guidance. When the District extended the invitation a second and third time to me to become the next executive, I turned them down three times! Then I began to realize that I was caught in my own trap! I had always taught that one should listen to the Holy Spirit and answer the call of service.

One day, a committee member called me and wondered out loud if I was resisting the Holy Spirit's nudge. Wow! In retrospect, I had to admit that I was! I then resigned the ministry at Mechanic Grove after thirteen great years there to take the position of District Executive of the Atlantic Northeast District of the Church of the Brethren with its office in Harrisburg.

* * * * *

Having agreed to begin my term as Executive on October 1, 1983, I suddenly received a double whammy when Harold Bomberger had a heart attack late in June and could no longer serve as Atlantic Northeast District Executive. The Mechanic Grove Church, in its typical and understanding fashion, negotiated with the District to allow me to spend two days a week in the Harrisburg office and the remainder of the week in the home office. It was understood I would be available only for necessities at the District office, and all pastoral placements, etc. were put on hold. Alma Herr, the capable administrative assistant, coordinated the District office work until I arrived on the scene fulltime in October.

* * * * *

Harold and Betty Bomberger in 2003. Harold preceded Earl as Atlantic Northeast District Executive.

Edgar and Gladys Ridinger were members of the Mechanic Grove Church, and Ed had cancer. About every third week, he would stop by my office for what he called his "spiritual booster shot." Consequently, as his condition worsened, I visited him frequently in his beautiful gray stone rancher in Lampeter. Often I would come home and share with Vivian how much I admired their home.

After Edgar passed away, in time, his widow, Gladys, remarried. The house was offered at public sale but was withdrawn, because the price wasn't right. We didn't attend the sale, but heard "through the grapevine" that it hadn't been sold. After some negotiating, we were able to buy it, and renters lived in it for several years. When I resigned from Mechanic Grove in 1983, we moved into *our own* home for the first time in our married life.

Front view of our stone house at 1720 Pioneer Road in Lampeter, 1983-2002.

From Lampeter, I commuted west to Harrisburg to the District Office and Vivian went south to Swift Middle School where she continued her job as middle school librarian. She felt so fortunate in that she commuted to Swift for over ten years with a fellow faculty member, Jim Martz from Strasburg, and although they took turns driving, they had the understanding that whenever it snowed or the roads were slippery, Jim would drive!

* * * * *

The task of the District Executive was to be a "pastor to pastors" to about 150 ministers in the seventy-five churches of the Atlantic Northeast District of the Church of the Brethren. Most of the churches are east of Harrisburg and in Pennsylvania, but a few are scattered in Maine, New York, New Jersey and

Delaware. The main office was in Harrisburg, and I was assisted by Associate, Dave Markey and later by Bob Kettering, plus the help of Mrs. Carl (Alma) Herr and Mrs. Russ (Gail) Martin as our secretaries. My duties included the installation, ordaining, licensing and placing of pastors and ministers, as well as counseling pastors and/or congregations when they encountered problems. I was also an interpreter and communicator between individual pastors and the national denominational staff in Elgin, Illinois.

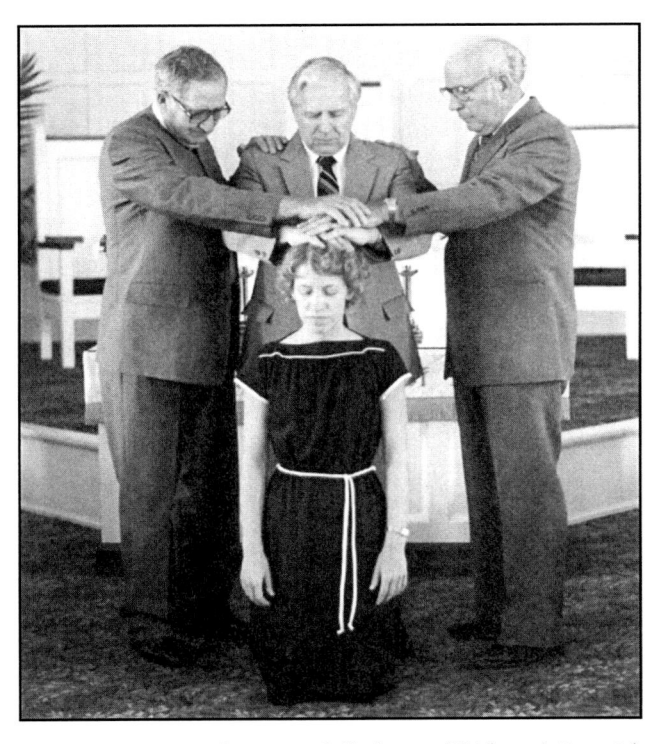

* * * * *

Consecration service for Nancy Sollenberger (Heishman) June 14, 1985, in the Annville, Pennsylvania, Church of the Brethren. Standing, left to right: Norman Gingrich, Earl Ziegler, the Atlantic Northeast District Executive, and Jim Tyler, pastor of the Annville Church.

The Gap Fellowship was born out of the crowded worship space in the Mechanic Grove Church, which sponsored it. Begun the first Sunday of June 1983, the Fairmount School on Simmontown Road was the worship location for the summer months under the internship of Joel Nogle as student intern pastor. In the fall, the move to the Gap Lion's Club house was followed that year by the calling of Jim and Tami Davis as pastor and spouse. April 28, 1985, was Charter Sunday when Merle Crouse, from the national staff for church planting, spoke, and 28 persons (25 that day and 3 the next week) were received as charter members

Vivian playing the organ at the Pequea Valley Church of the Brethren (formerly the Gap Fellowship) in 1994.

of the new district plant known as "The Gap Fellowship." (It later became known as the Pequea Valley Church of the Brethren.) Fifty-six was the average attendance.

After moves to the Old Laycock Presbyterian Church and the Intercourse Fire Hall, a beautiful house was built at 3926 East Newport Road with the generous aid of Carlos Leffler. The basement served as the sanctuary with other rooms used for Sunday School classes and fellowship dinners. Luke and Anna Brant served as pastor and wife until Luke's retirement, and his leadership was followed by that of Bryan and Janice Dever.

The last few years were difficult in that the frequent pastoral and lay changes of leadership, moves of location, and conflicts about the direction of the ministry, especially related to future building plans, became divisive. The Pequea Valley Church celebrated its seventh year of ministry in the area with a final service in July 1990. Later, the District sold the building, and the majority of its members joined neighboring Churches of the Brethren.

*****

The Church of the Brethren denomination was founded in 1708 in Schwarzenau, Germany, by Alexander Mack. Because he and his small circle of believers were being persecuted, they emigrated to America and founded the Germantown, Pennsylvania, Church of the Brethren in 1723. In the years since that time, Germantown, a suburb of Philadelphia, has evolved into a mostly black community, and the church, continuing to serve its closest neighbors, also has in it a black majority.

In 1988, the Germantown Church was without a pastor. Nationwide, the Church of the Brethren has very few black members, so I knew that finding someone willing to be their pastor and move into that urban black neighborhood would not be easy.

Mary Jane Myer, had just received her degree from Lancaster Theological Seminary and hosted a party to celebrate. Among her guests were several of her classmates, family members and she invited me as her District Executive. After introductions were made all around, the guests mingled and enjoyed the refreshments.

During the first break, one of her graduating classmates, a man from Ghana named Richard Kyerematen approached me and asked, "You are a member of the Church of the Brethren?"

"Yes, I am," I responded.

"Tell me, what does the Church of the Brethren believe?'

Although I was somewhat surprised, I answered, "Well, we believe that Jesus Christ was the Son of God and that He died for the sins of the world, rose again and lives today."

"I believe that, too."

"We also believe in a believer's baptism, in trying to live like Jesus, in promoting peace rather than engaging in war, and in living a simple life."

"I believe that, too."

"We practice feet washing as taught in John 13, and anoint people with oil for healing."

"I believe that, too."

Suddenly, I had an idea as though a light bulb went on. I looked him in the eye and asked, "Are you looking for a church where you could become pastor?"

With a wide smile, Richard admitted, "Yes, I am."

After more discussion, we decided to drive to Germantown the following Tuesday for Richard to see the church and meet with several of the leading people there.

During our conversation in my car on our way there, I thought the whole prospect was doomed when Richard raised the question, "How many black pastors does the Church of the Brethren have in this district?"

The answer was none.

Richard had no comment.

Walking into the church, I introduced candidate Richard to Patricia, the search committee chair. As I continued to talk with her, the nursery school teacher brought a small group of children into the sanctuary for a story. On seeing this, Richard meandered over to the children, got down on his haunches and began chatting with some of the children.

"Look at that!" exclaimed the woman to whom I was speaking. "Just look at that! *There's* our man!"

She was so impressed with the humility and caring attitude that was shown by this specific action of Richard's. And that is how Rev. Richard Kyerematen from Ghana became the pastor of the Germantown Church of the Brethren, and the first pastor from outside the United States called to a Brethren

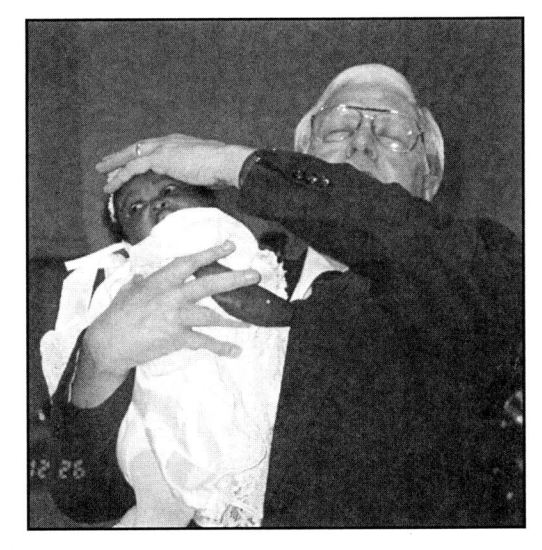

Earl dedicating the daughter of Pastor Richard and Elizabeth Kyerematen in the Germantown Church, 1999.

pulpit here. He continues serving there to this day, twenty-four years later.

* * * * *

As District Executive, one of my jobs was matching pastors and churches. When a church was seeking a new pastor, I would often accompany the candidate to the church where the prospective pastor would give a "trial sermon" so the congregation could assess his style, theology, etc.

On one such occasion, after the sermon, the pastor and his family were asked to "get lost" to the church basement while the congregation considered their call and voted. When they re-entered the room and came forward, they stood in front of the congregation as I explained the procedure to everyone. During this time, I heard the little daughter ask her father, "Do you think they want us?" (I always thought that was such a precious way of asking a very pertinent question.)

The congregation *did* want them, and the pastoral family moved into the Royersford parsonage.

* * * * *

As District Executive, I looked out of my Harrisburg office window and dreamed about the need of our district youth to be exposed to poverty and a third world culture. Jan (Glass) King was on the district staff as part-time youth director. Planning together, we arranged for a trip to Puerto Rico the fall of 1988 with our spouses to explore mission trips for our district youth. Flying to San Juan and hosted by Pedro and Magda Bruell, the Puerto Rico Island executive and his wife, we saw firsthand the progress

Left to right: Pedro Bruell, Thom Keller, Earl Ziegler, Jorge Toledo in Puerto Rico in 1994.

of the work in Puerto Rico and also the needs. As a result, Jan did plan for 40 district youth to go on a mission trip to Puerto Rico in 1989, serving in several locations, and introducing them to a far different culture.

    One evening we were invited to dinner in the home of Pastor Jaime Riviera and his wife, Rosalita. While we were there, two unexpected guests, Jorge Toledo and Victor Jorge, walked in and showed us pictures of work in the Dominican Republic as a follow-up to the 1986 hurricane David that devastated the Dominican Island. Baptisms of Dominicans in the triune immersion mode indicated a possible connection to the Brethren. The goal that night for Jorge and Victor, members of the Vega Baja Church of the Brethren near San Juan in Puerto Rico, was to attract support from someone who would lobby on their behalf to begin a Church of the Brethren in the Dominican Republic.

To understand their passion, one must understand that the Brethren, in 1981, had sent two female volunteers to work in the Viajames area. Large tarantula spiders frightened the workers who left and never returned to the island. Following the 1986 hurricane, Jorge Toledo began working in that area, taking in needed clothing and food supplies, and holding evangelistic meetings, and it was those converts that he was baptizing.

"In whose name and by whose authority are you baptizing these people?" I asked him.

Jorge answered, "In the name of the Church of the Brethren." He continued, pleading, *"I've tried to get the Brethren to help me, but no one will listen. I want you to help me."*

The challenge of starting a mission field in the Dominican Republic was a daunting one. In June 1989, Thom Keller (whom I invited personally, a member of the Midway Church of the Brethren and staff volunteer for "Passing on the Promise"), and I visited the Dominican Republic as guests of Jorge Toledo and Victor Jorge. We met Pastor Santos Mota of the Los Toros Church and through Jorge Toledo promised to secure $15,000 to finance the building of a growing church in Los Toros.

To receive blessings for this adventure from the denomination was important, and National staff member, Yvonne Dilling, joined in the support of the project. A proposed new item of business, co-sponsored by the Northern Indiana District and Puerto Rico Brethren, to start missions in the Dominican Republic appeared in the 1990 Annual Conference agenda and was passed for immediate implementation.

The necessary funds for building the church in Los Toros were received, and in November 1990, Thom and Sue Keller, Harlan and Shirley Keener from Lampeter, Vivian and I flew to Santo Domingo for the dedication of the new Los Toros Church building. We took along a large candle as a symbolic gift of a mutual sharing of the Light of the world from the Lampeter Church. The crowd in the hundreds was packed so tightly, the excitement so contagious, the oxygen so thin, that the candle literally could not burn! A child actually fell asleep standing up, so sandwiched were the people in the sanctuary! In addition, the windows were hanging full of hopeful and curious worshippers.

Following the dedication, the six of us were introduced by Jorge Toledo to many other leaders who wanted to join the Church of the Brethren. What a golden opportunity to share the Gospel with a spiritually hungry and waiting world!

During our wanderings that November with Jorge Toledo, also known as "The Saint Paul of the Caribbean," we met Diamera, a woman pastor with a large vision. We visited with her in her bare, ground-floor house where she revealed her dream to us. North of Santo Domingo, in the Guaricano community where she lived, was a garbage dump for sale. Her unique proposal to us was, "I want to erect a church building on this garbage dump. I'll buy the land and grow a large church here if you'll fund the building for me." Her challenge was framed by a contagious commitment to Jesus and the great commission. I promised her nothing, but said I'd take her request back home and act on it.

Contacting the General Board of our denomination through Dale Minnich, I received a letter authorizing the soliciting of funds for the Guaricano Church project. It took $48,000 and two one-week mission trips to complete the building, which included a large balcony. In August of 1997, Galen Hackman and I went to the Dominican Republic to the Guaricano Church where I preached the dedication sermon with translator, Jorge Toledo, by my side. Over 700 persons joined in the celebration.

The following chart reveals the building projects for which I secured the funds and the laborers in cooperation with Church of the Brethren National Staff and Brethren World Mission, a Brethren related agency whose mission is to help in fulfilling the Annual Conference mandate to become a world church.

WORK CAMPS IN THE DOMINICAN, ORGANIZED AND FUNDED BY BRETHREN WORLD MISSION

Year	Month	Church	Cost of Project	# of U.S. Workers
1996	January	Pariaso (country)	$15,000	11
1997	February	Guaricano	$48,000	20
	October	Guaricano (to finish 2nd story)	$14,000	8
1999	February	Tabara Abajo	$25,000	16
	June	Bastidas	$20,000	Dominicans
2000	November	Fondo Negro	$35,000	17
2001	December	San Luis	$50,000	17
2002	January	San Luis (to finish)		21
2012	Feb./March	Sabana Torso	$30,000	12

At Guillermo Encarnacion's invitation and hosted by Milciades and Lucy Mendez, I taught several courses on the New Testament and Church of the Brethren ordinances and doctrines to the pastors in the Dominican Republic. A summer Vacation Bible School, for which I organized and recruited leaders, was held there in July 2008, at three different churches with a nine volunteer U.S. staff.

Earl leading an outdoor Bible Study at the Sabana Torsa Church in the Dominican Republic.

The Dominicans themselves provided the teaching component of the schools. I was in the Dominican Republic in some leadership role during sixteen visits there including the one in February 2011, when I was the guest preacher at the Annual Conference of the Dominican Church of the Brethren. Held in a Mennonite site, Camp Hebron, near San Juan, the conference witnessed again to the powerful Holy Spirit-led vision of the now deceased Jorge Toledo.

* * * * *

One day I was approached by Dr. Gerhard Spiegler, president of Elizabethtown College, asking my thoughts about a possible Anabaptist Center on the college campus. "What an exciting dream!" I thought.

Dr. Spiegler pursued the dream through the Church-College Mutual Expectations Committee who appointed a committee composed of the College President, Vice President for Development, the College Chaplain, and two District Executives: Warren Eshbach of Southern Pennsylvania, and myself of the Atlantic Northeast District. The idea of building a meetinghouse modeled after the Germantown Meeting House was adopted with Ed Nace of the Black Rock Church as the builder.

The naming of the building was of historic significance. Having lived in "Rufus P. Bucher" country and experiencing the legacy of this noted preacher and national leader in the Church of the Brethren, I suggested naming it after him. I was given the privilege of contacting each of the children of Rufus Bucher for permission to use his name and to solicit financial aid.

Groundbreaking for the Rufus P. Bucher Meeting House was ceremonialized on Saturday, April 23, 1988. I was chosen to preside at the Groundbreaking Ceremony and also was privileged to present a ten-minute historical perspective at the Dedication Ceremony on October 15, 1988. What an honor it was to share in these two events!

* * * * *

Other high moments for me were to be the Sunday morning worship speaker at Annual Conference in 1986 and being the opening worship speaker at the Pennsylvania State Farm Show in January 1989.

In my tenure as District Executive, I placed forty-two pastors in my first two years.

At one point, there were fourteen pastoral vacancies that needed to be filled.

* * * * *

One of those vacancies happened in the Lampeter Church when their pastor, Curtis Dubble retired on August 31, 1988. (He was later elected to be Annual Conference Moderator-Elect in July 1989, and served as Moderator in 1991 in Minneapolis, Minnesota.) J. C. Wine, a former missionary to Nigeria and a retired professor of psychology at Millersville University, agreed to serve as interim pastor beginning on October 1, 1988. (It was the fourteenth interim pastorate for him!)

During the following months, I submitted several names to the Lampeter Pastoral Committee, but for one reason or another, all were rejected. Meanwhile, some Lampeter members and others suggested that since our home was in Lampeter, I should submit an application for myself and resign from the District Executive position.

To accomplish my Executive duties required me at times to drive long distances, especially at night. Hospitable members kindly invited me to their homes as a "Bed and Breakfast" stopover whenever necessary, and I frequently did that. However, when I am tired, I have the dangerous tendency to fall asleep at the wheel when driving alone.

One night, while driving home from a meeting in the Philadelphia area, I suddenly realized I was driving in the opposite lane and heading toward a ditch! This frightening experience was the clincher that helped me decide to leave this job, which I had enjoyed, and return to the pastorate.

In addition, I am very much a "people person" and I greatly missed interacting with people on a personal level. At my age then of 60 and having accomplished the goals given to me by the District Search Committee, I felt I could serve some congregation well for at least ten years. So, for all these reasons, I felt called to resign as District Executive, submit my name to be Lampeter's next pastor, and I was accepted.

When I began my second pastorate with them on Sept. 1, 1989, we didn't even have to move to a new residence!

RETURNING TO THE LAMPETER CHURCH, 1989-1999
CHAPTER SIXTEEN

> "I have found that there are three stages
> in every great work of God:
> First, it is impossible; then, it is difficult; then, it is done."
> *(J. Hudson Taylor, missionary to China)*

Earl –

After serving as the District Executive of the Atlantic Northeast District of the Church of the Brethren with offices located in the United Church Center, Harrisburg, Pennsylvania, for six years, I returned to Lampeter, arriving on the scene on September 1, 1989, after the call of the search committee and approval by the congregation. Charles Bieber, a personal friend representing the district, presided over my installation.

The November 12, 1989, groundbreaking for a $250,000 project in which a Christian Education wing was to be built, extending east from the sanctuary and wrapping around the north side, was the first big event in my pastoral ministry at Lampeter. A one bottom plow with an attached single tree was used in the groundbreaking, allowing over one hundred persons to pull together as a symbol of unity. That wing was dedicated on June 3, 1990.

* * * * *

On the day after Christmas, 1989, Lloyd Kreider's barn burned down. While Lloyd and his wife, Dottie, Lampeter Church members, had both been away on separate errands that morning, a malfunction in the electrical heat tape on the barn's water pipes started a fire. Neighbors and passers-by sprang into action and in spite of burning debris falling all around them, were able to rescue the livestock—heifers, mules, and a bull. Firefighters from twelve surrounding communities battled the blaze, but in a short time the barn was gone as well as numerous implements, farm equipment, and hay, straw and corn that had been stored there. A neighbor offered to give the livestock a temporary home.

Two days after the fire, Lloyd met with an Amish contractor, John Ebersole, who agreed to head a crew to rebuild the barn. The announcement was spread around that a barn-raising would be held at the Kreiders' on January 9, 1990. On that morning the volunteers poured in. They came in the latest model cars, in old pick-ups and in buggies pulled by horses. About seventy-five men and teenage boys, bringing their carpentry tools, made up the workforce at the barn site. Bearded Amish in plain clothes mingled with the Brethren, Mennonites, United Methodists and United Church of Christ members (UCC's). Women bringing baskets of food gathered in the house to help fix dinner.

As the barn was raised, differences in dress, ideologies, and lifestyles were leveled as the volunteer labor force sweated and toiled, following the directions of Mr. Ebersole, yelling above the whistling wind, "Together, hoist!"

Interestingly enough, the basic barn frame was constructed according to the century-old style of barn-building, using wooden pins (instead of nails), mortise and tenon joints, and tongue and groove boards. Not a nail was used in the basic structure. The beams were fitted into place with the workers' "Heave-ho!" at the crucial moment. Each piece of lumber fit a specific place.

The work went on for three weeks until the last partitions were built, the last doors were hung, the cattle stalls were in place, and the livestock were returned to their new home. Touched by the generosity and neighborliness shown, Dottie asked, "How can I repay this kindness? I've always been on the giving end of things. It is so hard to receive."

The people kept coming with gifts of cheese, chipped ham, butter, pretzels, doughnuts, homemade bread, and more. One farmer arrived with a container of cookies saying, *"If everybody gives something, nobody has much to do."*

The prevailing spirit of unity and the joint efforts of their surrounding community folk made the words of I Corinthians 12:12 take on new meaning: "The body is a unit, though it is made up of many parts; and though all its parts are many, they form one body. So it is with Christ." (NIV) All were working together "for the glory of God and their neighbor's good."

Whenever John Ebersole wanted the work crew to lift the load together, he shouted, *"Together, hoist!"* That could also be a good motto to inscribe over the doors of our churches!

* * * * *

Vivian –

From the beginning of the Gap Fellowship in 1983 until its demise as the Pequea Valley Church of the Brethren in 1990, I attended there, serving as one of the adult Sunday School teachers and as the organist. I also joined others in supplying flowers from our garden and occasionally made banners to decorate the worship area. During our entire marriage, it has been a rare privilege to sit with my husband during Sunday morning worship, but for these years, we didn't even attend the same church!

A little outreach project which I had at Gap was the "Less and Less Club," a weight loss group, which met once a week for about two and one-half years. Our theme verse was John 3:30: "He must become greater and greater, and I must become less and less." (TLB) We were aware that we had altered its original meaning, but this interpretation was motivational. We enjoyed encouraging one another by saying, "We hope to see less of you next week!" Unfortunately, very few of us were successful at losing weight, but we did teach one another about healthier nutrition and had fun doing it.

After the Pequea Valley Church closed, I began attending Lampeter where I frequently taught Sunday School and Wednesday night classes, took my turn as organist, played the piano for

The Lampeter Church library.

one of the contemporary service worship teams and organized and built up their library until we moved to Brethren Village in January 2003.

* * * * *

Earl -

In my 3rd year as pastor at Lampeter, the Church of the Brethren National Church called me to be the Moderator-Elect of the Annual Conference for 1993 and then to follow in the role of Moderator in 1994 when the conference was to be held in Wichita, Kansas. That conference was rife with discord over the homosexual issue. In my year as Moderator, I had to put out many fires related to that subject, thus blunting my vision to grow the ethnic ministry potential of our beloved denomination. I did succeed in convincing the delegates to "put on hold" the issue for the next five years so as to allow a cooling-off period.

Beginning July 1, 1993, the Lampeter Church hired Mark Cunningham, a recent seminary graduate, as half-time Associate Pastor, allowing me to travel more freely as Moderator. After Mark resigned in 1997, Mike Fletcher was hired as part-time Associate Pastor. Brian Flory, a student at Bethany Seminary, assisted me as an intern during two summers at Lampeter.

* * * * *

During my tenure, in 1990, the Lampeter Church organized its first summer Vacation Bible School, in 1992, its first Wednesday Nights Happenings, which combined a communal supper followed by Bible studies for all ages 2 through 92, choir practices and small group discussions, in 1995, a community theatre group called "The Promise Players" was begun. In September 1996, we started having two Sunday morning services, one traditional and one contemporary, and a pre-school nursery school which we began in September 1997, was filled during its first month of existence.

Interestingly, in their first sixteen and one-half years, "The Promise Players" have produced thirty-three dramas and/or musicals and have donated over $100,000 to thirty-seven different charities as they strove to further the name of Christ through dramatic arts.

Since Doreen, our daughter, was the drama director of Promise Players, when an older male actor landed in the hospital the afternoon of a performance, she persuaded me to come, pinch

Earl and Vivian and their grandchildren at Christmas 1996. Standing in back, left to right: Marianne Zimmerman, Rebekah Miller, Matthew Zimmerman, Jeremy Ziegler. Middle row: Michael Berces, Rikki Berces, Anna Ziegler, Tim Creighton, Lena Ziegler. Front row: Carrie Ziegler, Earl Ziegler, Ben Creighton, Vivian Ziegler holding Kara Berces, Sarah Ziegler and Emily Creighton.

hit and be an old grouchy man in that play—for a three-night run! I had no time to memorize my lines, but managed to read them as subtly as possible with many whispered and body language cues from the sympathetic cast. Wow! Never again!

*****

My ministry at Lampeter began in 1989 with the building of a $250,000 Christian Education wing, and when I left 10 years later, the church was in the midst of an $800,000 construction project, including three new church offices, a library and eleven new classrooms which were completed in June 2000. Within three years, the Lampeter Church had paid its debt in full. What an amazing accomplishment, all done without reducing its outreach giving!

John H. Hostetter followed me as pastor of the Lampeter Church fifteen days after my final day on August 31, 1999. To prepare the congregation for the transition, I took off my shoes during that final Sunday morning service, placed them on the altar and said, "These are my shoes. I walked in them with you for the past ten years. We have been faithful together in serving the Lord and this community. Thank you so much for your nurturing, for our mutual ministry together. Now comes a change."

Taking my shoes from the altar, I replaced them with a pair of John Hostetter's shoes (by pre-arrangement). Then I continued. "These shoes belong to your new pastor, John H. Hostetter. They belong to *him*. I do not fit into them. He is a unique individual who will fill his own shoes. Allow him to walk in them with his own skills and gifts for ministry. Support him like you supported me in the role of pastor." I then led in a final prayer for Pastor John, the congregation and their future together.

Then I walked away from the Lampeter Church knowing that the best was yet to come.

*****

Vivian –

By the way, in 2011 Earl finished writing *The History of the Lampeter Church of the Brethren, 1978-2010* and had it published. It provides more details, stories and photos than we've included here.

*****

We had reservations for the two of us to leave the week after Earl's final Sunday at Lampeter in August 1999, to travel (just as a couple—a very rare experience) to Spain for a rest and relaxation (R&R) interlude before the next chapter of our lives. Interestingly enough, that first Monday as Earl was carrying a file drawer out of his office at the church, intending to put the drawer in his car, he tripped on the sidewalk and fell with the heavy file drawer on top of his arm, breaking his arm! What a way to end a pastorate—or to begin our mini-vacation! Consequently, when we flew to Spain, he had his arm in a sling!

AT THE HELM OF THE 1994, WICHITA, KANSAS, ANNUAL CONFERENCE
Chapter Seventeen

"Come . . . Drink the Living Water"
(From John 7:37, 38 – The theme of the 1994 Conference)

Earl –

Having served as a volunteer in the Annual Conference bookstore for many years, I was serving as a cashier there in 1992 in Richmond, Virginia, when someone came and informed me that I'd just been elected by the delegates to be the Moderator-Elect of the Annual Conference for 1993 and Moderator for the 1994 Conference.

On Sunday, June 27th, 1993, after the Moderator Consecration ceremony in Indianapolis, Vivian and I drove straight to Richmond, Indiana, to perform my first big task as Moderator of the National Church. The event was a groundbreaking at the site of the new campus for Bethany Theological Seminary there. Along with other representatives of the larger church, I turned over a shovel of dirt to begin the building project.

During my year as Moderator, I traveled many miles across the country, visited mission points in Maine, Puerto Rico and India and spoke in sixteen of the twenty-three districts of

Earl, in his first act as Annual Conference Moderator, spoke at the groundbreaking service in July 1993, for Bethany Seminary in Richmond, Indiana.

the denomination. During the same period, I preached twenty-six Sundays at the Lampeter Church where I continued as pastor.

An especially memorable journey was to the island of Puerto Rico where about a dozen healthy churches were flourishing. Visiting them twice during my moderatorship as an ambassador of reconciliation, it was a joy to help them achieve resolution and harmony among the leadership. They became some of my best friends and cheerleaders during conference.

* * * * *

The theme of the 1994 conference held in Wichita, Kansas, June 28–July 3, 1994, was "Come, Drink the Living Water" based on John 7:37-38. As prompted by the theme, representatives from every congregation in the U.S. brought small containers of water to the opening session, dumped the water into a small waterfall exhibit symbolizing a sense of unity and oneness. Water was brought by Brethren from the Sea of Galilee, the Jordan River, the Eder River in Schwarzenau, Germany, (where the first Brethren were baptized in 1708), the Wissahickon Creek, near Germantown, PA, (where the first baptism in America took place in 1723) and from Nigeria and Puerto Rico. The waterfall flowed all during conference and at departure time, all delegates took some of the water back to their home congregations. Attendance registration revealed a total of 4,062.

My sermon for the opening service at the conference on Tuesday night was titled, "Come to the River of Life." Audrey, our Korean exchange student and known professionally in Korea as Hyun Joo Yun, had lived with us at Black Rock in 1964-65. Now a Ph.D. professor of music at Seoul National University, she flew from Seoul, Korea, to give a vocal concert that week with Nancy Sollenberger Heishman as her piano accompanist.

At the business session on Saturday morning, the conference presented to Vivian and me a quilted wall hanging that represented the many phases of my life and ministry and had been sewn by conference goers. What a gift! It is hanging on my office wall today. Composed of 15 patches, it tells my life story recognizing my birth family, my nuclear family, the churches I have served, the institutions from which I graduated plus two special colorful patches from friends in Puerto Rico. Appropriately, the very center patch proclaims the symbol and message, "Come, Drink the Living Water." (See pages 190 and 191.)

Having received the gavel from the 1993 Moderator, Charles Boyer, I gladly handed over the gavel to Judy Mills Reimer, the 1995 Moderator. As I pounded the gavel on the table signifying the close of the 1994 Annual Conference in Witchita, I remember the sigh of relief expressed in an inaudible, "Praise the Lord!"

* * * * *

Here are some brief comments of encouragement from a lengthy letter received a week following conference from a Standing Committee delegate. "I want to extend my congratulations and deep appreciation for your large contribution to the successes of the week. My guess is that it had 'its moments' for you, but you always approached every issue from a position of fairness and openness. One could not ask more from any leader. I'm aware how difficult it is at times to desperately try to keep personal biases invisible, but you were able to pull it off with impartiality and a spirit of Christian graciousness. There were those times when none of us really knew where things were headed, but you patiently, yet firmly, steered us through some choppy waters . . . ."

While not everyone would have agreed with the spirit of the letter, I was very blessed with the overwhelming support of the conference officers, the delegates and conference goers, an amazing feat accomplished through prayer and trust in God.

* * * * *

As the 1994 Moderator of the Church of the Brethren, I was privileged to visit India during their celebration of the One Hundredth Anniversary of Missions in India. In 1894, the Meyersdale, Pennsylvania, Annual Conference had called and sent three missionaries to India: Wilbur and Mary Stover and Bertha

Ryan. They had landed in Bombay in December and began working in the Bulsar area, in the Gujarat State.

One hundred years later, who would have thought of receiving from the Bishop the bronze cross which symbolized his ordination and leadership in the large protestant Church of North India? What a kind and intimate gesture on his behalf, and what a humbling moment it was for me! If you were to visit the office in my home today, you would see the personal cross of Bishop Paul Chauhan who presented it to me on the last day of my visit to the Indian Churches as I was about to depart for the Bombay airport to fly back to the United States.

Partnering with me on this twelve-day venture were Joan Deeter, national executive of the World Ministries of the Church of the Brethren, and Lamar Gibble, staff for the denomination's Asian missions. On March 7, 1994, we flew on Trans World Airlines from Harrisburg, Pennsylvania, to Kennedy International Airport and then directly to Amsterdam on KLM (Royal Dutch Airlines).

Having boarded the KLM flight for New Delhi after a six-hour delay, I was relaxing in my economy seat (separate from Lamar and Joan) when the airline purser came by to chat. The plane was not full. Our conversation led me to explain that as Moderator, my purpose for going to India was to celebrate the one hundredth anniversary of the founding of missions there. When he understood my role as Moderator represented the entire denomination, he invited me to come to the first class upper deck section of this 747. I felt like royalty on that flight as I was given the special attention and service of a head of state!

Upon landing in New Delhi, India, on March 8th, we were met at the airport by Bishop Paul Chauhan of the Gujarat State, and his assistant who accompanied us to the administrative suites of the Moderator of all of India, Dr. V. S. Lall, of the Church of North India. A leader with a vibrant, sensitive and forward-looking attitude, Dr. Lall explained that their theme for the anniversary year was "Toward a Holistic Understanding of Mission." Through him, we were introduced to the various ongoing ministries in medicine, education, social services with an emphasis on AIDS, ecology and leadership development. We learned that the Church of North India operated sixty-one hospitals plus many schools and village clinics. As an example, we visited one of their seminaries, the Gujarat United School of Theology (G.U.S.T.) where we met a senior student and his wife, the only Christians in their family, whose house had been burned to the ground by their own family members on the day after their baptism.

After the official greetings and the floral lei ceremony, we were given an orientation of Indian culture and church life. The main points were that one must recognize the caste system into which people are born, the sacredness of animals, especially the cow, the fact that Indian culture does not have an emphatic "yes" or "no" in casual conversation, and the poverty of the people. It was also explained that the Church of North India (CNI) was created in 1970 out of the merger of six Protestant denominations: The Church of the Brethren, the Lutheran Church, the Baptist Church, the Church of England (Episcopalian), the Reformed Church and the Presbyterian Church. This merger, approved by the Annual Conference, was the official entity with which the U.S. Church of the Brethren related.

We visited three judicatories: The Agra, the Gujarat and the Bombay Dioceses. The concentration of our visits and contacts were in the Gujarat area where the Brethren influence was most obvious with 150 congregations composed of 35,000 members. The outdoor baptisteries, the love feasts and the contagious joy revealed the continued nurture of the Christians. After I had given a sermon to the church assembled in Anklesvar, one Indian brother grabbed the mike from me and charged me in front of his congregation, "Tell the church in America that we are so grateful the missionaries were sent one hundred years ago and that today you are witnessing the fruits of their labors."

* * * * *

However, some Brethren congregations, (about 5,000 in membership, mainly Anabaptist in origin), slowly withdrew from the Church of North India over theological issues. Eventually, as history reveals, division of property was difficult, conflicts arose, and it was not until 1998 that the separated group of Brethren was recognized by the Annual Conference as a legitimate group. Today (2012), the U.S. Brethren relate to both groups.

* * * * *

One high moment among many was the dedication of a new church building in the Agaswan congregation. Although our arrival was two hours late, the members welcomed us by forming a long line along both sides of a path that led to the door of the church and placing a floral lei around the necks of Bishop Chauhan and myself. Twelve hundred persons, who had waited for two hours, then entered the church with the women sitting on the floor on one side and the men on the other.

As we walked into the church building, the Bishop whispered to me, "They're expecting you to preach the dedication sermon." While they engaged in lively singing and Lamar and Joan brought greetings, I was frantically searching for a nudge from the Holy Spirit. And I wasn't disappointed.

On the ceiling were many crepe paper streamers of all colors. I felt led to use those celebrative streamers as a basis for my remarks about 1 Corinthians 12:1-27 where the apostle Paul describes the church as the body of Christ, one body composed of many members. I simply compared those colored streamers to a rainbow where each color is needed. One color does not make a rainbow, and neither does two. It takes all seven to make a rainbow. So it is with the body of Christ at Agaswan. The object lesson was clear, visual and Biblical, and the audience responded enthusiastically.

Immediately following the service, a love feast for the twelve hundred members was held in an open courtyard, including the meal, the washing of feet and the communion. What a foretaste of heaven!

* * * * *

Early in the morning on another day we traveled to a small village and laid the cornerstone in a new building that was being erected for worship because the congregation had outgrown the old one. Later, in another village, I laid a cornerstone for a new fledgling church just being born. While traveling to a third village to participate in a groundbreaking, I met the energetic young pastor, a recent convert from Hinduism, who in 1994 envisioned the goal of reaching 99 villages plus his own for Christ as the outreach challenge of the one hundredth anniversary.

In the past, the Brethren had a significant medical ministry to the community surrounding the Dahanu Road Hospital. Although it was once vibrant, effective, and well-staffed with the latest technology, on our visit we found it to be much inferior to its earlier days, having become a government-run hospital.

In Bulsar, we experienced both a high moment and a low moment. I was scheduled to preach at the local Church of the Brethren and when we arrived in the afternoon, the church was filled with worshippers. I soon discovered why. Earl M. Zigler from Virginia and his wife, Rachel, had spent many years on the mission field in Bulsar. Having heard that Earl Ziegler was returning to visit with them, the local members came in droves expecting to welcome their old friend back to their church. When I arrived and was introduced as Earl Ziegler, one could feel a huge wave of disappointment come over the crowd. They had not received the word that Earl M. Zigler had died shortly before my visit. Most of them were gracious, however, and stayed for the sermon, but after the service, many of them departed and didn't stay for the evening service.

The next day, at the invitation of the Mayor of Bulsar, we experienced a high moment when we joined a group of believers gathered at the corner of a main road in Bulsar to unveil the name of the street and dedicate it in memory of Wilbur B. Stover, the first missionary. He and his wife, Mary, and their friend, Bertha Ryan, had come to Bulsar to share the gospel of Jesus Christ in 1894. Today the Wilbur B. Stover Road is a prominent street in the bustling metropolis of Bulsar, India.

We also were privileged to accompany the local Bulsar church leaders to visit the grave of Ida Shumaker, an early missionary from Western Pennsylvania, who gave her entire life to the Indian people. Although she had returned to the United States to retire, she missed her Indian friends so much that she decided to go back to die among the people she loved so dearly. She is buried in Bulsar as she had wished.

* * * * *

Not all of our destinations in India were church-related. Although I'd visited India before in 1970 as leader for an around-the-world tour group, it was a special joy to travel by train north from Dehli to view again the magnificent Taj Mahal, sometimes included as one of the seven modern-day wonders of the world. What an amazing architectural feat it is! What a gift from the king who commissioned this building to his bride! It truly is a marvelous structure of beauty!

* * * * *

One of the tragic social ills in India is the plight of orphans. Numerous families, too poor to provide for their children, abandon them or give them away. Consequently, parentless and "throwaway" children populate the hostels administered by the churches and other charities. To give us an idea of the magnitude of the problem, one hostel administrator described four other hostels which *each* served one thousand children between the ages of three through college age. In our visits to three different hostels, we were entertained by the children in each one with a beautiful and creatively done program. How sad it was to see these dear children, so obviously bright and with such potential, yet with so little chance to blossom. In addition, illness ran rampant among the hostel children.

* * * * *

One of the scariest moments of our trip occurred the night I was preaching in the Vyara Church where there was serious conflict between the Christians and the community. Believing that the culprits might take advantage of disturbing the large crowd of over five hundred persons who had gathered in the church building, the local Christians had warned us of possible trouble.

When I was about one-third way through my sermon, the sound of shooting suddenly erupted in the street right outside the sanctuary. At the same time, the lights went out. Total darkness as well as sounds of shooting enveloped us. No one moved. After a brief time, I was instructed to continue preaching in the dark, so that is exactly what I did. Eventually, the light again pierced our dreaded darkness and the shooting subsided. The service finished without any further incidents.

* * * * *

As I recall this trip, I realize that the faith and faces of the Indian people plus the unique sights, smells, and sounds linger in one's heart and mind long after the jet lag is gone. As I look at the bishop's cross in my office, I'm daily reminded of his country of India with its teeming millions with only 2.3% of them Christian. The words of Jesus in Luke 10:2 (NIV) are still so true today: *"The harvest is plentiful, but the workers are few. Ask the Lord of the harvest, therefore, to send out workers into his harvest field."*

IN JOY AND IN SORROW
Chapter Eighteen

*"Weeping may go on all night,
but in the morning there is joy."*
(Psalms 30:5b TLB)

"The joy of the Lord is your strength."
(Nehemiah 8:10 TLB)

Some of Our Sorrows:

Earl –

A defining incident in my ministry came in my third year as pastor of the Black Rock Church of the Brethren. It was the closest I ever came to leaving the ministry.

In an Official Board meeting, one member raised a business item in which I was accused of "running around" with another woman. That week was the first I'd heard the rumor, and I promptly dismissed it as just another bit of untrue gossip. However, when it came up in the Board meeting, I was in shock and asked, "Where is this originating? Who is the woman?"

Silence followed because most of the Official Board were also stunned. I raised more questions in defense of myself and proceeded to categorically flat out deny the accusation. The devastating clincher came when the chair of the board turned to me and questioned, "How do we know it isn't true?" I felt absolutely no support. They never told me who the woman was. When the meeting ended with no resolution, I went home and told Vivian. I was so angry and overwhelmed that I sat outside on our front step until 1 a.m. struggling with my future.

The next morning the moderator came to see me and explained that the rumor was fed by jealousy. A very small group of persons had voted against the "full time pastor" position and some of them were on the "official board." Since the disgruntled group gained no traction for their rumor, the leader of this minority group, a deacon, left the church.

Out of this incident, the unity was rekindled, and the church began to grow!

* * * * *

Vivian –

When we moved to Mechanic Grove in 1960 [1970], our youngest son, Mike, was eleven years old and in sixth grade. He soon made a whole new circle of friends, but the one with whom he felt closest was Dave Cunningham. Although Dave was two months younger and Mike was a grade ahead of him in school, they were in the same Sunday School class and both loved sports. Dave went along for a family camp weekend with us, and these two boys remained close friends all through high school.

Mike graduated from Solanco High School in 1977 and began attending Millersville College that fall. With Mike gone, Dave needed someone to "pal around with," and although Randy was almost five years older, these two boys discovered they had many common interests also. Together, they co-managed the

Mechanic Grove Church's junior softball team which, in the summer of 1979, had an undefeated season.

Although Dave worked at a tire shop in Lancaster, many nights he would show up at our house while we were eating supper. He seldom would join us in eating, but would sit or stand at the side and he and Randy would banter smart remarks back and forth to the amusement and delight of Konnae, Earl and me, and anyone else who happened to be there. Of course, on those weekends when Mike would come home, the *three* boys together were hilarious. What one didn't think of, another would. All three were lightning quick with quips, and Dave became like one of our family. Earl and I grew to love him and talked to him, gave him advice, or admonished him, just as we did our own sons.

David Ray Cunningham, son of Amos and Ruth Cunningham, November 24, 1959-September 23, 1979.

On Sunday, September 23, 1979, the Mechanic Grove Church had a combined Sunday School so that everyone, from youth to seniors, could view a film. After the early church service, everyone walked down to the basement where they'd be able to see the movie more clearly with less natural light coming in the windows. While I was standing near the sanctuary door, the youth filed by me. As Dave went past me, he gave me one of his tricky, naughty smiles as he asked, "Are we gonna see cartoons down here?"

We both had a good chuckle.

That was the last I ever spoke to him.

That afternoon he offered to take a friend, who had been home for the weekend, back to the University of Delaware where she was attending. On his return home on a back road, he rounded a curve, lost control of the 1977 Chrysler he was driving, and turned sideways in the road. An oncoming truck, unable to stop, struck the right side of Dave's car causing it to immediately burst into flames. Dave was nineteen.

Amos and Ruth Cunningham, Dave's parents, were not home that afternoon but someone notified Ruth's sister, Lucy de Perrot in Lititz about the accident. Lucy phoned Earl and asked him to break the news to Dave's fifteen-year-old brother, Mark, who was home alone and to stay with him until she got there.

What I did next is something I have regretted ever since. While Earl was gone, I phoned Mike at Millersville College and told him his best friend had died. When he realized I was serious and the import of what I was saying, he had a sickening feeling. I was still sharing what I knew about the accident when Mike suddenly said, "Mom, I don't want to hear anymore," and hung up. I was so wrong in how I handled that. Even during the next day or two, we failed Mike by not going to him and letting him express his grief with us face to face. He had to suffer alone.

Dave's younger sister, Joan, and her good friend, Beth Hershey, were students at Messiah College in Grantham, Pennsylvania, so after Aunt Lucy arrived at the Cunningham home to be with Mark, Earl left with Beth's parents, Earle and Joanne Hershey, to tell Joan and Beth about the tragedy and to bring Joan home.

Randy was almost inconsolable. He secluded himself in his room and finally was able to express his feelings in a poem which he simply titled, "Dave."

Dave

Born the son named David in the autumn '59,
Growing up so fast that he hardly had the time
To reach his goals, to help all those around him that he loved
Before he was called home by his Father from above.
The concern he showed for others, helpful acts he would engage,
Showed that through his Christian learnings,
he was just coming of age.
Although his work on earth is over, his life having just passed,
The memories of those whose lives he touched,
I know will always last.
Helping Dad around the house, assisting Mother Ruth,
Active in the church he was, 'specially with the youth.
Catching chickens, chopping wood, Dave found no chore too small,
Singing in the local choir, looked up to by us all.
He often spoke of sister Joan, how proud he was of her!
"I wish I could be more like she," his words often were.
The pride he had in brother, Mark, was surpassed by none,
He often said, "In playing sports, my brother's Number One!"
I loved Dave for many reasons, things he did for me,
Coaching softball, when in season, a success he was tru-ly.
He'd cheer me up when I was down, a friend he always was
Laughing, joking, all fun poking. I loved him much because
His will to please and work for others was outshone by none.
When God reviews his life, He'll say, "My child, a job well done!"
Born the son named David in the autumn '59,
Growing up so fast that we hardly had the time
To thank him for his kindly deeds, for all to us he's giv'n;
We'll get our chance to thank him when we meet someday in heav'n.
Dave, we'll always love you, and we'll miss you very much,

Thanks from those you've left behind,
And all of us you've touched.

Randy E. Ziegler

Dave's sister, Joan Cunningham (Kaba Kjian), also had a hard time accepting his sudden death and she too found consolation in writing poetry. Here are two of the poems she wrote concerning her brother:

His memory is sharp and clear; it cuts my very soul.
Waves of pain wash over me, the grief has made me old.
No more carefree childhood days when we were young and brave.
I must face the future now, and I must face it without Dave.

I feel numb. It can't be real! He meant so much to me!
Gone in an instant. Gone forever, Consumed in flames was he.
I'd give almost anything to have him walk right in that door.
I want to scream! It seems I just can't stand it any more.

I'll never hear him laugh again; I'll never see him smile.
All I have is a memory of when he was with us for a while.
He was special in so many ways, at work, at church, at home.
And he's special now in heaven . . . but it's lonely here alone.

Joan L. Cunningham 9/25/79
(Used by permission.)

* * * * *

I hate waking up in the mornings knowing he isn't there.
Our relationship as brother and sister was so special and so rare.

The more I love him, the more it hurts,
and the more I want him back.
I feel peaceful inside, but then it hits,
and something within me cracks.
This morning at ten we'll bury him.
He's in heaven; I'm going through hell.
Putting him in that cold, dark earth, the earth he loved so well.
It's final now. He's dead. He's gone, and I can fantasize and yearn
For him to come back to me, but he'll never ever return.
Is there anything worse in the whole wide earth
than burying one you loved?
My only solace, my only joy, is that he's gone to his Father above.

Joan L. Cunningham 9/26/79
(Used by permission.)

* * * * *

Dave's remains were buried prior to his memorial service which was held on Sunday, September 30, one week after his death. Ironically, this was also our son, Mike's, twentieth birthday! This was the most difficult funeral Earl ever conducted in his ministry because of how close we and our sons were to Dave.

Because Dave grew up in the church and was such an active member, his sudden death hit the youth group hard. On Sunday morning, September 30, Earl, as the youth teacher had their Sunday School class, including many members of the undefeated baseball team which Dave had co-managed, walk out to the cemetery next to the church and form a circle around his grave. There they shared memories, grieved together, sang together and prayed together. One of the youth in that circle was fifteen-year-old Doug Smith, son of Barry and Janet Smith.

The following week was a sad one as the Cunningham family, Mike, Randy, the junior high softball team members, the youth group, and Earl and I adjusted to and accepted our loss. Dave's untimely passing had left us with "holes in our hearts," but we found solace in sharing our faith and our memories.

* * * * *

Earl –

Late that next Thursday night I received a phone call from Barry and Janet Smith. Their son, Doug, had been at school that day and on the way home was so very tired that he stretched out on a seat on the school bus to rest. On entering his home, he told his mother that he was so tired, and he took a nap before supper. He ate very little and a short while later threw up what he had eaten. His lethargy, so atypical for him, soon began to concern his parents who then phoned their doctor.

When he was admitted to the St. Joseph's Hospital in Lancaster about 10:00 p.m., Barry and Janet called me to meet with them there. Around 1:00 a.m., Doug slipped into a coma. Tests showed that he was stricken with acute leukemia, and he died at

Douglas Wayne Smith, son of Barry and Janet Smith, June 10, 1964-October 5, 1979.

five o'clock Friday morning. In less than fifteen hours after Doug had come home from a day at school, he was dead.

Exactly one week and a half from the time that Doug Smith had stood in the circle of youth around Dave Cunningham's grave, his own memorial service was held at the Mechanic Grove Church! Our youth group was struck with a double shock! No one expects a healthy-appearing ninth-grade wrestler and star baseball player to suddenly die in that short amount of time from acute leukemia, but it happened.

Again, this was a hard blow for Randy. To lose Dave, his close friend, cohort and softball team co-manager, and then Doug, one of his best players, within a two-week period was almost more than he could bear. But once again, he found an avenue for his expressions of grief in poetry:

A Tribute to Douglas Wayne Smith

First base is a tough position, few can play it well.
It takes a sense of dedication, as anyone can tell.
Doug always tried, he gave his best, from game to game I saw.
Compared to others in the league, Doug was best of all.
In practice, Doug took extra time to improve upon his skills.
The extra time was not required; it was only just Doug's will.
Doug moved from left field to first base,
when I asked him if he would.
His concern was just to help the team any way he could.
With Doug's help, the team lost none and ran away as champs,
He always knew what he could do; he seldom took a chance.
The younger players' admiration showed just how well he fit.
For his hitting, they nick-named him after Philly slugger, Schmidt.
The older players respected Doug for the efforts that he made,

His attitude, the ways he shared, reflected in how he played.
The team will miss Doug's laughter, the smile across his face.
They'll also miss his leadership, and the way he played first base.
Doug would want his life to be a lesson to us all,
That winning through the game of life
comes through answering God's call.

Randy Ziegler, Team Manager 10/6/79
(Used by permission.)

(A tragic addendum to Doug's death is that his parents, Barry and Janet Bollinger Smith, were left with one child, their daughter, Marjean. She grew up, married Kenneth Harnish, became a beautician and the mother of two children, Debra and Doug. At the age of twenty-seven, after a year-long battle with *acute leukemia*, she died on June 14, 1995.)

* * * * *

Vivian –

This *double* tragedy weighed heavily on Randy's mind. He still lived at home with us, worked the third shift (11:00 p.m. to 7:00 a.m.), daily at Donnelly Printing Company in Lancaster and slept during the day. About two weeks after Dave's death, Randy was sleeping one morning and woke up because he thought he heard someone call his name. He looked around the room and saw Dave standing at the foot of his bed. This was not unusual, because Dave would often enter our house without knocking, walk into Randy's room and even sometimes jump on him while he was sleeping, just to startle and heckle him. However, now he was dead . . . but there he was! Wearing a long-sleeved shirt, Dave smiled and said, "Randy, don't worry about me. I'm happy here." Then he disappeared.

After that, Randy finally felt peace.

* * * * *

I confess that I'm a pack rat, and I believe it is hereditary. My mother was one, and some of our children have that tendency. I also *love* going to garage sales, especially when I have a purpose. When our church packed layettes to send to needy areas of the world, I enjoyed buying baby clothes, blankets, and other needed items at garage sales. How thrilling it was to find some beautiful hand-crafted item, donate it to the Disaster Relief Auction and watch it being bid up to triple the amount I had paid for it. I considered that a win-win situation all around. Even the grandchildren benefited when they were small, and I bought them many like-new clothes at very economical prices.

Sometimes I'd find antique toys, ceramic dishes, glassware, and other collectibles and stash them away thinking that in time they would become more valuable. In addition, my mother had given me an old chest filled to the top with the correspondence of my great-grandfather, Samuel Ruhl Zug (1832-1926). He had been an active church leader in the Mastersonville area helping to establish a number of Church of the Brethren congregations, Sunday Schools, Elizabethtown College and also Brethren Village. In addition to being a minister, he was versatile in that he also was a surveyor and justice of the peace. Consequently, his chest also contained many wills, surveyor charts, and deeds. He must have been a pack rat too, because he had documents from earlier than his birth, dating back into the late 1700's and early 1800's, and we felt they may be of some value to someone.

Earl and I moved to the Brethren Village near midnight on New Year's eve of 2002 so that we could begin New Year's Day in 2003 by waking up in our new home, Cottage 203, on Fieldcrest Drive. In order to make that move, we had to sell our home in Lampeter and go through the painful process of down-sizing. Some items of sentimental value we gave to family members, and of course, we brought with us whatever we needed here. However, to get rid of the bulk of the "stuff" we had collected through the fifty-three years of our marriage (at that point), we decided to have a public sale.

Again, our timing was *not* the most brilliant decision of our lives. Because our house was sold, we had to empty it. Since we didn't know where to store our things until spring, we saw no alternative except to have our sale during winter and chose January 18, 2003. I was fearful that if there were a blizzard, people would not be able to come. Our auctioneer assured me that "sale-goers are even more faithful than postal carriers: they'll go through snow, sleet, rain, or any weather conditions to get to sales!" We debated moving everything to a fire hall or community fair building, and again were advised that would be too costly and bothersome. Since our auctioneer had a large tent, if the weather would be inclement, the sale would take place within it. We were assured the tent came equipped with heaters in case the weather would be especially cold.

We had high hopes for some of our items. I had several dozen very old green glass Atlas and Ball canning jars and had seen similar ones sell for four and five dollars *each* at other sales. One old document, which had on it a hand-drawn eagle and fancy calligraphy, had been appraised to be worth between $1,000 and $1,500.

Unfortunately, the morning of our sale was windy and bitter cold, the coldest day of the winter, with a near-zero temperature. We discovered the heaters in the tents only threw heat about three feet directly in front of them. The ground was frozen and even when people wore layers of warm clothing, the cold penetrated through their shoes and/or boots, and their feet were uncomfortably cold. At the fullest point, there may have been sixty people at our sale. Most of the time it was twenty-five or even less, and some of those were our own children. The sale was a disaster. Our stuff was virtually given away.

The green jars were sold for one dollar for a box of a dozen. When Earl belatedly saw that the eagle drawing was only selling for $300, he was about to bid on it himself when it was pronounced, "Sold!" A few valuable items were stolen. We asked the auctioneer at one point if we could stop the sale due to the extreme conditions and lack of people, and he said that since the ads said it was an "absolute sale," that wasn't possible. We got through it by putting on a brave front, but it was one of the worst days of our lives. After many hours of preparation, cleaning, polishing, sorting and displaying everything, we felt as though we had been plundered and financially raped. And it was really nobody's fault, except for some poor decisions we had made in planning, choosing that time and place.

A number of friends came but stayed only a half hour or so. As they left, they apologized because they had intended to stay for the entire sale, but it was just too cold, and we understood. We felt lots of love and support, not only from them but also from our loyal family and our wonderful neighbors who outdid themselves by purchasing many items.

For a few days, I could think of nothing else. Finally, I decided to write the following poem, and in doing that received consolation and resolved my grief.

* * * * *

The Death of a Dream

The mother remembered her childhood so poor—
Being cold, without money and toys.
She vowed she would teach her own children to save
For their future with all of its joys.
She taught them to save pretty things and to see
The value in keeping things old.
"Just store them away and some day they will be
Your income," her children were told.
Her little girl listened and hoarded away
Glass dishes, and pictures and such
A number of bells, fans and pitchers and birds
No one ever had seen quite so much!
She kept wooden boxes and green canning jars
And programs from days of the past,
Her grandmother's handwork, and postcards galore,
She learned to make everything last.
At garage sales she bought this and that just to add
To her future whenever she'd sell.
These things were her "nest egg," her dream,
So when she'd be old, she'd live well.
The little girl lived beyond seventy years,
Retiring and settle-ing down.
She decided that NOW was the time to have sale
To live in a nice house in town.
But the day of the sale was the coldest in years
And people stayed home in their bed.
No one wanted the things that the woman had saved
And her dreams of wealth became dead.
The moral to learn from this sad tale is

*That treasure does not come from "things,"
But love in a fam'ly and love from our God
Can sustain whate'er futures may bring.*

(By Vivian S. Ziegler after their disappointing
personal sale on Jan. 18, 2003.)

* * * * *

Earl and Vivian –

Among the saddest times of our lives would also be the deaths of many friends, our parents and our siblings. For Earl, the deaths of his sister, Mae, and her husband, Wayne Patches, his sister Verna's husband, Norman Kline, and his brother, Victor. Victor had been the best man at our wedding, was a frequent visitor, and was not only Earl's younger brother but also his best friend.

For Vivian, the loss of her younger brother, Charles B. Snyder, was hard to accept, as he had traveled with us on several tours and would frequently stop by at our house to ask a question or just to heckle us. In addition, she also especially missed these friends: a co-teacher at Swift, Dan Gaido, who died suddenly at an early age, a college friend, Nancy Seldomridge Ginder, who always made her laugh and was a major supporter of the Lampeter Church library, and Mary Beth Bieber, (wife of Rev. Charles Bieber), a former missionary to Nigeria who was very outgoing, brilliant and a tireless game-player.

Vivian also grieved over the passing of family pets, especially "Sparky," a Pomeranian whom we had for 9½ years. He was an intelligent and beautiful little friend and although he died four years ago, she still misses him greatly.

* * * * *

Pastors' families also have their heartaches. Sadly, we admit that three of our six children and one of our grandchildren have experienced divorce. Some married young, were betrayed, chose poorly or too quickly. However, there is only so much parents and grandparents can do. After they reach twenty-one, the choices they make are their own, and they must live with them. When there is brokenness, all we can do is help them pick up the pieces, and continue to love them, no matter what. But it is heartbreaking, and drives us to our knees in prayer.

* * * * *

Some of Our Joys:

Vivian –

On the other hand, our children and grandchildren have also always been a source of much joy. In their early years, when they would make interesting observations or say funny things, I tried to record most of them on 3"x5" cards. Some day, they may even appear in another book!

While we were at Woodbury and had three children under the age of four, Earl and I attended a Family Life Institute held at Juniata College. In a small discussion group, someone asked, "What is the main thing you would like to teach your children?" One woman immediately responded, "Self-reliance."

That sure sounded good to me, as at that point, I felt swamped with diapering, tying shoes, combing hair and wiping faces, and it seemed like these would be my main occupations *forever*! One woman pointed out that the "diaper stage" is really very short when you consider it from the perspective of your lifetime.

However, at that time, I couldn't see the "light at the end of the tunnel." (Now, I would totally agree with her!)

We did try to teach our children to be self-reliant, though, and as they got older, we sometimes felt we had done too good a job! They seemed to get along so well in life without us that sometimes we didn't hear from them for weeks!

Let me add, that if I were answering that question today, I would not say "self-reliance" was my *top* priority of what I wanted my children to learn. Instead, I would want to teach them the Christian faith, the way to salvation, the attributes of God, and the treasures in God's Word. I would make a greater effort to have them memorize scripture, which can provide comfort throughout one's life as well as an effective tool in fighting spiritual warfare. Of course, we did do this and tried to model it, but we should have done more.

* * * * *

What a joy it is when your children show their love by sharing their unique gifts with you! For example, in 1979 I had major surgery, and when I was still not fully awake, Randy came to my hospital room and sat with me for several hours and spent that time writing a poem. Again, in the mid-1980's, I couldn't go to church one Sunday morning because I was hemorrhaging, and Doreen came over and sat by my bed so I wouldn't be home alone. These demonstrations of love-in-action meant so much.

One year for Christmas, Karen gave us ten pints of frozen corn. What a gift of love that was! She probably remembered that cutting corn is not one of my favorite things to do, and to think of the work she did, probably on a hot summer day, and her willingness to share the fruits of her labors with us, was much appreciated.

In our cottage today we have at least five pieces of furniture that were made by our son, Mike. The most recent thing was a beautiful and practical kitchen island, which we love and use every day. What wonderful reminders these are of his skills and his love!

* * * * *

On our trip to Europe in July 2010, we toured a Bohemian glass factory in the Czech Republic. While there, we bought a lovely cobalt blue vase with the intent of donating it to the Brethren Disaster Relief Auction in Lebanon that September.

Unwrapping the Bohemian cobalt blue glass vase that had been bought in the Czech Republic by Earl and Vivian in July 2010, donated to the Brethren Disaster Relief Auction in September 2010, and bought by Randy there to surprise his mother, Vivian, by giving it to her that Christmas.

I thought it was so beautiful, and was very tempted to keep it and not donate it after all. However, with mixed feelings, we did donate it, with the understanding that we would not let it be sold for less than we had paid for it.

At the time the vase was auctioned, Earl was not present, and our son, Randy, was sitting with me. During the bidding, I bid it up to our purchase price, but then stopped. When it was sold, I couldn't see who had purchased it, but I was glad that it had brought a nice contribution to the auction total.

At our 2010 family Christmas gathering, I received a large package, which had multiple layers. I unwrapped one box after another, as my and everyone's curiosity grew with each layer. Upon opening the innermost package, to my astonishment I discovered the blue cobalt Bohemian glass vase! Through special arrangements, Randy had given instructions to a friend to buy that vase to surprise me, and he sure accomplished that! I am pleased to be able to display it in our china closet today.

* * * * *

After Earl's ordination on Feb. 18, 1950, during his 62 years of ministry to 2012, he performed approximately 350 or so weddings. Interestingly, he officiated at the weddings of three couples who were over 80 years old: Goldie Baugher and Paul Sterner (Black Rock), John Kreider and Bertha Welch (Mechanic Grove), and his own mother, Rhoda Keller Ziegler to his uncle Levi H. Ziegler (in Chiques Church of the Brethren). He had the privilege of marrying all six of our children, and one of our grandchildren—Marianne Zimmerman to Gary (Chip) Smith.

One couple he married twice—to different people! He married Terry and Ginger Kreider and also Mary Ellen DeLong and Tom Peffley. After each couple was married 25 to 30 years, Terry and Mary Ellen were both widowed. In time, a romance developed between them, and when they decided to get married on May 17, 2008, they asked Earl to officiate as he had married both of them in their first marriages.

Earl's most distant wedding was near Portland, Maine, where he married Ray Leach, a member of the Holsinger Church of the Brethren, and Dorothy Bold. His most distant marriage re-dedication was that of Byron and Delma Over in February 1993, on their 38th wedding anniversary in the Fiji Islands. He had officiated at their marriage in January 1955, when we were living at Woodbury.

Some unusual happenings at his weddings included:

- The time the wedding ring was dropped and rolled across the floor under a heater on the one side of the church.
- When the groom's father (from another state) discovered ten minutes before the wedding that he had no shoes except a pair of sneakers. Fortunately, he and Earl wore the same size shoes, our home was next door, and Earl quickly loaned him a pair.
- At an *outdoor* wedding, the maid of honor collapsed while walking down the pathway to the altar. Someone called 911, an ambulance came and took her to the hospital, and after that sudden interruption, the wedding resumed.
- When he was informed that the bride's mother's bra strap tore, Earl was able to get a safety pin which he happened to have in his desk drawer in the church pastor's office and send it to her dressing room.
- Partway through one ceremony, Earl remembered that the couple being married wanted to have the communion service

In Joy and in Sorrow 355

as part of their ceremony, and he had forgotten to bring the bread and the grape juice from the church kitchen. After their vows, during a vocal solo, Earl quietly walked out and returned with the bread and the cup up the sleeve of his clerical gown. He placed the missing items on the altar and resumed his place in front of the couple who were the only two people who realized why he had gone. By the time the solo was finished, everything was in its proper place.

- After his wedding, one young groom asked Earl what the charge was for his services. Earl said that because he feels that is a part of his pastoral service, he doesn't charge a fee, but each couple can give whatever they wish. The groom smiled and said, "Thank You." (And that was what Earl received!)
- Just a day or two before our daughter, Doreen's, wedding to Ken Creighton, Ken's dad stepped off a curb in Elizabethtown and fractured his leg. The break was such that the leg had to be in a cast and perfectly straight, so at the wedding, the father of the groom was brought down a side aisle lying on a hospital cot. He was also on the cot for the family photos afterward.
- At one wedding, one of the groom's relatives arrived dressed in black and wearing heavy makeup. We were told she was a Satan worshipper and practiced witchcraft. When she was asked if she would like to be introduced to Earl, the officiating minister, she declined saying, "I know he is a spiritual and righteous man as I can see an aura of light surrounding him, protecting him." *"Everyone who does evil hates the light, and will not come into the light for fear that his deeds will be exposed."* John 3:20 (NIV)
- For one wedding, the pre-ceremony music was provided by a string quartet which included our daughter, Karen, playing

the viola. Several selections were played without incident, but during the classical number being played as the bride's mother was escorted down the aisle, it sounded as though each member was playing from a different page! The result was a cacophony of sounds similar to an orchestra tuning up. Each one continued playing with a serious expression of concentration on his/her face, but it was difficult for the wedding party and guests to keep from giggling!

- In addition to being the bride and groom in our own wedding and Earl performing weddings, we have experienced being the parents of the bride, parents of the groom, grandparents of the bride, grandparents of the groom, son of the bride, brother or sister of the bride/groom, uncle/aunt of the bride, best man, maid of honor, attendant, usher, parent of the soloist, Vivian as pianist, organist, and soloist, both of us singing as a vocal duet, and being the only Caucasians ("grandparents" of the groom) at the large Korean wedding of Jimmy & Joanna Choi.

- In order to not show favoritism, we tried to give the same wedding gift to all the couples Earl married. For years, we gave a picture of Sallman's head of Christ. Then we gave a picture of "Grace," the old couple or old man seated at a table with an open Bible in front of them and with their head bowed in prayer. For nieces and nephews, we usually gave two folding chairs. In lieu of an engagement ring, Earl gave me a set of silverware for six in a lined wooden chest, and as a wedding gift, he gave me a cedar chest made by Rev. Henry King from the Heidelberg Church of the Brethren near Reistville, Lebanon County.

* * * * *

Among our joys is the fact that we have been privileged to celebrate numerous August 12 Wedding Anniversaries . . . in very unique places! To illustrate:

1966 — 15th — Switzerland, climbing a 7,000-foot mountain in a cable car
1970 — 19th — Tiberias, in Israel
1980 — 29th — Heidelberg, Germany
1984 — 33rd — Innsbrook, Austria
1988 — 37th — Leningrad, USSR
1995 — 44th — Glacier Bay, Alaska
2000 — 49th — Prague, Czecheslovakia
2004 — 53rd — New York City with John and Audrey Choi
2005 — 54th — Italy
2006 — 55th — Banff, Canada

For our 35th Anniversary, we invited our original wedding party to a dinner at the Bird-in-Hand Restaurant and took photos lined up as we had been thirty-five years earlier. Dale Hylton couldn't attend that day, but all the other members of our wedding party were present and still married to their original spouses! (See photo on page 182.)

In August 2001, Earl and I celebrated our 50th wedding anniversary, and although we heard from many of our friends, we didn't hear from Audrey and her husband, John Choi. We were surprised but not concerned, because we knew they were very busy people.

In December, we received a phone call from Audrey in Korea in which she began, "I'm a very bad daughter."

We said, "Why do you say that? What do you mean?"

"You had your 50th wedding anniversary, and I didn't call you or even send you a card."

"That's okay, Audrey. We know you're busy. We love you anyway."

"No, I'm a very bad daughter," she insisted. "I want you to come and visit me here in South Korea."

"Oh, we can't do that," we replied. "That would be too expensive."

"No, I want you to come. Could you come and visit me in April? That's when the spring flowers are blooming, and it shouldn't be too cold," she continued. "If you can come, I will get your plane tickets and make the travel arrangements."

We said, "What? You're offering to pay for us to come to South Korea?"

"Yes, would April be a good time for you?"

"Well, yes. We could come, but . . ."

"Okay, you reserve those dates, and I will make the arrangements," she promised . . . and she did!

From April 29th to May 12th, 2002, Earl and I were in South Korea. John Choi, Audrey's husband, met us at the airport and drove us to Seoul University where Audrey was a faculty member, and we stayed in one of their guest suites. On the way, Earl asked John if he would please stop at a bank so we could get some American money changed into Korean currency.

"No, we've taken care of that," he replied, handing us a bank envelope of Korean bills worth approximately $1,000. "You can spend that while you're here."

We discovered they had thought of everything.

When Audrey was busy teaching her voice students at Seoul University, the "Harvard of Korea," she arranged for different friends of hers to take us sight-seeing or to programs, and we had a wonderful time. She even took several days of vacation and accompanied us on a train ride to the southern end of the country to view the sights there and visit a charity which she helped support.

During our visit we asked her what ever happened to U Gene. She said, "I know where he is, and I will contact him."

It turned out that he is the owner of the largest Hilton Hotel in Seoul. When he heard that we were in Korea, he insisted that Audrey bring us to his hotel for our last two nights and also share a meal with him. In his deluxe hotel we stayed in a swanky VIP suite, complete with fruit and fresh flowers, and located on the top floor. On the morning we left, we checked with the clerk at the desk about our bill and were told, "There is no bill for you."

* * * * *

In December 17, 2005, Audrey and John's son, Jimmy Choi, was married to Joanna, a beautiful Korean girl, in a church in Virginia and we attended. How surprised we were when they insisted on including Earl and me as Jimmy's "grandparents" on their wedding photos! Being the only Caucasians in the group, we felt highly honored.

How blessed we were that the ICYE in New Windsor had called us in 1965 about hosting an exchange student. Because we opened our home, we received a wonderful daughter who brought to our family a son-in-law and two grandchildren whom we love dearly. We always enjoy joking about how much Audrey's children look like their American grandparents—us!

Jimmy and Joanna welcomed baby Bethany into their home on December 1, 2009, so we now have a Korean great-granddaughter. Today Jimmy is the Minister of Music and Worship in a large Presbyterian church in Virginia.

Audrey's lovely daughter, Jacqueline Choi, an accomplished cellist, completed her Bachelor of Music degree at the New England Conservatory in Boston, her Master of Music degree at the Juliard School in New York, and is currently pursuing her Doctor of Musical Arts degree at the Manhatten School of Music. She has been called "an emerging star" by Richard Dyer of *The Boston Globe*, and already is an active soloist, recitalist and chamber musician sought after in the United States and abroad. Her family has given her tremendous support, and she is constantly practicing and working to improve her performances.

As their American grandparents, we are so proud of the achievements of our Korean grandchildren. Through the years this whole family has brought us so much joy. Look what we would have missed had we said, "No."

* * * * *

Celebrating our Sixtieth Wedding Anniversary August 2011. Standing: Doreen and Ken Creighton, Mary and Mike Ziegler, Karen Ungemach, Audrey Choi (Hyun Joo Yun), Konnae Berces, Randy and Linda Ziegler. Seated: Earl and Vivian Ziegler. (Absent were Grant and SuLien Markley, John Choi, and George Ungemach.)

Konnae and her three children, April 2012. Left to right: Kara, Taylor, Konnae, Luke Berces, all living in Key West, Florida.

In August 2011, we celebrated our 60th Anniversary by taking the family on a "Heritage Tour." Boarding an Elite bus, complete with driver, twenty-five of us attended morning worship at the Black Rock Church after which we toured the parsonage. It was especially poignant seeing the powder room door which still had some markings and indentations on it showing the height of our children at various ages. We then drove around the South Western High School in Hanover where Karen had graduated, and we ate our pre-packed bag lunches there.

Next we drove by the Manheim Elementary School near Glenville where Karen, Randy, Doreen and Mike had attended. Returning to Lancaster County, we walked through the old parts of the Mechanic Grove Church, through the former parsonage (now a day care center), and visited the cemetery. These visits brought back many memories for us and our children and gave the grandchildren a chance to see where their parents had grown up. We drove around Swift Middle School and around Solanco

High School, past the Lampeter Church and the house we once owned on Pioneer Road.

At Brethren Village, we dismissed the bus and driver, got in our own cars, and traveled ten minutes to the home of our nephew and his wife, Dean and Carole Ziegler, who are caterers, and had a delicious hot meal outdoors in their lovely backyard with a gazebo and scenic view. It was a day of warm fellowship, family love, and picture-taking, one that everyone will remember. Not only were we blessed with perfect weather and the participation of most of our children and grandchildren, but Audrey was here from South Korea and also our daughter, Konnae, and her three children who now live in Key West, Florida, were with us. That helped to make the day *extra* special! What a joyous time!

* * * * *

ENJOYING "RETIREMENT"
Chapter Nineteen

"Retirement is when you don't have enough time to get everything done!"
(Unknown)

Earl –

Two months into retirement, I was called to be the interim pastor of the Florin Church of the Brethren in Mount Joy, Pennsylvania, beginning December 1, 1999. The church had just dismissed its young pastor after a 2½-year conflict over leadership style. That dismissal action created conflict among the membership, a majority in favor of the decision and a minority opposed. More than fifty members left the Florin Church and attended elsewhere, but a few returned . . . in time. The congregation sought out professional assistance to resolve the conflicts, reviewed the congregation's organizational structure, held intentional conversations among its membership, experienced a candlelight forgiveness service, all of which contributed toward the healing process. After two years, I concluded my work at Florin in October 2001 when Eric Anspach was installed as the new pastor.

* * * * *

How well I remember sitting in my office at Florin on September 11, 2001, and receiving the frightening phone call from Ricki Grubb that the two World Trade Center buildings in New York City were burning due to two large airplanes used as missiles flying into the Towers. "Turn on the television and see this horrible picture," Ricki alerted me.

A worship service addressing this national emergency was hastily planned for that very evening with the result that the sanctuary was quite full of anxious people trying to make sense and find peace in the midst of this national tragedy. Old Testament and New Testament scriptures as well as the prayer of Saint Francis of Assisi were read, punctuated by moments of meditation. The service ended with the congregation singing, "Let There Be Peace on Earth," and each person holding a lighted candle for peace.

* * * * *

The first fair sponsored by the Florin Church for the community and coordinated by Joe Wolgemuth was held on the church parking lot with more than six hundred persons attending. Its purpose was to be an outreach to the community through various displays highlighting ministries of the church. Food stands were popular as was a "water dunk tank" where I was one of several victims, including the mayor of the town.

While the healing process was stressful to plan and lead, my two-year tenure at Florin was great and established some lasting friendships.

* * * * *

Vivian –

Being at the Florin Church was very nostalgic for me because that church building stands on land that was part of our apple orchard when I was growing up. Our house, barn, hired man's house and what had once been a cold storage and a few other buildings are still there, but in poor condition. Having spent most of the first twenty-one years of my life there, I have many memories of that area and its people.

* * * * *

Earl –

Galen Hackman began as the new pastor of the Ephrata Church of the Brethren on January 1, 2002. Needing a temporary staff member to assist in the pastoral duties while he prayerfully surveyed the leadership styles and needs of the congregation, I was invited to join the pastoral team on June 1, 2002, on a half-time basis. My duties were basically the ministry to Senior Adults, hospital calls plus general visitation, including the families of newborn children. My tenure was to be for six months.

In the initial interview for the interim position, I was asked, "Since you were always the senior pastor, will you find it difficult to work under another person . . . and one younger than you?"

What an excellent question! I knew I could. My reply was, "Yes, I can. I know who the boss is. Just wait and see!" Galen and I had a super working and personal relationship during my two and one-half years of service at Ephrata.

I found this axiom reaffirmed again and again in my time at Ephrata: *"If a pastor wants his/her spiritual well to be filled, all he needs to do is visit the older folks, sit at their feet and listen."*

366   Enjoying "Retirement"

Earl and Vivian often shared the podium at speaking engagements. This example was at a Sweetheart Party at the Ephrata Church of the Brethren in 2003.

The day I began working at Ephrata, I counted more than eighty senior adults on the roster. (Note: the church also had many children, teenagers and young adults.) I finished my work in November 2005, with several creative and exciting retirement parties.

Great joy and a good learning experience were my rewards in serving on the team with Pastor Galen, a visionary leader, Carol Bowman, a competent administrator, and the other part-time paid and volunteer staff. Galen has the gift of bridging the old and the new into one whole where harmony is experienced in the midst of differences. His extraordinary gifts as a teacher were evident in his preaching ministry as well.

* * * * *

Following Pastor Jim Rhen's very successful twenty-year ministry at the East Cocalico Church of the Brethren, Reamstown, a new church plant in Lancaster County, was both a blessing and

Still dedicating babies! At the East Cocalico Church, Earl dedicated Andrew Ensinger, son of Dan and Ralyssa Ensinger on March 5, 2006. Left to right: Dan, Breana, Ralyssa, Andrew and Pastor Earl.

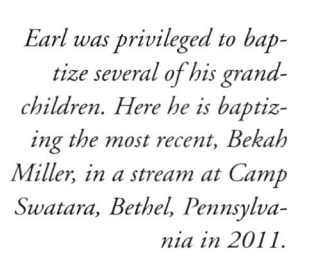

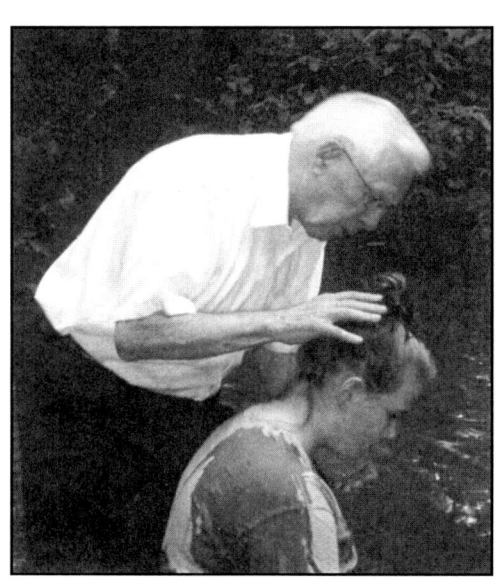

Earl was privileged to baptize several of his grandchildren. Here he is baptizing the most recent, Bekah Miller, in a stream at Camp Swatara, Bethel, Pennsylvania in 2011.

a challenge. The East Cocalico Church, in a grieving mode, found it difficult to transition to new leadership and rightly so. Interims exist to address those issues. I began as their half-time pastor on January 1, 2005.

The church rather quickly accepted my leadership, albeit with some reservation. In my one year and four-months interim with them, the church repaved their entire parking lot and erected a church steeple to communicate their purpose and establish a greater presence in the community. Change was crucial but difficult for the leadership. Annually, the church invited the community to a block party on the premises and also conducted Vacation Bible Schools that local children loved to attend.

*****

As the next invitation to serve an interim parish was given, it was easy to decline, for when I completed my ministry with the East Cocalico Church, I had completed serving the Lord and His Church for fifty-five years of active ministry. My next step was to become a layperson in the home church.

*****

Vivian –

In the late 1950's, when we were serving at Woodbury, the pastor of the neighboring New Enterprise Church of the Brethren was Wayne Dick. In a conversation I had then with his wife, Hazel, she said, "When I pass from this scene, I want people to remember more about what I've done than simply that 'she kept a clean house.'" As a young mother and pastor's wife, I agreed completely, and through the years I have had a similar goal for my own life.

In July 1993, I retired as Swift Middle School librarian after serving twenty-five years in the public school system. That September, on the first day of school, it seemed strange to see the yellow busses heading for school and I wasn't there among them, going toward school to greet the students and anticipating another year of school. However, after about five minutes, that feeling passed!

* * * * *

Since our home in Lampeter was only about a mile from the Lampeter Church, we had a growing feeling that it would be best to move from that community so that our presence would not interfere in any way with the work of the next pastor, John Hostetter. I still continued to teach the Lampeter Church's Founder's Sunday School class now and then for twelve more years, while Earl was involved with interim pastorates, teaching, and serving on committees in our new home church, the Lititz Church of the Brethren.

In discussing our alternatives, Earl favored moving to an over-55 community for the next ten years or so and then moving to a retirement village. I wanted the security of knowing that if anything happened to either of us that we would be assured of continuing care. In addition, I said to Earl, "I do not enjoy moving and only want to move one more time, and that's it!"

I felt strongly about that because after our marriage in August 1951, we had moved to Bethany Theological Seminary on West Van Buren Street in Chicago, living in an apartment with Monroe and Ada Good. In the middle of that year, Earl and I moved to a room on the second floor of the Wieand-Hoff building. For the summer of 1952, we lived in a room in Mrs.

Dunlap's mansion directly across from Earl's parents' home near Myerstown, Pennsylvania.

In the fall of 1952, we moved to the second floor of 408 Homan Ave. on the Bethany campus, sharing a bathroom with Maurice and Jean Strausbaugh and their family. Kremlin, Montana was our home during the summer of 1953, followed by our return to Bethany for Earl's senior year and moving to the third floor at Homan Ave., sharing a bathroom with Wayne and Gwen Miller and their three children. Upon Earl's graduation in 1954, we then moved to the parsonage in Woodbury, Middle Pennsylvania, completing seven moves in the first three years of our marriage. After that we moved to the Black Rock parsonage, the Mechanic Grove parsonage and then into our own home at 1720 Pioneer Road in Lampeter. Actually, it wasn't as bad as it sounds, as we didn't have much "stuff" in those beginning years to move! However, I did *not* enjoy moving. Each time it got harder!

In 2002, after discussing various options with Scott Wissler, head of marketing for Brethren Village, we decided to purchase a brand new cottage, one of about twenty being built that year. When Earl inquired who our new neighbors would be, Scott replied, "Oh, you wouldn't know them. They're from California."

Hearing they would be Wayne and Gwen Miller, we had broad smiles as we shared with Scott that we sure *did* know the Millers. We had even shared a bathroom with them for our last year in seminary! Even though they spent most of their lives in the West, we had maintained our friendship and visited one another several times through the years. In the early 1970's, they had lived in Pennsylvania and Wayne served as Dean at Elizabethtown College. When they moved from Elizabethtown in 1975, we bought their home at 18 Meadowbrook Lane. We

Enjoying "Retirement" 371

Our present home at 203 Fieldcrest Drive within Brethren Village.

Earl likes to keep busy. Here he proudly shows some of the 200 quarts of strawberries he picked at a neighboring fruit farm in 2010 to give away or sell (at cost) to residents of Brethren Village.

loved that home and its location and had dreams of retiring there some day. However, our plans changed and we sold it about five years later when we bought the house at 1720 Pioneer Road in Lampeter.

So it was that on December 31, 2002, Earl and I and Sparky, our Pomeranian, moved into a brand new duplex cottage at 203 Fieldcrest Drive within Brethren Village, north of Lancaster and along route 501. We chose that date because Earl wanted "to wake up in our new home on the first day of the new year, January 1, 2003."

We have no regrets and we love our home here. In our 1,275-square foot cottage, we have two bedrooms, two full baths, a large living-dining room, a sun room, kitchen, utility room, a patio and an attached single garage. We have converted one of the bedrooms into an office for Earl and my "office" is complete with a desk and computer in our utility room.

Since we enjoy watching things grow, we've planted flowers at the front, side, and back of our house and also have a small strawberry patch (where we picked fifteen quarts this year), four or so tomato plants, Swiss chard, brussels sprouts, peppers, egg plants, spearmint tea, parsley, basil and other herbs. By living here we never have to mow lawn, rake leaves, shovel snow, or even pay for repairs within our house. Our home gets a free complete house-cleaning once a year and when we go away, we know that the security staff will be watching and checking our home. Among the amenities here are free in-village mail, on-campus pharmacy, beauty shop, bank, restaurant, grocery store, gift shop, thrift shop, podiatrist services, craft room, chapel, swimming pool, fully-equipped exercise room, workshop, one-day trip options, clubs interested in model trains, gardening, writing, and investing plus interesting speakers and frequent top-notch vocal and instrumental musical programs. If one is bored here, it's his/her own fault!

No wonder we like it here!

* * * * *

Vivian –

The Church of the Apostles on Marietta Avenue in Lancaster, Pennsylvania, offers a series of classes for five weeks each spring and fall. During the fall of 2002, I took a course there about Alternative Medicine. Each week featured a different teacher—one spoke on massage, one on aroma therapy, one on yoga, and two weeks were devoted to acupuncture, taught by Dr. Alma Schwartz. I had never been to any doctor other than an M.D., so when I heard that Dr. Alma is an M.D., she had my attention.

Among her remarks that aroused my interest were these: "Chinese medicine has been practiced with good results for over 4,000 years. When we consult a western-trained doctor, they listen and really *want* to help and bring relief to us. So they give us a drug in a pill. If that doesn't help, they increase the dosage or change the drug. If that still doesn't help, they suggest surgery. They do this because they are treating the *symptoms*. The Chinese approach is entirely different. After they listen to our complaints, they begin to treat the *cause*. Surgery and/or drugs are their very *last* options."

I thought this was very interesting, but never expected to see her again.

In November 2002, a routine blood test revealed that I had extremely high, off the chart, numbers for certain enzymes in my liver. My family doctor sent me to an internal specialist whose first order was eliminate the VIOXX which I was taking for arthritis pain. However, that didn't bring down the numbers, so he referred me to another specialist. The resulting diagnosis was to wait a few more weeks, and if the numbers didn't improve, surgery would be required.

"I've had three major surgeries already, and I don't want another one," I told Earl.

Then I remembered what Dr. Alma had said in the class and felt I had nothing to lose if I went to see her. In addition to the liver concern, I had reflux digestive problems, sleeplessness, high blood pressure, a life-long weight problem, plus a painful lump on my left foot and painful hands due to arthritis.

Dr. Alma and her husband, Dr. Stephen Schwartz, are both M.D.'s, trained in *both* western and Chinese medicine techniques, and they share the same office and are equally good. Her first response to my complaints was to say, "Vivian, you didn't get this way overnight, and you won't be cured overnight!" She added that I needed at least ten weekly treatments, and after that should come back at two or three-month intervals for "tune-ups." At the end of ten weeks, I had lost thirty pounds and no longer had arthritis pain in my foot or hands. I was able to cut my blood pressure medicine in half, but it took a year and a half before my liver numbers were in the normal range but they did come down—without drugs or surgery! The arthritic lump on my foot disappeared, and my family doctor was amazed. "I honestly thought you would have that lump the rest of your life," he admitted.

I have continued going to Drs. Schwartz for tune-ups about once a quarter ever since, and although I am now ten years older, I am virtually pain-free. During 2011, I didn't get any acupuncture treatments at all and felt great all year. However, because of tingling in my right hand, I consulted them again in 2012.

Years ago, I never would have dreamed that I would become an advocate for acupuncture, but I do feel that God led me to meet Dr. Alma and Dr. Stephen as I did, when I needed them, and that acupuncture makes sense and has been very helpful for me. Since then, I have encouraged friends to see her and some have amazing stories of how they have been helped.

John Becker of Ephrata had periodic totally debilitating cluster headaches for over twenty years. He tried everything including very expensive treatments, and nothing brought him relief. On a fishing trip with him, Earl and I saw his pain and pitied him, but hesitated giving him advice. Finally, wanting to help him, I told John of my experience with acupuncture. Feeling it was worth a try, he went. Dr. Alma told him she was sure she could help him but he needed to come about ten times. However, after the fifth treatment, she said she thinks he is healed, and he was! His headaches left and he didn't have one for almost fourteen months. Now, when he gets a flare-up, he knows where to go to get a treatment and have immediate relief.

Honestly, though, it doesn't seem to work for everyone. I don't know why it works for the majority of people but not for all. When one gets tired of experiencing pain, before that person gets desperate, I feel acupuncture is at least worth a try.

* * * * *

Earl –

One day while visiting the Sight and Sound theater near Strasburg, Pennsylvania, I unexpectedly met Glenn Eshelman, the co-owner with his wife, Shirley. Glenn had been a Church of the Brethren minister in the Middle Creek congregation when I was the District Executive. I long had admired his gifts as an artist and photographer. In fact, he had been the photographer at the wedding of our daughter, Karen.

After chatting about mutual interests, he looked at me and asked if I would be interested in being on his team, traveling one day a week visiting churches and sharing information about the opportunities to bring groups to see the two and one-half hour Bible-based musical dramas at Sight and Sound. The result of that conversation was that I spent one day a week for the entire year of 2008 on the Sight and Sound team. Although I enjoyed it immensely, because of my busy schedule and the downturn in the economy, it was best to conclude my services at year's end.

* * * * *

Vivian –

I have always enjoyed writing. In high school, I served on the staff of the school's paper, *The Beacon*, and at Elizabethtown College was elected editor of the 1951 *Conestogan* yearbook my senior year. Together, in 1957 Earl and I wrote a booklet for junior highs entitled, *"So You Want to be a Christian?"* In the 1960's I wrote for the *Biblical Studies* (Sunday School Quarterly) and *Leader* several times, plus some magazine articles. Together we wrote "Day by Day," a two-page devotional for families, appearing in the bi-weekly denominational magazine, *Messenger*, from January 1965, to May 1, 1967. During the years of raising a family and being a librarian, I simply had neither the time nor the energy to write more.

Earl's brother, Victor, had the type of personality that was the "life of the party." He was *never* at a loss for words, and was full of stories, often humorous, sometimes inspirational, but always interesting. I often said to him, "Victor, you ought to record your stories and have them put into a book."

He would agree, "Yeah, I guess you're right. I should do that sometime."

But that's as far as it got, and our busy lives went on.

In January 2004, at the age of 71, Victor was diagnosed with lymphoma. In April he phoned me to ask if I'd be interested in recording his stories because he has the time now. That began my two-hour twice-a-week visits with him when I would interview him and tape our conversations.

I had hoped to transcribe and put these stories in order in a book manuscript that Victor could read and make revisions, if he so desired. However, as time progressed and his condition worsened, I only had completed two chapters by the time of his death at age 72 in December, 2004.

In mid-2005, the book, *On My Way to Heaven—Traveling with Grace*, was finished and printed by Masthof Press, and to date about 1,200 copies have been sold. The greatest compliment I received was when I was told that one young man, perplexed about what career to pursue, was given this book and for him, it was life-changing. In reading it, he felt the Lord speaking to him, calling him to become a minister, so he went to college to start toward that goal.

On a Friday in December 2005, Brethren Village held its annual cookie and craft sale, and I rented a table to try to sell copies of my book about Victor. One buyer, riding by on a scooter, was Anna Buckwalter, a 93-year-old resident of our village. (Her son, Glenn, had been a member of the Mechanic Grove church in the 1970's when Earl had been pastor there, and in the early 1980's we had taken a one-day Mennonite Historical Society sponsored Lancaster County Amish Tour and Anna had been our guide. So, I knew who she was but that was the extent of my knowledge of her since I had had no further contacts with her.

That Sunday night I received a phone call from Anna stating that she had finished reading *On My Way to Heaven* (all 431 pages!) and had enjoyed it very much. As a result, she wanted to meet with me to request my help on a project she had in mind. It turned out that she had written an essay about what it was like growing up almost 100 years ago. Her goal was simply to inform her grandchildren about the comparisons between "then and now."

During my first meeting with her, I quickly noted that Anna had a magnetic personality, a quick wit, and was also full of stories. She had been a nurse for 70 years, Lancaster County Fresh Air program coordinator for 32 years, an Amish tour guide for 36 years, an Amish taxi driver for 16 years, and had hosted around 700 international students, military officers, and refugees in her home during her long life. At her request, I took her essay home and read it and made minor corrections.

When I met her next, I said, "That was interesting, Anna, but you only wrote about your first ten years of life. Don't you think your grandchildren would like to know what you did the next 84 years?"

She laughed. "I guess they would," she agreed, "but I couldn't write it. Typing is difficult for me, and I don't want to begin a big project like that. I don't want a big fuss made over what I've done."

I still felt tired from writing the first book, so I didn't particularly want another big project either. However, I felt she had a story to share, so I offered to help her if that's what she'd like to do. "Let's both pray about it, and I'll visit you next week and see what you've decided."

The next time we met, we were both excited about the project, and that began a series of meetings with her, interviewing her and recording her stories. Next I had to transcribe them from

The five books we've written before We Remember It Well!"

the tapes and then polish and organize them. The completed book, *Look Who Just Came in my Door,* was published in 2006, and about 1,200 copies of that book have been sold also. Anna celebrated her 100th birthday on January 15, 2012.

* * * * *

Earl –

About seven years ago I began noting that many of my traveling clientele were becoming more interested in one-day tours than the longer tours. About that same time, the Atlantic Northeast District's Christian Education Commission approached me and asked me to specifically offer more one-day

When Vivian's book, Look Who Just Came in My Door, *the story of Anna N. Buckwalter, was published in 2006, Brethren Village hosted a book signing with Anna, 94, left, and Vivian, right.*

trips. Since we live in the heart of Lancaster County Amish country, I started including the option of taking local tours.

Through writing her book about Anna Buckwalter, Vivian discovered that Anna had the experience and the stories to conduct those tours, so I enlisted Anna's help. On the very first one, we were amazed at her knowledge of all of the back roads. Her years of taxiing the Amish had embedded the road maps in her brain, and she directed the bus driver as the professional that she is. Difficulties in walking mandated that she stay on the bus at our various stops, and I did all the running.

This led to conducting numerous Lancaster County Amish Tours in later years with Anna as our guide. However, as Anna approached the century mark in years, each tour became more tiring and difficult for her. One day she suggested, "Earl, why don't you write down our routes and our stories so that you can do this yourself?"

At 98, she conducted her last tour for me, but she graciously had introduced me to a number of Amish people and got me started so that I now host two or three of those tours each year by myself.

* * * * *

Vivian —

The Brethren Disaster Relief Auction (BDRA) was begun in 1977 and is an annual tradition held at the Fairgrounds in Lebanon, Pennsylvania, each September. Volunteers who work hard all year growing produce, making quilts, baking, preparing Share-A-Meals, planning, raising animals, auctioning, setting up and tearing down, do it all for the glory of God and to help persons caught in the destruction and tragedies of natural and manmade disasters. In its first thirty-five years, by the end of 2011, the Auction had raised almost $13,000,000.

In 2008, the Board of Directors of the Auction approached me and complimented me on the two books I had written. Because of the success and interest in those books, they inquired if I would be willing to write a history of the Auction including many of the unique stories, "God-Moments," that had occurred at the Auction through the years. As time passes, these precious stories could become lost and/or forgotten, so it was their desire to have them collected and saved for posterity in a book. Earl and I had started writing this book together and were about two-thirds finished. I was reluctant to put this on the "back burner" and take on another huge project. However, the more I prayed and thought about it, the more I felt this was something I should do.

Jay Witman, a very successful auctioneer from the Manheim area and a member of the White Oak Church of the Brethren, had been one of the three originators of the BDRA and in the last two decades had become its leading spokesman and motivator. However, Jay was afflicted with Crohn's Disease and had serious struggles with his health through the years.

I began by meeting regularly with Jay to glean information and stories from him, for he knew all the facts. However, Jay was also recovering from a stroke and had difficulty speaking. He knew what he wanted to say, but couldn't express it, so he often would point at a name or a picture to identify the person about whom he was speaking. Finally, as he became weaker, I began interviewing others.

After his death on June 7, 2009, and when I had the manuscript completed and photos chosen, the Board decided to follow Jay's wishes and have the book printed on quality glossy paper with the photos in color. The printing was completed and we picked up the books entitled *The Story of an Auction: For the Glory of God* at the printer's on Thursday, the day before the BDRA weekend of 2009. In order to save money per book, we printed 12,000 copies in the first printing, and to date about 8,000 copies have been sold.

* * * * *

When I had completed *The Story of an Auction*, I was tired. Friends, relatives, fellow travelers and former parishioners kept asking, "When are you and Earl going to finish compiling and getting your own stories published?"

After two years of procrastination, we again determined to make 2011, the year of our 60th Wedding Anniversary, our goal for completing it, and this manuscript was finally sent to the printers in October of 2012.

LIFE GOES ON . . .
Chapter Twenty

"Lord, keep us alive as long as we live!"
(Unknown)

Earl –

After four hurricanes ravaged the island of the Dominican Republic in 2008 and the devastating earthquake that shook the neighboring country of Haiti in January 2010, it became apparent to the Brethren disaster workers that much help was needed. In September of 2010, nine of us from the Lititz Church of the Brethren formed a work team and spent one week in Haiti in the city of Gonaives, installing electricity in houses, teaching the women to sew and finishing the building of a sanctuary.

Because of the lack of adequate facilities there, I had not shaved for a week and planned to shave off my growing beard at the Miami airport on the way home. However, the fellows challenged me to continue to let my beard grow. When needled sufficiently, I responded, "How much will you give me for the Lititz Church of the Brethren's Building Debt if I keep it on?"

Ken Hess responded, "Three hundred dollars!"

I thought a moment and retorted, "That's not enough."

"Well then, $500—for the church debt," Ken countered, adding this stipulation, "but you must wear the beard at the Atlantic Northeast District Brethren Disaster Relief Auction this coming weekend at the Lebanon Fairgrounds and to church on Sunday morning." (They wanted me to be embarrassed!)

I replied, "It's a deal."

That Sunday night, with thirty people present as witnesses, Ken Hess handed me a check of $750—and on Monday morning, the beard was gone.

What a hair-raising experience!

* * * * *

Vivian –

Two statements with a similar theme that have always inspired and challenged me in teaching Sunday School classes are these:

"You can't lead anyone in your teaching any closer to God than you are yourself." (Said in a Christian Education workshop)

"You can't expect your light to shine unless you have filled your lamp with oil." (Harriet Bright, a retired missionary to China)

* * * * *

Brethren Village is blessed to have an inter-village television system that broadcasts chapel services, special music programs, and daily announcements into the living quarters of its 1,025 residents. Every morning there is a brief devotional program, with prayer, and announcements. Village pastor, Mark Tedford, or associate pastor, Dana Statler, are the usual leaders. Exceptions are on Thursday mornings when Charles Bieber has the devotions, and beginning about six years ago, they asked me to be the worship leader on television every Saturday morning, relieving them of that early morning task. I count it a privilege, and have received many compliments from village residents.

* * * * *

Earl –

Although I have never spent a night in the hospital and do not take any prescription medications, I am currently facing a challenge to my health. In mid-April 2011, I noticed my urine was pinkish for a few days, and I thought it was because I had eaten red beets. It soon appeared normal.

Several weeks later, it colored again, but this time it was bright red like beet juice, and although I felt no pain whatsoever, I decided to see a urologist. I shared my problem and my frustration with my long-time friend and next door neighbor, Wayne Miller, who suggested that I contact his urologist, Dr. Michael Rommel, whom he felt was very knowledgeable.

I called Dr. Rommel's office and after his secretary checked his schedule, she said, "How about tomorrow?"

Without ever having met me before, on my first visit with Dr. Rommel, he spent almost three hours with me, working over his lunch hour! He ordered one test after another and didn't like what he was finding. Finally, he examined me internally and found a large tumor growing inside my bladder.

In about ten days, the tumor was removed and found to be cancerous. Dr. Rommel prescribed a very concentrated vitamin capsule daily to strengthen my bladder walls. In September, an internal examination, including biopsies from various parts of the bladder, revealed no cancer cells and Dr. Rommel declared me

"Cancer free," and we rejoiced.

As a precaution, Dr. Rommel examined me every two months, so when he checked me in November, he was surprised to find five tumors growing now in my bladder! In December, those were removed, and he started me on a three-year maintenance program to rid my body of cancer.

When the Great Physician and an excellent doctor are on the same team, this surely is a winning combination!

Goin' fishin'—one of the joys of retirement, May 28, 2004.

* * * * *

"You shall have what your faith expects," were the words of Jesus to two blind men in Matthew 9:29 (Moffat Translation). These words are a challenge to the potential within each of us, to have a faith that conquers, a spirit that soars. *Between the possible and the impossible is the measure of one's will.* This sums up my life's philosophy.

* * * * *

Believing the axion, *"When you stop growing, you start dying,"* our visionary spirits continue to propel us into new adventures. At age 81, Vivian took her first art classes, and at age 83, I spearheaded a group of twelve persons on another mission trip to the Dominican Republic (my sixteenth trip there!) to erect a church building for the people in Sabana Torso. Short courses at local universities, educational seminars, marriage enrichments and family life institutes were always a part of our yearly professional growth experiences. As someone penned, *"If it is to be, it is up to me."*

Another saying that inspired us through the years is *"Lord, give me a dream that allows me to fly and the faith to pursue it no matter how high."*

* * * * *

Vivian –

If I were going to summarize with a Bible verse the way God has planned and molded our lives, I would choose Ephesians 3:20, 21. Paul uses a literary style here of "stacking" his superlatives. I especially like the way it is translated in the KJV. As you read the next statements, stop after each sentence and think what a blessing <u>just that</u> <u>statement</u> of faith is.

> First of all, God is able. (Do we *really* believe that?)
> Then, God is able to do. (to act)
> > God is able to do what we ask.
> > God is able to do what we think.
> > God is able to do what we ask or think.
> > God is able to do (not some of, but) **all** that we ask or think.

God is able to do **above all** that we ask or think.

God is able to do **abundantly above all** that we ask or think.

God is able to do **exceeding abundantly above all** that we ask or think! (with NO limits! Nothing is impossible!)

That's the way God has blessed our lives. To Him be the glory. He's certainly allowed us to see, do, experience, and travel to an extent that is *exceeding, abundantly, above all* that we would have ever asked or thought back in 1951 when we got married.

Earl and Vivian Ziegler, July 9, 2010.

WHEN IT ALL HAPPENED!

CHRONOLOGY FOR EARL & VIVIAN ZIEGLER'S JOURNEY

1929, Mar. 4	Earl K. Ziegler is born to Abraham Hoffman Ziegler and Rhoda Bucher Keller Ziegler at Sheridan, Lebanon County, Pennsylvania.
1930, June 29	Vivian Z. Snyder is born to Elmer Rupp Snyder and Kathryn Eshelman Zug Snyder at St. Joseph's Hospital, Lancaster, Pennsylvania.
1941, May 11	Death of Vivian's father, Elmer Rupp Snyder, 45, within 24 hours after experiencing a cerebral hemorrhage.
1946	Earl's parents move from the farm at Richland to the Villa Pine Farm on Weavertown Road, Myerstown. Earl transfers from the Richland High School to the Newmanstown High School.
1947, May	Vivian graduates with honors from East Donegal High School, Maytown. Earl graduates as salutatorian from Newmanstown High School.
1947, Sept.	Vivian enters The King's College, New Castle, Delaware. Earl enters Elizabethtown College, Elizabethtown, Pennsylvania.

1948, Aug. 2	Earl is licensed as a minister in the Church of the Brethren.
1949, Sept.	Vivian transfers to Elizabethtown College as a day student.
1949-50, 1950-51	Earl is part-time pastor at the Springfield Church of the Brethren, Coopersburg, Pennsylvania.
1950, Feb. 18	Earl is ordained as a minister in the Church of the Brethren.
1951, May	Earl and Vivian graduate from Elizabethtown College with BA degrees. His in Social Studies and English. Hers in English, Social Studies and Spanish.
1951, Aug. 12	Earl K. Ziegler and Vivian Z. Snyder are married in the Elizabethtown Church of the Brethren by brother-in-law, Rev. Monroe Good.
1951, Sept.	Earl and Vivian move to Van Buren St. in Chicago where Earl enters Bethany Biblical Seminary full-time and Vivian part-time.
1952, Dec. 19	Birth of Karen Louise Ziegler (Ungemach) at Bethany Hospital, Chicago.
1953, June-Aug.	Summer Pastorate in the Milk River Valley Church of the Brethren, Kremlin, Montana.
1954, May	Earl graduates from Bethany Biblical Seminary and becomes pastor of the Woodbury Congregation with churches at Woodbury, Curryville and Holsinger.

1955, Jan. 23	Birth of Randall Earl Ziegler at Nason Hospital, Roaring Spring.
1957	Publication of *So You Want To Be A Christian?* A manual for prospective and new church members of the junior high age written by Earl and Vivian.
1957, Mar. 15	Birth of Doreen Kay Ziegler (Creighton) at Nason Hospital, Roaring Spring.
1958	Earl is elected to Standing Committee as a Middle Pennsylvania delegate.
1959, Sept.	Earl is Moderator of the Middle Pennsylvania District, Church of the Brethren.
1959, Sept. 30	Birth of Michael Wayne Ziegler at Nason Hospital, Roaring Spring.
1960, Apr. 1	Earl leaves Woodbury and begins pastorate at the Black Rock Church of the Brethren, Brodbecks, Pennsylvania.
1961	Earl directs the first Eastern Regional Family Life Institute, Elizabethtown College.
1962	Earl is elected to Standing Committee from Southern Pennsylvania distrtict.
1963	Earl is director of the Black Rock/Lineboro Community Chorus Easter cantata, *Behold Your King*.
1963	Earl is Moderator of the Southern Pennsylvania District, Church of the Brethren.

1964, Apr.	Earl receives a citation from Elizabethtown College for Outstanding Achievement in the Field of Christian Service.
1964	Earl directs the Black Rock/Lineboro Community Chorus Easter cantata, *No Greater Love*.
1964	Earl directs the second Regional Family Life Institute, Juniata College.
1965, July	Earl & Vivian escort a group to Ecuador . . . their first overseas trip.
1965, Aug. to July 1966	Hyun Joo Yun (Audrey) from Korea is an exchange student in the Ziegler home for one year.
1965	Earl becomes a member of the Elizabethtown College Trustee Board.
1965	Vivian is elected president of the Southern District Women.
1966	Earl directs the 60-voice Black Rock/Lineboro Community Chorus in the Easter cantata, *The Glory of Easter* over WBAL-TV, Baltimore, Maryland.
1967, July	The Ziegler family takes 5-week cross-country trip to Annual Conference in Eugene, Oregon. John Willis, exchange student from New Zealand, accompanies them making 7 in the car!
1967, Sept.	Vivian begins public school work as a year-long substitute librarian at South Western High School in Hanover.

1970, May	Karen graduates from South Western High School, Hanover, and begins attending summer classes at Elizabethtown College.
1970, July	The Zieglers leave Black Rock and Earl and Vivian go on a 33-day around-the-world tour.
1970, Sept.	We begin our ministry at Mechanic Grove Church of the Brethren, Quarryville, Pennsylvania.
1971, Sept.	Vivian is hired by the Solanco School District to be the librarian at the Swift Middle School.
1972, Aug. 20	Konnae Lee Ziegler (now Berces) arrives from Korea and joins our family.
1972	Earl serves as Moderator of the Atlantic Northeast District.
1973, Jan.	Karen marries James Zimmerman in the Mechanic Grove Church and they live in Campbelltown.
1973, May	Mike "graduates" from Middle School, Randy from Solanco High School, Karen from Elizabethtown College. Vivian gets her M.S.L.S. degree from Shippensburg University, and all of this happened 50 years after Grandma Kathryn Zug Snyder graduated from Elizabethtown College in 1923.
1975	Doreen graduates from Solanco High School and begins college at Shippensburg University in the fall.

1976, July 5	Hyun Joo Yun (Audrey) marries Yong Suk (John) Choi.
1976	Vivian is elected to Standing Committee from the Atlantic Northeast District.
1977	Mike graduates from Solanco High School and begins attending Millersville State College that autumn.
1978	Vivian is elected as Chairperson of the Standing Committee Nominating Committee of the Church of the Brethren.
1978	Vivian is co-chair (with Esther Landis) of Mechanic Grove's committee for a 430-page cookbook, *Our Daily Bread II*.
1978, July	SuLien Nicodemus (now Markley) comes to live with us and becomes a part of our family.
1979, Dec.	Doreen graduates from Elizabethtown College with B.S. in Math.
1980, June 15	Doreen marries Ken Creighton in the Mechanic Grove Church, and they begin living near Princeton, New Jersey.
1981, June	Konnae graduates from Eastern Mennonite High School in Harrisonburg, Virginia.
1981, Dec.	Mike gets his B.S. in Industrial Arts from Millersville State College; Earl receives his D. Min. degree from Lancaster Theological Seminary.

1982, Jan.	Earl and Vivian begin an 8-month sabbatical and for 3 months Earl serves as the first Pastor-in-Residence at Bethany Theological Seminary, Oak Brook, Illinois, and Vivian takes seminary classes. From Jan. 1, 1982 – Aug. 31, 1982, Wilbur & Evelyn Martin serve the Mechanic Grove Church and live in the parsonage.
1982, Apr.-June	Earl and Vivian conduct a tour to Australia and New Zealand. After the group leaves, Earl and Vivian tour New Zealand and have a 3-week pastorate on Stewart Island.
1982, Aug. 28	Marriage of our son, Mike, to Susan Koziol in Levittown, Pennsylvania.
1982-89	Mechanic Grove plants a new church at Gap and Vivian attends there as teacher and organist.
1983, Aug. to 1989	Earl leaves Mechanic Grove to become the District Executive of the Atlantic Northeast District. We move to 1720 Pioneer Road, Lampeter, Pennsylvania.
1985, Apr. 1	Death of Abraham H. Ziegler, Earl's dad.
1985, Oct. 5	Our son, Randy, marries Linda Neese in the Mechanic Grove Church, and they live in Hessdale, Pennsylvania.
1985, Oct.	Our daughters, Karen, Doreen and Konnae travel in Europe for two weeks.
1986, Mar. 15	Our daughter, Konnae, marries Ronchai Manatrakoon from Thailand, in the Mechanic Grove Church.

1986	Vivian's mother, Kathryn Z. Snyder, moves to Brethren Village.
1987	Earl performs the wedding of his mother, Rhoda Ziegler, 80, to his uncle, Levi Ziegler, in the Chiques Church of the Brethren.
1988	Vivian's camera was stolen while we were in Puerto Rico (but we did get it back!).
1989	Earl preached at the service opening the Pennsylvania Farm Show in Harrisburg.
1989	Both Karen and Konnae separated from their husbands and were later divorced.
1989	Earl becomes pastor of the Lampeter Church of the Brethren.
1991	We took Konnae, our Korean daughter, to visit South Korea.
1993, June 30	Vivian retires from being librarian at Swift Middle School in the Solanco School District after 25 years in education.
1993	Earl serves as Moderator-Elect of the Church of the Brethren.
1993	Death of Earl's mother, Rhoda Keller Ziegler, 87.
1994, Feb.	Karen marries Andy Miller, and they live in Palmyra.
1994	Earl serves as Moderator of the Annual Conference of the Church of the Brethren assembled in Wichita, Kansas.

1995, Aug. 27	Konnae marries Chris Berces, a Filipino, in Virginia, and they live in Alexandria, Virginia.
1995, Sept. 18	Death of Vivian's mother, Kathryn Zug Snyder, 94.
1996, Sept.	A contemporary service is begun at Lampeter Church of the Brethren.
1999, July 3	Mike marries Mary C. Weckesser in Conyngham, Pennsylvania.
1999, Aug. 31	Earl retires from being pastor at Lampeter Church of the Brethren.
1999, Dec. to Oct. 2001	Earl serves as Interim pastor at Florin Church of the Brethren.
2000, June 17	SuLien and Grant Markley are married in an outdoor setting in Marietta, Pennsylvania.
2001, May 19	Karen marries George Ungemach in an outdoor wedding and they live on a farm near Palmyra, Pennsylvania.
2002, Apr. 29 to May 13	We are gifted a trip to Korea by John & Audrey Choi for our 50th Wedding Anniversary (August 12, 2001).
2002, June to Dec. 2004	Earl begins an interim at the Ephrata Church of the Brethren as halftime Visitation Pastor.
2003, Jan. 1	We move to Cottage 203 on Fieldcrest Drive in Brethren Village, 3001 Lititz Pike, Lancaster, Pennsylvania 17606-5093.

2003-2008	Earl serves as chair of the Annual Conference Council.
2005	We join the Lititz Church of the Brethren, our home church now.
2005, Jan. to June 2006	Earl is interim pastor at the East Cocalico Church of the Brethren, Reamstown, Pennsylvania.
2005, Sept.	Publication of Vivian's first book, *On My Way to Heaven—Traveling with Grace, the Life of Victor K. Ziegler*.
2006, Sept.	Publication of Vivian's second book, *Look Who Just Came in My Door—The Life of Anna N. Buckwalter*.
2008	Earl works for the Sight and Sound Theatre for one year.
2008, Oct. 1 to Sept. 30, 2010	Vivian is elected to serve as the Resident Representative to the Brethren Village Board of Directors.
2009, Sept.	Publication of Vivian's third book, *The Story of an Auction—For the Glory of God*.
2011, Aug. 12	60th Wedding Anniversary of Earl and Vivian Ziegler.
2011, July	Publication of Earl's book, *History of the Lampeter Church of the Brethren, 1978-2010*.
2012, Oct.	Publication of *We Remember It Well! Stories from Our Lives*.

INDEX OF NAMES

Albright, David, 26
Alderfer, Rev. Alvin, 34
Amspacher, Karen, 186
Anderson, Marian, 45
Ankeny, Jacob, 28
Ankrum, Edith, 274
Anspach, Eric, 363
Apostle Paul, ix, 387
Audrey (Hyun Joo Yun) Choi, 126, 128-132, 129, 138-139, 146-147, 161, 187, 326, 357-360, 360, 362, 392-394, 397
Bachman, Elmer and Susan, 27, 102
Bachman, Roland, 27
Baker, Grace, 147
Barnhouse, Donald Gray, 13
Barrows, Cliff, 24
Baugher, Goldie Wolf, 143, 353
Baugher, Joel, 118
Baugher, Stanley, 79,138
Baughman, Bill and Liz, 264-265
Beahm, William H., 43, 255
Bechtel, Glenn and Tina, 80
Beck, Dennis, 294-296
Becker, John, 375
Becker, Miss, 7
Becker, Sadie (Mrs. Henry), 36
Beckner, Curry, 98, 142
Beckner, Joan, 186
Beckner, Linda, 114, 186
Beckner, Lucy, 98
Berces, Chris, 397
Berces, Kara, 321,361
Berces, Konnae Lee Ziegler, viii, 149-154, 149, 153, 154, 156, 167-172, 178, 187, 257, 274-275, 360, 361-362, 393-397

Berces, Luke, 361
Berces, Michael, 321
Berces, Rikki, 321
Berces, Taylor, 361
Berlin, Irving, vii
Bieber, Charles, 188, 272, 316, 384
Bieber, Mary Beth, 272-273, 349
Biggy, 91-92
Bingham, Roland V., 13
Blattenberger, Ben and Florence, 80
Bold, Dorothy, 354
Boldosser, Frank, and Esther, 138
Boldosser, Shirley Baughman, 186
Bomberger, Betty, 300
Bomberger, Harold, 188
Bomberger, Harold Z., 239, 298-299, 300
Bowman, Carol, 366
Bowman, Dr. Rufus, 52
Boyer, Charles, 188
Boyer, Charles (Chuck), 326
Bradfield, Bobby, 12
Bradford, Richard and Carla, 270-271
Brant, Connie, 186
Brant, George, 119, 120, 130
Brant, Luke and Anna, 304
Brant, Martha, 119, 120, 139, 137
Brant, Randy, 186
Brant, Randy, 186
Brant, Sandi, see Keller,Sandi
Brant, Sue, 130-131
Breneman, Cathy, 118
Brenneman, Michael, 186
Bright, Harriet, 384
Brown, Bobby, 12
Brown, Dale, 188

Index of Names

Brown, Tim, 245
Brubaker, J. Omar, 102
Bruell, Magda, 307
Bruell, Pedro, 307-308,308
Brumbaugh, Melvin and Lucille, 73-74
Bucher, Dr. Henry, 29
Bucher, Naomi, 239
Bucher, Rufus P., 238-239, 313
Buckwalter, Anna N., 377-381, 380
Buckwalter, Glenn, 377-379
Burkholder, Evie, 247
Burkholder, John, 247
Bush, Warren and Hazel, 80
Bushong, Joyce, 240
Calvin (not his real name), 86-87
Campbell, Don and Arlene, 31
Campolo, Tony, 173
Carson, Johnny, 112
Chauhan, Paul, 328
Chavez, Annie, 152-154, 153
Chinworth, Jim, 247
Choi, Bethany, 161,359
Choi, Hyun Joo Yun, "Audrey", 126, 128-132, 129, 138-139, 146-147, 161, 187, 326, 357-360, 360, 362, 392-394, 397
Choi, Jacqueline (Jackie), 360
Choi, Jimmy, 187, 356, 359
Choi, Joanna, 356, 359
Choi, John (Yongsuk), 161, 357-360, 394, 397
Christ, 13, 24, 35, 47, 90, 129, 207-209, 236, 265, 272, 281-282, 318, 321, 331-332 (See also Jesus)
Christophel, Todd, 189
Clinton, Bill, 225
Clouse, Hannah, 233
Cooper, Pat, 230-231
Creighton, Ben, 177, 280, 284, 321
Creighton, Doreen Kay Ziegler, viii, 36, 70-71, 115, 115, 126, 137, 143, 145, 152, 153, 157, 159, 163, 170-171, 177, 187, 239, 257, 267, 277-280, 284, 321, 355, 360, 351, 361, 391, 393-395
Creighton, Emily, 284,321,351
Creighton, Ken, 36, 187, 267, 284, 355, 360, 394
Creighton, Tim, 227-229, 228, 284, 321
Crouse, Arlene Ziegler, 3
Crouse, Jean, 89
Crouse, Merle, 89, 193, 303
Cunningham, Amos, 152, 242, 249, 338
Cunningham, David Ray, 336-345, 337
Cunningham, Joan, 338-342
Cunningham, Mark, 247, 320, 338
Cunningham, Ruth, 152, 338
Curtis, Dr. Gordon, 24
Davies, Professor Robert, 20
Davis, Jim and Tami, 303
Dean, John, 82
Deeter, Joan, 328, 331
DeLong, Ervin, 244
DeLong, Mary Ellen, 353
DeLong, Pat, 251
de Perrot, Lucy, 338
Dever, Bryan and Janice, 304
Dew, Honey, 161
Diamera, 310
Diamond, Bush, 161
Diamond, Fairy, 161
Diamond, Honey Dew, 161
Dibert, Don, 282
Dibert, Doris, 282
Dick, Wayne and Hazel, 368
Diller, Ann, 214, 244
Diller, Carl, 214-215, 244
Dilling, Yvonne, 309
Do, Chau Viet, 248

Dole, Bob, 225
Dourte, Lamar, 226
Drescher, Rev. John M., 38, 182
Dubble, Anna Mary, 40
Dubble, Curtis, 40, 188, 314
Dundore, Susan, 188
Dunlap, Mrs., 47, 370
Duvall, Evelyn, 141
Dyer, Richard, 360
Eberly, Bill, 188
Ebersole, John, 317-318
Eby, Jim, 189
Eckman, Marlene, 255, 257-258
Eisenhower, Dwight D., 44
Elijah, 76
Encarnacion, Guillermo, 311
Engle, Dale, 226
Englert, Mr. 291
Ensinger, Andrew, 367
Ensinger, Breana, 367
Ensinger, Dan and Ralyssa, 367
Erb, Chester, 181
Eshbach, Warren, 313
Eshelman, Glenn and Shirley, 375-376
Eshelman, Jim, 181
Favie, 152
Fidler, John, 6
Fike, Earle, 188
Finkbinder, Audrey Wagner, 247
Fitzkee, Nancy Swope, 18, 36, 182
Fletcher, Mike, 320
Flory, Brian, 320
Foard, Dr. Wilbur, 86, 115
Ford, Don, 52
Ford, Wilma, 52
Forney, Glenn Y., 84
Forney, Maria , 15
Forney, Mary Snyder, 62, 100, 101
Forney, Rev. Roy S., 35
Forney, Rev. Roy, 62
Forney, Roy, Jr., 37, 182
Frederick, Warren and Mary, 80

Fuhrman, Dale, 165, 186
Fuhrman, Ronald, 186
Fuhrman, Suzanne, 186
Gaido, Dan, 349
Gantz, Bobby, 12
Garner, Cheryl, 189
Garner, Scott, 189
Garvick, Brenda, 186
Gebhart, Bobby, 12
Geisert, Wayne, 188
Gertrud, guide in Rothenburg, Germany, 211
Gibble, Lamar, 328, 331
Gibbs, Edward, 83
Gideon, 249
Ginder, Nancy Seldomridge, (Mrs. Stanley), 349
Gingrich, Hiram, 33, 59-60,
Gingrich, Lloyd, 37, 182
Gingrich, Norman, 302
Gish, Roy, 282
Glisson, Anna Jane, 233
Good, Ada Ziegler, 5, 6, 8, 10, 37, 41, 45, 278, 369
Good, Geraldine, 50
Good, Monroe Crouse, 33, 37, 41, 47, 278, 369
Good, Roy, 50, 51
Goodman, Clair (not his real name), 63
Graham, Billy, 24
Green, Misty, 137
Groff, Charles, 265
Grubb, Jeff, 189
Grubb, Ricki, 364
Guest, Edgar A., 162
Guhl, Bill, 257
Guttmacher, Dr. Alan, 141
Guyer, Jay, 181
Guyer, Risa, 71
Guyer, Robert (Bobby), 71
Guyer, Robert, 70, 230-231

Guyer, Rodney, 70
Guyer, Ruth, 70-71
Hackman, Galen, 310, 365-366
Harnish, Debra, 344
Harnish, "Doc" and Helen (Sealover), 218
Harnish, Doug, 344
Harnish, Kenneth, 344
Harnish, Marjean Smith, 344
Harnish, Wilmer and Martha, 80
Havergal, Frances, 37
Heaton, Dr. 61
Heinly, Diane Lehman, 186
Heisey, Peter, 33
Heishman, Irvin, 188
Heishman, Nancy Sollenberger, 302, 326
Helman, Blair, 188
Helser, Albert, 13
Henry, Mr., 244
Hepburn, Audrey, 129
Herr, Alma, 299, 302
Herr, Glenn, 246
Herr, John, 89
Herr, Mary Jane, 246
Herr, Theresa, 89
Hershberger, Charles and Dolores, 81
Hershberger, Dan and Gayle (Brubaker), 109
Hershey, Beth, 338
Hershey, Earl and Joanne, 338
Hershey, Harold, 189
Hershey, Milton, 33
Hershey, Ted, 255
Hess, Ken, 189, 383-384
Heyerdale, Thor, 232
Hollinger, Anna Garber, 12
Hollinger, Charles Arthur Shearer (CASH), 18-20
Hollinger, Don, 247
Holt Adoption Agency, 148

Hoover, Annie, 54, 66-67
Hoover, Bob, 66-67
Hoover, Carol, (Mrs. Gordon Hoover), 137
Hoover, Dr. Paul and M.E., 118-119
Hoover, Herbert Clark, 1
Hoover, James, 66
Hope, Bob, 147
Horning, Dr. John, 89
Horning, Estella, 48, 89
Hostetter, John H., 322, 369
Hottel, W. S., 13
Hughes, Albert, 13
Hutchinson, Jim, 247
Hylton, Dale, 25, 37, 182, 357
Hylton, Gladys Stehman, 26
Ingrid, guide in Innsbrook, Austria, 207
Ironside, Harry, 13
Jacoby, Paul and Anna, 29, 40-41
Jerry (Not his real name), 95-96
Jesus, 32, 64, 171, 196, 209, 236, 242, 265, 276-277, 281, 284, 286, 305, 310, 332, 334, 386 (See also Christ)
Jim (Not his real name), 103
Jimmy, guide in Thailand, 221-226
Johnny, Diamond and Angel Kenneth, 160-161, 293-296
Jonah, 94
Jones, Tim, 246, 247
Jorge, Victor, 308-310
Kabakjian, Joan Cunningham, 338-342
Karner, Heinz, 237, 237
Kauffman, Stuart, 181
Keane, Bill, 162
Keener, Harlan, 201-202, 245-246, 309
Keener, Shirley, 309
Keeney, Del, 247
Keeney, Walt, 297

Kegarise, John, 6, 181
Kell, Bill, 26
Keller, Alice, 2
Keller, Chris, 3
Keller, Ethel, 3
Keller, Harold, 2
Keller, Sandi Brant, 186
Keller, Sue, 309
Keller, Thom, 308, 308-310
Kenneth, Angel, 160-161, 293-296
Kettering, Bill, 189
Kettering, Robert, 226, 238, 297, 302
King, Rev. Henry, 9, 49, 356
King, Jan Glass, 307
Kipple, Esther, 186
Kipple, Glenn, 186
Kline, Norman, 277-280, 278, 349
Kline, Verna Ziegler, 1, 2, 6, 10, 26, 277-280, 278, 349
Knaub, Art and Pauline, 168
Knepp, John, 189
Koch, Calvin, 40
Kocher, Judy, 247
Kofroth, Alicia, 219-220
Koziol, Susan, 395
Krall, Melvin, 6, 181
Kramer, Gerald, 29
Kramer, Grace, 29
Kramer, Leroy, 27
Kramer, Nina, 27
Krantz, Miriam, 255
Kreider, Art, 189
Kreider, Clayton, 199-200, 249
Kreider, Irvin, 36, 278
Kreider, John and Bertha W., 353
Kreider, Lena Ziegler, 6, 10, 36, 182, 277-280, 278
Kreider, Lester, 258
Kreider, Lloyd and Dottie, 317-318
Kreider, Sadie, 199, 243
Kreider, Terry and Ginger, 353

Kreider, Terry and Mary Ellen Peffley, 354
Kreiner, Faye, 201-202
Ku, Bway Hser, 161
Kurtz, Earl H., 247
Kyerematen, Elizabeth, 306
Kyerematen, Richard, 304-307
Lai, Dan and Lai, 247, 252
Lai, Tuyet Thi, 248
Lall, V.S., 329
Lam Quang Nguyen, 247, 252
Lamborn, Dora, 60-61
Lamborn, Elmer and Mary Alice, 58
Landers, Ann, 177
Landis, Esther, 152, 273, 394
Lauver, Alice Dourte, 226
Lawler, Ruth, 133-135
Leach, Ray and Dottie, 534
Lee, Kyung Ae, see Berces, Konnae or Ziegler, Konnae
Lee, U Gene, 131, 359
Leffler, Carlos, 304
Lehman, Karl, 186
Lehman, Kevin, 186
Lehman, Sharon Sunday, 186
Lengle, Dean, 188
Lionel, 156
List, Florence, 93
Livingstone, David, 41, 93
Lockamy, Norma, 186
Lucabaugh, William Jr., 118
Ludwick, Ron, 225
Mace, David, 141
Mace, Vera, 141
Mancha, Debbie, 186
Mack, Alexander, 304
Manatrakoon, Ronchai, 395
Mantle, Micky, 172
Margolies, Marjorie, 147
Marian (not her real name) 234-235
Markey, Dave, 302
Markle, Emory, 133

Markley, SuLien Marie Nicodemus, viii, 154-156, 156, 187, 360, 394, 397
Markley, Grant, 360, 397
Marta, 157
Martin, Carl, 189
Martin, Gail (Mrs. Russ), 302
Martin, Leroy, 247
Martin, Wilbur and Evelyn Zuck, 266, 395
Martz, Jim, 301
Mauer, Alberta, 92-94
McCardell, Annetta, 255
McComsey, Edna, vii
McComsey, Ethel, vii
McCree, Avon, 124, 124-127, 161, 187
McElrath, Jennie, 186
McElrath, Robin, 186
McGibbon, Walter, 286
McMahon, Ed, 112
Measley, Jim and Marian, 125
Measley, Tony, 186
Meckley, Connie, 186
Mendez, Milciades and Lucy, 311
Meyer, Gertrude (Mrs. Ephraim G.), 37
Michael, son of Marta, 157
Michelle, (Not her real name), 154-155
Miller, Andy, 396
Miller, Chris, 53
Miller, Glenn, 118
Miller, Gwen Studebaker, 52, 53, 370
Miller, Henry, 114, 115, 118, 138
Miller, Kevin, 53
Miller, Rebekah (Bekah), 188, 290, 321, 367
Miller, Terrie, 53
Miller, Wayne, 52, 53, 370, 385
Minnich, Dale, 310

Mock, Bob, 135-136
Morphew, Tim, 247
Mota, Santos, 309
Mow, Anna Beahm, 43-44
Mueller, Warren, 101, 102
Mull, Earl, 189
Mummert, Sue, 186
Mundell, George, 13
Murray, Andrew, 44
Myer, Mary Jane, 305
Myers, Gloria Bortner, 138
Myers, Isaac, 136
Nace, Ed, 313
Nace, Pearl Diane, 186
Nadia (Not her real name), 292-293
Neese, Linda (Ziegler), 360, 395
Nelson, Ricky, 140
Ney, Gladys Blessing, 101
Nicodemus, SuLien Marie (Markley), viii, 154-156, 156, 187, 360, 394, 397
Nogle, Joel, 303
Nyman, Barry, 98
Ohman, Marjorie Siddron, 181
Over, Byron, 62, 354
Over, Delma, 62, 230-231, 354
Over, Ed and Roxy, 71
Patches, Mae Ziegler, 6, 10, 39, 277-280, 278, 349
Patches, Wayne, 39, 277-280, 278, 349
Patricia of Germantown Church, 306
Pauley, 239
Peffley, Tom, 353
Peifer, Chris, 189
Peifer, Mark, 189
Peters, Ira, 188
Petry, Rev. Wilmer, 78-79
Pettingill, William J., 13
Phillippe, 158
Pletcher, Ordo and Margaret (Peg),

75-76
Pletcher, Randy, 75
Pletcher, Reid, 75
Pletcher, Trent, 75
Plowfield, Kathryn, 213-214
Popenoe, Paul, 141
Powers, Paul, 82
Rabin, Izak, 286
Ramsey, Dwayne, 188
Rappoldt, Barbara, 186
Ream, Matthew, 188
Ream, Sue, 188
Regula, 237
Reid, Don "Buckets", 26
Reider, Fanny Ruth Snyder, 14, 19, 31, 32, 36, 137, 182
Reider, Paul, 36
Reimer, Judy Mills, 326
Rhen, Jim, 251, 366
Ridinger, Edgar and Gladys, 300
Riebling, Sandi, 186
Ritchey, Beverly, 230
Ritchey, Bud, 220-221
Ritchey, Herman, 230
Ritchey, Sarah, 220-221
Riviera, Jaime and Rosalita, 308
Roberto, 156-157
Robinson, Dr. Paul M., 53
Rohm, Dr. Curtis, 273
Rommel, Dr. Michael, 385-386
Rosario, Arial, 188
Rowe, Donald, 188
Royer, Lydia, 5
Royer, Russell, 79
Runk, John, 79
Russell, Iola, 81
Ryan, Bertha, 327-328, 332
Sackett, Paula, 186
Sadd, Tracy Wenger, 247
Saint Francis of Assisi, 364
Saint, Kathy, 90
Saint, Marjorie, 90

Saint, Steve, 90
Sally (Not her real name), 122-123
Saylor, Eugene, 17
Schlicter, Rev. Harvey, 121
Schlosser, Dr. Ralph, 9, 10, 31
Schwartz, Dr. Alma, 373-375
Schwartz, Dr. Stephen, 374-375
Sealover, Helen, 218
Sell, Lester, 54, 160
Sell, Sarah Pepple, 54
Sellers, Noah S., 116, 118
Sepulveda, Robert, 274
Shearer, Fannie, 39, 137
Shearer, Henry, 39
Shenk, Beth Hershey, 338
Shenk, Ernest, 34
Shenk, Marian Stauffer, 34
Sho, Bway Hser Ku, 161
Sho, Ester, 161
Sho, Michel, 161
Sho, Mu Mu, 161
Sho, Poe, 161
Sho, Shee, 161, 293
Shoemaker, Jesse, 65, 66
Shumaker, Ida, 332-333
Siddron, Marjorie, 181
Slaybaugh, Dr. Warren, 52
Small, Dean and Jeanne, 260-261
Small, Marjorie, 260-261
Smith, Barry and Janet, 342-345
Smith, Douglas Wayne, 342-344, 342
Smith, Gary (Chip), 353
Smith, Genive, 181
Smith, Marianne, 221-226
Smith, Marianne Zimmerman, 187, 321, 353
Smith, Marjean, 344
Snyder, Carol, 276-277
Snyder, Charles Bertram, 14, 19, 349
Snyder, Dean, 181, 276-277

Snyder, Elmer Rupp, 11, 11, 21, 389
Snyder, Emma Rupp, 11, 13, 192
Snyder, Ida Rupp, 192
Snyder, Kathryn Eshelman Zug, 11, 11, 19, 21, 108, 196-198, 238, 254, 256, 257, 389, 393, 396-397
Snyder, Paul Zug, 14, 19, 21, 32
Snyder, Ross, 159
Sollenberger, Elaine, 188
Sollenberger, Susie, 60
Sorel, Julia, 100
Sparky, 111, 285, 349, 372
Spiegler, Gerhard, 312-313
Stambaugh, Ida, 113, 136
Statler, Dana, 384
Stauffer, Dorothy Hershey, 77, 81
Stauffer, Gail, 77
Stauffer, Mark, 76-77, 81
Stauffer, Mary, 76-77
Stayer, Paul, 57
Stayer, Vernon and Estella, 80
Sterner, Goldie Wolf Baugher, 143, 353
Sterner, Paul, 353
Sterner, Sally, 186
Stone, Dr. Robert and Catherine, 226-227
Stone, Phil, 188
Stoner, Jeannine Roth, 101
Stover, Wilbur and Mary, 327, 332
Strausbaugh, Connie, 47
Strausbaugh, Dennis, 47
Strausbaugh, Maurice and Jean, 47, 370
Strawbridge, Kate Ruhl, 135
Stremmel, Barry, 186
Stremmel, Randy, 186
Stultz, Owen, 44
Sunday, Bill, 137
Sunday, Terri, 186
Swindoll, Chuck, 1

Taylor, J. Hudson, 316
Tedford, Mark, 384
Thierut, Richard, 234
Tina (Not her real name), 292-293
Toledo, Jorge, 307-312, 308
Tran, Duc, 248-252
Tran, Dung (John), 251-252
Trang, Christine, 252
Trang, Cynthia, 252
Trang, Gia, 252
Trang, Phat, 248, 252, 253
Trinh Family, 247
Tyler, Jim, 302
Underwood, Genive Smith, 181
Ungemach, Karen Louise Ziegler, viii, 48, 49, 53, 61, 62, 68, 71, 75, 79, 87, 108, 114, 115, 137, 139, 143, 145, 163-165, 167, 170-171, 178, 186-188, 194, 196, 239, 254, 256, 257, 351, 355, 360, 376, 390, 393, 395-397
Ungemach, George, 360, 397
Vasco, Betty, viii
Walker, Bob, 159, 160
Walker, Delena, 233
Walker, Mabel, 159, 160
Walker, Preston, 233
Walker, Raymond, 159, 160
Warren, Rick, ix
Wayne (Not his real name), 122-123
Weaver, Jason, 257
Weckesser, Mary Conahan (Ziegler), 178, 290-291, 360, 397
Weik, Harvey, 6, 181
Welch, Bertha (Mrs. John Kreider) 353
Wenger, Blaine, 247
Wenger, Irvin, 25
Wenger, Megan, 188
Wenger, Molly, 188
Wenger, Nancy, 189

Index of Names

Wenger, Naomi, 245
Wenger, Todd, 247
Wentz, Dean and Frances, 98-99
Wentz, Rodney, 186
Werner Family, 160
Werner, Annabelle, 98, 231
Werner, Gladys, 118
Werner, John, 186
Werner, Sharon, 186
Wesley, Charles, 121
Wieand, Dr. 48
Wildasin, Sallie, 120-121
Williams, Bobby, 12
Willis, Glenda, 140, 141, 161, 267, 282
Willis, Helena, 141
Willis, John, 139-141, 141, 161, 267, 282, 392
Willis, Jonathan, 141
Willis, Melanie, 141
Willis, Tony, 141
Wilson, Dave, 30
Wine, J.C., 314
Wissler, Scott, 370
Witman, Jay, 381-382
Witman, Paul and Arlene Weidman, 26
Wolgemuth, Joe, 364
Wood, Jesse, 105, 252
Wood, Ruth Ann, 105
Yohn, Larue, 28
Yohn, Sam, 28
Young, Bob and Dorothy (Longenecker), 196
Yudarin, Mrs., 90
Yun, Hyun Joo, (Audrey), 126, 128-132, 129, 138-139, 146-147, 161, 187, 326, 357-360, 360, 362, 392, 394, 397
Zeigler, Rev. Carl, 151
Ziegler, Abraham Hoffman, 1, 4, 6, 10, 191, 389, 395

Ziegler, Anna, 321
Ziegler, Bob, 37
Ziegler, Carlos, 3
Ziegler, Carrie, 321
Ziegler, Dean and Carol, 362
Ziegler, Earl, 188
Ziegler, Earl Keller, vi, 6, 10, 25, 28, 38, 53, 118, 127, 138, 145, 153, 181-182, 188-189, 228, 255, 256, 257, 262, 267, 278, 302, 306, 312, 321, 325, 360, 366-367, 371, 386, 388
Ziegler, Glen Keller, 5, 6, 10, 278
Ziegler, Jeremy, 291, 321
Ziegler, Konnae Lee, viii, 149-154, 149, 153, 154, 156, 167-172, 178, 187, 257, 274-275, 360, 361-362, 393-397
Ziegler, Lee, 1
Ziegler, Lena, 189, 321
Ziegler, Levi Hoffman, 396
Ziegler, Linda Neese, 360, 395
Ziegler, Levi Hoffman and Rhoda, 353
Ziegler, Mary Conahan,178, 290-291, 360, 397
Ziegler, Michael Wayne, viii, 81, 113, 115, 124, 137, 143, 145, 149, 152, 159, 163, 169, 171, 178, 187, 240, 254, 257, 259, 268, 290-291, 336-342, 360, 361, 391, 393-395
Ziegler, Randall Earl, viii, 61-62, 71, 75, 70, 81, 87, 113, 114, 115, 118-119, 124, 137, 142-143, 145, 152, 162-167, 170-173, 178-179, 186, 187, 239, 254, 256, 257, 336-345, 351-353, 360, 361, 391, 393-395
Ziegler, Reba Copenhaver, 278
Ziegler, Rhoda (Bucher) Keller, 1, 4, 6, 10, 353, 389, 396

Index of Names

Ziegler, Samuel and Bessie, 3
Ziegler, Sarah, 321
Ziegler, T.Grace Cox, 152-153, 189, 278, 287-289
Ziegler, Victor Keller, 6, 6, 10, 37, 152-153, 182, 217, 262, 277-280, 278, 287-289, 349, 376-379
Ziegler, Vivian Zug Snyder, vi, 14, 19, 25, 38, 111, 127, 145, 152, 177, 181-182, 228, 256, 257, 278, 302, 321, 352, 360, 366, 380, 388

Zigler, Earl M. and Rachel, 332
Zimmerman, Jim, 187, 257, 393
Zimmerman, Marianne E., (Mrs. Gary Smith), 187, 321, 353
Zimmerman, Matthew Earl, 321
Zook-Jones, Jill, 246, 247
Zuck, Rev. Nevin, 26
Zug, Kate Eshelman, vii, 39
Zug, Nathan Shelly, 33
Zug, Samuel Ruhl, 345
Zytkowiak, Adam, 252-253